Two thousand sons

Cal and Mimi Farley . . . 1965

Two thousand sons

the story of Cal Farley's Boys Ranch

By
Cal Farley
and
E. L. Howe

PHOENIX PUBLISHING
Canaan, New Hampshire

P E R M I S S I O N S

The passage on page 24 by Justin Isherwood, as quoted from the Wall Street Journal, *is reprinted with the kind permission of the author.*

The passage on page 181 is reprinted from 1984 Revisited *by Malcolm Muggeridge, copyright 1964 by the author.*

Farley, Cal, 1895-1967.
  Two thousand sons.

  Includes index.
  1. Cal Farley's Boys Ranch (Tascosa, Tex.) — History. I. Howe, E. L. (Elvon L.) II. Title.
  HV885.T3F37   1987   362.7'4'09764824   87-14040
  ISBN 0-914659-23-5

Copyright 1987 by Elvon L. Howe

Printed in the United States of America

To Diana

Contents

Preface

O NCE EVERY now and then a story comes along that refuses to let a man rest until he sees it in print. Once in a fortunate lifetime occurs a friendship so sinewy and instructive as to sustain the survivor years after his preceptor and soul mate has taken leave of this planet. Once and only once in our time has arisen a prophet of such unorthodox credentials whose vision arcs across intervening cacophonous decades of electronic turmoil to prescribe, with simplicity and the force of unassailably demonstrated success, remedies for the most poignant ailments of today's American society.

This book presents such a story about such a prophet, Cal Farley by name. It is the product of a friendship that took instant root in those dimly remembered but acutely envied days just after the close of World War II, when the American West was on a roll and a now long departed lusty humor was abroad in the land.

Two-thirds of this book—the first thirteen chapters, plus elaborations withheld from this first edition—were first offered to a series of New York publishers in 1950 and 1951 under the title *Six Hundred Sons*. Initially planned as an autobiography with Cal Farley as sole narrator, the tale gravitated early into a tripartite dialogue interspersed with scene-setting by the co-author at appropriate intervals.

The results solicit of the reader a bit of indulgence. As befitting the only book ever personally authorized to bear the name of the founding genius of a transcontinentally revered American institution now approaching its fiftieth anniversary, those major portions of this text which were studied, discussed, and ultimately approved by Cal Farley himself have been preserved verbatim as faithfully as possible. Should the reader thus find himself caught in a time-warp occasionally as incidents and comments valid thirty-five years ago are set forth as if in the present, it is our hope that he too will understand and appreciate our maintaining manuscript authenticity as an overriding consideration.

All but one of the vicissitudes which again and again over so many years postponed the completion and publication of this book are sketched briefly in the narrative and need not be synopsized here. The missing reason I as co-author must concede as a literary defeat still unerased—my apparently congenital incapacity to transliterate to the printed page with proper vividness the one-of-a-kind Farley wit and speech patterns. Ever since our first tour of publishers proved unavailing, this manuscript has been stored in Colorado. Periodically over busy decades of my sojourn on the East Coast, it would be pulled from its hiding place as vacation schedules permitted and studied, tinkered with, then shelved once more to await the greater leisure of my own retirement.

Always it has been the Farley speech—rapid, fluent, peppered with wry metaphor, warmly humorous yet impatient, saltily original yet never nudging the severest conversational conventions—my reproduction of the Farley speech, that to this day has proved a stylistic challenge beyond my capability to meet. Try as I might and did, I here acknowledge that oral rendition of the Farley-spoken anecdotes in this book often still do not quite "sound" like Cal Farley.

But I have done the best I could, and must leave to those with greater talent for conveying spoken words through ear and eye to typewriter fingers the task of rendering Farley speech patterns in more meticulous fidelity. To aid those so inclined, I have placed in permanent repository in the Farley collection at the Panhandle-Plains Museum at Canyon, Texas, a twelve- to fourteen-pound bundle of transcripts faithfully typed from the approximately eighty hours of interviews put on stenographic records during the many days and hundreds of hours of my talks with Cal Farley over the three-year period this original manuscript was in preparation.

Future probers of the Farley legend will be well rewarded. To Americans of the "era of the anti-hero" now drawing to its welcome close, I commend this book as an opportunity to revel in the company of one of the most productive and profoundly refreshing personalities of our century: Cal Farley, Citizen.

E. L. Howe

Miami, Florida
April 10, 1987

Two thousand sons

1

The First Wildcat

BY TEXAS STANDARDS or any other, this was a lot of man. Rocking along with the unmistakable stride of a horseman, he swung out of the hot sun and crossed the three rows of Phillips 66 gasoline pumps on the "front porch" of Cal Farley's store. His two hundred thirty pounds, six-three long and an axe-handle wide, shut off a lot of daylight as he paused in the doorway.

Yep.

After six years and one large war, the place was the same. Outside, the yells of the tire jockeys cutting through waves of gasoline vapor and the smell of the flat tires being fixed. Inside, the ranks of bicycles, refrigerators, and washing machines. A table piled high with radios "special" at 30 percent off, this week only. The credit desk near the front. Four clerk-musicians already on the stage Cal Farley had built out into the main showroom back toward the ready-to-wear, tuning up "You Are My Sunshine" for the noon radio show.

Customers in small clots all over the place, joshing away with passers-by in from the sidewalks. Customers with coin-purses, in Levis and cottons, visibly unrich, needing Cal Farley's easiest credit in town but the kind who pay up somehow. The kind of people you see at the wrestling matches and the Tri-State Fair and the football games of the mighty Golden Sandstorm team of Amarillo High School.

Customers who enjoy the things they buy and like to enjoy the people they buy from, many of them hanging around here now only in the hope

1

of being personally insulted on that crazy radio show coming up. Customers of a fellow who liked to see them coming in bunches, let the rich ones go to Neiman-Marcus and welcome. Like Cal had said a hundred times: "Look at 'em. There's nine million of 'em. With them a fellow can do business and have fun at the same time." Always had more damn fun somehow, that Farley did.

Let's see, now.

If things are going as usual, he's outside the door of his office behind the stage there, joshing half a dozen customers, woolling the heads of a couple of kids, and wrapping up a pair of socks all at once. A speed merchant, that Farley, a top-speed merchant whose head and feet had been whirring even before he got himself all tangled in the job of raising several hundred kids out there at Tascosa. And right there back of the stage he stood for sure, razzing the customers, woolling the kids, wrapping up a pair of red-over-green cowboy boots, size three and a half.

"Hi, Mr. Farley."

"Spud! Where you been?"

"A long ways from Amarillo, Texas."

The right hand his visitor extended, Cal Farley noted, had grown to be about the same size as the banjo twanging behind him. The rest of him, behind the hand, called for a slow and careful going over: ninety-dollar boots shined to a brown blaze. An elm-trunk torso lightly carried and exuding hairspring power, a tailored gabardine shirt lying glossy over tremendous shoulders. Jaw and eyes of a man who is liable to get where he aims to go. A face mostly determination, with a little humor in it — but maybe not quite enough, just yet.

"Look what I got here, Mr. Farley."

An interesting little package carried like a sack of sugar under his left elbow came into full view. She was also blonde, curly-haired, two years old — sassy type, smug as a mahout nudging instant lofty obedience from her Stetson-hatted elephant.

"My gosh, Spud, she's wonderful." Cal Farley touched a suddenly reflective forefinger to a tiny snub nose. "Come into the office here and let me shut this door."

Seated and bouncing his girlchild with the astonished clumsiness of a Great Dane, the man called Spud told Cal Farley with schoolboy pride about his new job as foreman and general manager over one hundred thousand Arizona acres. He talked about the bright little missus he had found and married in Brooklyn after he got back from the war, how crazy she was to learn everything at once about the ranch and the outdoors, how she skinned herself up in no end of foolish scrapes, how every sagebrush she saw in the desert was a new wonder and a thrill.

He told how she had popped the whip and made him sit up nights studying away on a string of university correspondence courses she had laid out for him. He talked about their plans for a new house and, eventually, a small cattle spread of their own.

All the news was good news, but as it rolled on in the quiet speech of a man happily on his way, Cal Farley wasn't listening too closely. Vivid in his mind was the savage scene that had taken place almost exactly eleven years before when this same young fellow had paid his first visit to this office. Let Cal Farley tell the story.

✴ Ralph Dykeman had telephoned from the Maverick Club, Amarillo's athletic center for underprivileged boys.

"Cal," he asked me, "are you ready to send some kids out to that new ranch of yours at the Old Tascosa courthouse?"

"We're just opening up the place, Ralph. Alton Weeks and his wife are out there now with the first five boys in tow."

"Good. I've got a wildcat for you. No father. Mother hangs around the beer joints mostly. A smart kid but really rugged."

Within the hour a stringy-haired woman of sharp features, alcoholic breath, and slept-in clothes pushed the boy Spud through the office door. He was a defiant beanpole of thirteen, with bristling hostility and a thicket of hair that had not seen soap or barber shears in six months. This was the boy, Ralph Dykeman had said, who persisted in smoking, cussing, breaking all rules, gouging and kicking other boys unmercifully during Maverick Club games, hooting loudly at all attempts to civilize him.

"You want this no-'count kid?" the woman barked, without preliminaries. "Well, take him! I don't care if I never see him again."

The boy turned and stared at his mother, a strange look of almost fright pushing the cockiness off his face. He had heard her pop off like this many times before, but now she sounded as if she meant every word.

She did.

Then, in a manner I had never heard from a mother before and have not heard since, that woman set about verbally cutting the boy to pieces. He was ignorant, and he wouldn't try to learn or listen to nobody. He was a thievin' little punk. He was a scrub who would eat more'n he was worth. He was headed for reform school sure.

No protest from me could stop that woman, though her tirade was plainly doing to her fatherless boy a thing as brutal as if her dirty fingernails

4

Roy Williams, the "first wildcat" in the original Boys Ranch family, on a return visit to see Maud Thompson, housemother for many years to the earlier boy residents of the Old Tascosa courthouse. Felled by a heart attack at 54, Roy became the first alumnus to be buried at his own request in the ranch cemetery at the foot of Boot Hill.

were tearing at his face. The boy Spud took it standing up and without a word. But his tough-guy swagger was gone, and his whole body sagged. Once I saw him make a quick, involuntary start toward the woman who was his last slipping anchor of normal security in this world. But the blue ice in her eyes told him she wasn't his mother anymore.

I was suddenly angry, as furious as ever I was in my life.

My jaw clamped tight, I stepped between my two visitors and stared down at the woman while she was rasping an announcement that she was leaving for Galveston that same afternoon and that she wasn't gonna buy that boy no ticket. No sense monkeying with him no more. He could just make out by himself, and he'd damn quick find out he'd 'a' better listened to his mother.

I ordered her out of my office and told her she'd find it advisable to BE on that southbound bus within the hour. She stalked out, and neither Spud nor I ever heard from her again.

Complete silence settled on this place for two or three long minutes.

I was in a strange way—a fast-talking tire salesman who couldn't find a word fit to start a conversation with this boy. Ignoring the chair I offered him, Spud stood in a daze in the center of the room. His chin was down, eyes half-closed, dirt-crusted fingers wriggling tensely among the holes in his shirt, the skin of his neck showing yellow-pale from long diet of cigarettes and stolen candy bars, his clothes an alley urchin's tatters of this or any other century—a spectacle still distinct among memories of the two thousand other boys in trouble who over the years would find their way into my office. Our newly opened Boys Ranch had acquired its first real wildcat.

From the start, we seemed to do quite well by the boy, physically. Baths and haircuts spruced him up notably. Good food filled out his scrawniness at the rate of a pound a day. To our surprise, he obeyed the no-smoking, no-swearing, do-your-work rules fairly well, but always with the air of one who obeys only to purchase seclusion. In the din of the dining room of the Old Tascosa courthouse he ate aloof and quiet, never arguing to get his full share of the cookies.

A month later the superintendent remarked, "This boy Spud worries me. He's listless—doesn't seem to care much whether he dies or stays alive." Spud was a challenge.

We tried everything—baseball, basketball, wrestling, gardening, horseback riding, marbles. Nothing excited the slightest flicker of real enthusiasm in this boy. Instead, as his muscles filled out and his new energy had to find an outlet, he fought.

Never since have we had another fistfighter at Boys Ranch to surpass the boy Spud. He fought viciously and without anger, on any or no provocation, seemingly just to register upon any nearby living object his hatred of a world that had abused him. He would as soon kick another boy's dog in the belly, slap a younger lad around and send him squalling, or fly into a much older and larger boy than himself. Once or twice he launched himself in a small tornado of fists and feet upon fully grown men. An older boy named Martin, husky and pugnacious enough to fight Spud to a standoff, did so regularly during their prowlings of the timber down toward the Canadian River, both gladiators returning for meals with hides full of contusions and the burrs we call goatheads.

My arrival from town usually brought an armistice. Several times, the other boys told me, Martin and Spud halted their afternoon slugging match when my automobile came in sight on Boot Hill, scooped creek water on each other to wash off the nose-blood, then returned to the ranchhouse with composed faces and combed hair. That boy Spud—he was as impervious to physical beatings by the older boys as he was to explanations, pleadings, disciplinary chores.

Many hours the superintendent and I racked our brains for a possible key to his scarred heart, spending days and weeks tacking one way and then another. But no exhortation or punishment, no normal boy activities we urged upon him brought a noticeable change in that remote, what-the-hell look in his cold eyes. Finally our strategies were exhausted. With our new ranch barely started, we masterminds were stumped by the one boy we wanted most of all to reach. Nothing to do but wait and hope.

Eventually, in the normal rotation of jobs around the ranch, the superintendent assigned Spud to feed the hogs. A certain huge old sow, he cautioned Spud offhandedly, was due to farrow soon and should be closely watched.

For two days Spud puzzled over what that word meant. Finally he asked the superintendent one of the first voluntary questions he had been known to ask during his stay at the ranch.

"Mr. Weeks, what you mean saying that old sow is going to farrow?"

The superintendent was startled.

"Sorry I didn't explain, Spud," he apologized. "That old sow is due to have a litter of little pigs someday soon—maybe eight, maybe more. I want you to be sure to tell me right away when it happens. You see she's awfully heavy—about seven hundred pounds—and she might roll over on those pigs and kill them."

Deep in that boy's eyes, a distant spark glinted.

"You mean...," he murmured, "she's really gonna have a lot a' little bitty pigs?"

"Sure she is. That's the way we get 'em." Mr. Weeks laughed and consulted his records. "It ought to happen about Thursday."

During the next three days a certain astonished dowager of the pigpens grunted comfortably under a deluge of pampering. Every minute he could spare from his meals and his schoolwork the boy Spud spent in feeding her, brushing her, arranging her cornhusk mattress, tidying up the place. When nothing was left to do, he merely sat on the fence and watched.

Wednesday at supper, much worried, he hesitantly asked permission to stand guard all night over the proceedings. The superintendent sent Spud on to bed, promising to visit the "maternity ward" himself before retiring.

Thursday morning, Spud didn't appear at breakfast. His bunk was empty, still made up from the evening before. With little hesitation, Mr. Weeks took a stroll to the pigpens.

Events were on schedule. At the old sow's great, flabby belly eleven pink pigs were noisily consuming their first breakfast in a new world. Around the curve of her broad back lay the boy Spud, sound asleep on a blanket!

From that day the boy Spud, too, moved in a new, different world, and it was soon clear to us that he would never long desert the ranch life which had given him that world. He came along so fast that within two years we arranged a full-time job for him on one of the largest of the old-style cattle ranches that still exist in the Texas Panhandle. There he became while still very young a trusted top wrangler. And his combative masculinity found new release: two or three of his "vacations" were spent challenging the ruggedest bucking broncos New York's Madison Square Garden rodeo could offer.

Spud came back from World War II with a railroad of paratrooper's ribbons on his chest and the pert little wife from Brooklyn at his side. Now, as he bounced his baby and glowed with anticipation of his future spread in Arizona, I admit I was about to bust with pride in the fact that Boys Ranch's first wildcat had been somehow transformed into a citizen — all man and, for my money, one of America's finest.

Luckily for me, however, the circumstances of his rebirth forever thereafter prevented us from heaping too much credit on ourselves. All our concentrated efforts and ingenuity had not been enough to save this boy. But an aging, fertile, slab-sided old sow had done it!

2

Pictures on the Wall

P RIVATE CITIZEN Cal Farley lived the American life, man and boy, for seventy-one years. He did not waste his time

The pattern of those years was cut from traditional fabric. Farm boyhood, the one-room schoolhouse, a passion for championship athletics, doughboy shot and shell along the Marne, then a precariously tiny business made large and successful through relentless energy: this much of the story is essentially the same for thousands of American businessmen of the first half of this century. Other standard ingredients are here, too — the stunts of salesmanship, the noisy luncheon-club comradeship of other storekeepers, the good works, the speech-making, and by middle age a recognition truly nationwide.

Several distinctive characteristics, however, prevented Cal Farley from becoming just another ho-hum millionaire. Always inclined to quick impatience whenever the challenge of competition had passed and the game was in the bag, he was never a fellow to wait around for the distribution of trophies. He couldn't spare the time to make the "easy half" of his million because, as usual, he was already engrossed in another, bigger game.

Cal Farley's first love had been baseball. More than anything else, even in his later years, he regretted more than any other goal unachieved his failure to become a great second baseman in Yankee Stadium. But the fates were opposed. He wrestled instead, winning the Allied Expeditionary Force (AEF) and Inter-Allied championships in Paris in 1919 as a sergeant

8

of engineers with seven major battles behind him and a bad knee underneath. From the vagabond circuit of the wrestling arenas and the baseball parks, he gathered an unlimited store of congenial anecdotes and the thorough education in showmanship that permitted him, during his rare vacations, to relax in technical shoptalk with friends in the upper echelons of Hollywood showbusiness.

Public speaking was a challenge to Cal Farley, who was at first painfully self-conscious over his lack of schooling and his awkward athlete's tongue. Yet for two midcentury decades at least a hundred audiences a year—ranging from small-town chambers of commerce to the boiled-shirt crowds of the East—found him expert and irresistible in the high-spirited account of his workaday miracles among wayward boys. A chrome-plated radio microphone taunted him: he conquered it, too, to the extent that for fifteen years his customers must have wondered whether he was running the latter-day Texas version of a whittlin' general store or a rapid-fire comedy show.

The operation of a hotly competitive store held his interest for awhile. Athlete Farley, who intended always to have more fun than anybody, was merely making merchandising his postgraduate sport. His community labors and his prankish enthusiasm made him a district governor of Rotary International termed for years thereafter "the most popular man in Texas." Twice in the years after World War II he refused insistent urging that he enter politics—because there was still a job to finish for his boys.

His biggest challenge caught up with Cal Farley because never in his life had he been able to pass by any boy, particularly a dirty-necked ragamuffin, without looking twice and stopping to think. Boys, in fact, had been the one continuous thread through his multifarious existence, an ever-intensifying preoccupation that led his great friend and the famous editor of the *Amarillo Daily Globe*, Gene Howe, to chaff him observantly, "Cal, you could be a sure-enough Texas tycoon if you'd ever spend as much as twenty percent of your time on your business!"

The affairs of their boys finally became so ruthlessly demanding that Cal and Mimi Farley decided not to bother to make the rest of that traditional million. After all, they concluded, there was now enough money for them and their beloved daughter Gene (named for their friend Gene Tunney) to be comfortable, and more. It seemed time to be building something different and permanent. "I'm the selfish type," Cal remarked. "I couldn't see much fun in making a lot more money just to be left in a trust of some sort so that others could enjoy putting it to good use after I am dead."

PICTURES ON THE WALL

In 1947 the business was sold. By then the burgeoning city of Amarillo could and did take inordinate pride in providing for its youngsters a citywide program of youth athletics called Kids, Incorporated, of proportionate size probably never equaled before or since—enrolling in organized summer games three-fifths of all youngsters in the city between the ages of six and fourteen. By then a unique "home in the country" for more than 100 boys had been established—without public solicitation of any kind—at Old Tascosa, and several thousand visitors a year were traveling the narrow automobile trails over Texas's lonely uplands to that ghost town located beside a quicksand ford of the unpredictably captious Canadian River. There, around the stone courthouse on the plat of an ancient cattle town that formerly saw some of the wild West's wildest characters, they could observe a rapidly expanding Boys Ranch whose story had been told already in hundreds of newspapers, nearly all the national magazines, and in one feature-length motion picture.

A personal friend and admirer of the late Father Flanagan, founder of the world-famous Boys Town at Omaha, Nebraska, who came to Amarillo to speak on behalf of the infant Boys Ranch, Cal Farley sought to extend the state of the art in boy salvation one step further. This meant utilizing the distinctive locale and philosophy of the Texas ranch, not only to provide a home for the homeless, but also to reclaim the bright-eyed, precocious, truly dangerous lad who already had trodden far down the path toward big-time crime. Like the professional rodeo rider or horse wrangler who typically sticks to his bone-jolting trade long after his physical and financial interests point elsewhere, Cal Farley discovered his greatest earthly thrill in wrestling with a "real wildcat" of a boy until he had made a good and loyal American citizen out of him.

By the time the Flying Dutchman Wunstop Duzzit emporium at Fourth and Fillmore, Amarillo, had been sold in 1947, the cluttered, picture-strewn office behind the broadcast stage in ready-to-wear had been the scene of hundreds of boy interviews like that of the boy Spud, each tense with its own life-or-death drama. Carefully, Cal Farley would explain to the uncommonly penetrating visitor the pattern and critical purpose of these interviews.

* That boy is suspicious, wary, a lonesome coyote skilled in one thing—survival. He doesn't need me to survive—well, maybe, for a day or a week or two until he gets out of this particular jam. His chin is down, but his eyes are calculating. His frame is so thin and unsubstantial that I wonder our booming Texas wind hasn't whirled him off his feet during the

TWO THOUSAND SONS

hundred-yard walk from the Potter County courthouse to this office.

He smells.

Here is an undernourished young animal some of our Amarillo folks might vaguely remember having glimpsed on the streets. But to most of us he is not really a boy, a human being. We know he is there—he and his kind—but as a sort of immaterial presence, a wraith, a voice that is just another of the many sounds of a city.

That voice is not difficult to identify. It is a peculiarly high-pitched voice, heard during school hours or, late at night, to the accompaniment of foul language and the scamper of feet. It is strained and defensive and savage, like the cry of a wilderness beast hard-pressed to survive.

It is the voice of the alleys.

We would rather not hear that voice. All of us are busy and overwrought already. We have a living to make, our families' problems to conquer, automobiles to buy, taxes to pay, a troubled nation's welfare to worry about, and a lawless world to persuade—if we can—to let us live.

What about the ten percent at the bottom of our social barrel? Haven't many sincere and learned specialists devoted their lives to the problems of these people, and aren't we supporting huge government agencies created for the sole purpose of helping them? Don't we dig down and give money—if not our minds—to private humanitarian agencies every year, to a degree of generosity and social consciousness unparalleled in human history? "The poor we have always with us." What more can a fellow like me be expected to do? Why, under the circumstances of today, should I try?

Now that voice of the alleys speaks from that shuffling, sag-shouldered boy standing very much alone in my office. As dirtyneck kids go, he is just about as unattractive a creature as one could handily find. No tidy housewife would come near him. (Man, how this kid needs a bath!) We shake hands.

"Make yourself at home, son. I'll be through here in a few minutes."

With that I go on shuffling papers, telephoning, reading mail, going through a merchant's motions. Many minutes, perhaps, thus tick by, though the work is far from uppermost in my mind at the moment. This lad is wise and wary, and the busybody adult who seeks to negotiate with him will do very well to spar with him awhile as an experienced boxer feels out his opponent in the first round. This first talk is vitally important. It can make this boy either my genuine friend or a suspicious antagonist at least temporarily beyond my reach. My challenge of the moment in a way is tougher than that of a G-2 interviewer extracting information

PICTURES ON THE WALL

from an important defector: this lad has not yet "defected" from the world of the alleys.

While I'm making a show of working at my desk I know very well he's studying me as intently as I am studying him. He appears in almost every detail the perfect figure of a whipped human pup—until one notices his eyes. Those eyes are not whipped yet. They are furtive and old and smart. Having dissected other well-meaning adults before now, they are full of silent scorn for me. By turns they burn with rebellion like the eyes of a snared raccoon.

Except when I toss out an inconsequential remark, friendly but rather brief, to help him feel more at ease, he refuses to look directly at me. Instead, his gaze eventually strays upward from his shoetops and around among the dozens of framed photographs hung all the way to the ceiling on three walls of this office.

"Where does this mug Farley come off?" he is wondering. "Him and his big office by the stage where they put on radio programs every day—I reckon he's doing all right by Farley. So now I get a big spiel.... Well, why the hell doesn't he get started?"

Spiels he's heard aplenty, that much is certain. All his miserable little life he has been scolded, lectured, patronized, sympathized with, yelled at, and sermonized by adults of all descriptions. First there was his mother, who beseeched him tearfully to be good until she lost all control of him. Then there were overworked school teachers to whom he was another hopeless exasperation, but not for long. An assortment of adults followed, many of them kindly folks who genuinely tried to help this boy—for a little while. But they were all very busy and very, very well fed, and their continual exhortations never made much sense to him.

After that there were the cops, who chased him, warned him, perhaps bought him meals, then finally took him to jail. Finally there was the judge. Bound by laws that were out-of-date before they were written, the judge could do little to stop this boy's pilfering and other minor violations except to be lenient several times, thus merely instructing him to be more clever next time.

Today he could be lenient no longer. A few hours ago this boy had had only one destination, the reform school, until someone wondered aloud whether "Cal Farley might have room for this kid at Boys Ranch."

In some such manner as this the ball has been passed to me. Considering the extent of this boy's trouble with the law, which I have learned already, I wonder whether he is not too far gone to be reclaimed.

By now he is thoroughly impatient. I play the busy businessman to

A smiling Cal Farley and the pictures on the wall which so often stirred the restless curiosity of the raggedly defiant waifs brought to him. "Do you know all those guys, mister?"

a finish, probing gently for gaps in his tough armor, knowing very well that this man-to-man contest must end my way before I can have any real hope of successful dealings with this boy. And the kid, waiting sullenly for the preaching to start, is just as determined not to give way an inch, not to reveal the slightest sign of weakness or tractability.

My real leverage, however, is the fact that no boy can hold the bead of his antagonism on any one target for very long. This boy, like his predecessors, is defeated by his boy-curiosity and the pictures on the wall. The latter are many, hung there for just this purpose. Half a hundred famous athletes of the past thirty years grin down at him in clowning or

PICTURES ON THE WALL

handshaking poses. One photograph in particular catches his eye. It is pure horseplay, showing a burly man with a good-natured face that would be recognized almost anywhere on earth playfully engaged in breaking a little fellow in two.

The boy studies that big fellow, then the little fellow, then looks at me. Increasingly restless, he starts to speak but checks himself. He repeats the examination. At last his curiosity breaks the surface.

"Is Jack Dempsey really a friend of yours, mister?"

"Sure is—known him for twenty-five years. He stops by here once or twice a year—came in to see the boys just last month."

More playacting may be necessary, but the ice is broken. Soon the kid is wandering around the room, looking more closely at other pictures. Some are carefully inscribed: "Cal Farley winning the AEF wrestling championship, Paris, 1919," or "Cal Farley meets his old teammate Gene Tunney at Tunney's training camp the day before the Dempsey-Tunney fight." He studies assorted scribbled greetings from Babe Ruth, Lou Gehrig, Mildred (Babe) Didrikson, and others. Off slides his tough-guy pose like a muddy raincoat, and for a few unguarded minutes he is a boy again, considerably impressed.

"You know all those guys, mister?"

Gradually, he learns about my athletic career and how I tried to be a pro ball player but wasn't good enough for the big leagues.

"Like to play ball, son?"

"Never did, much."

"You've got pretty good shoulders on you. Ever box or wrestle?"

"Sure, I can fight like hell—uh—pretty good, sometimes. I ain't afraid of 'em."

So his story begins. It comes easily so long as the kid feels at ease. His head is up. His suspicion is suspended. Fewer and fewer questions are necessary as he recounts his life and his adventures. Some of this tale is truth; most of it is heroic imagination.

Details of this so-called case history don't matter much. Mostly the pattern is altogether too familiar before he starts. It's a ten-to-one chance, for example, that no father at all is present in whatever dismal shelter he may call home at the moment. His mother probably stays there because mothers, however sorry they may be as human beings, have a way of sticking by their children. But her working hours are too long, or maybe she is drunk too much.

School? That's a joke. In spite of our shiny buildings and stern truancy laws, this boy and thousands upon thousands of his kind across America have abandoned the three *R's* in the third, fourth, or fifth grade. *His* school has been the alley, the sidewalk in front of the poolhall, the shacks along the railroad. His teachers have been larger replicas of himself, older boys qualified by seniority to instruct apprentices in the relentless animal processes of survival.

The details, I repeat, don't matter right now. What counts is the fact that this boy is telling the story himself, of his own free will, to me, a stranger who has managed to gain his confidence.

But another rivet or two must be driven to bind tight a highly personal relationship between this kid and me. The next question jolts him.

"You've been in trouble quite a lot, haven't you?"

Down goes the kid's chin again. His mouth snaps shut, and out comes a defiant lower lip.

"Son, let me tell you something. . . ."

So now, he thinks, comes the sermon after all. With some effort he reconstructs a facsimile of his tough-guy sneer. Inwardly he is calling me every dirty name in the book for leading him on like that. But not for long.

"Let me tell you: I don't know all you've done, but I'll bet a dollar you're not in half the trouble I was in at your age."

The boy's head pops erect in amazement. It is almost as though no grownup ever before had climbed down off his pedestal of respectability long enough to talk to him on his own ground. Especially a regular businessman.

I'm not kidding you," I assure him. "Up in Minnesota I was about the toughest kid in town, in trouble all the time. Why, I don't know exactly why I didn't do something really bad and land in prison before I got straightened out. Guess I just didn't have the nerve."

That sally clinches the first small victory, almost without fail. The astonished kid usually has to sound me out further to be sure that this kind of talk is on the level. Then, with assurance that I am not just another agent of the law he hates, he tells me freely in confidence a fairly true account of his latest misdemeanor. Again it is strictly a man-to-man exchange. Never does he get the slightest impression of a "helping hand" reaching down to him from above. For the moment at least he is just a friend of mine on a common level, genuinely and, I hope, for keeps. That is exactly the way things must be.

"Ever hear of Old Tascosa?" I ask him. "That's a ghost town, seventy-five years old, that sits under a bluff beside the Canadian River about forty miles northwest of here. The big cattle drives of the early days used to stop there to water the longhorns at the fine deep springs. There's a big

PICTURES ON THE WALL

16   stone courthouse — all that's left of the old town. On top of the hill there's
a boothill cemetery where they buried the outlaws and the cowboys who
had what our boys call arthritis of the trigger finger. There were some
wild scrapes at Tascosa in the early days — four men were shot in one
afternoon.

"Well, son, nowadays we have a ranch out there, over a hundred acres
that's for nobody but boys. Besides the courthouse there's a big gymnasium, a schoolhouse, a mess hall, several good barracks to live in, even
a water tower. It's a regular town, with about a hundred and forty boys
living there right now.

"They have a herd of beef cattle to take care of, a string of good riding
ponies, saddles, ropes, irrigated gardens, cows to milk, pigs and chickens
to feed. The boys do just about all the work, and first thing you know
they have made real cowhands out of themselves.

"Out there you can eat a lot of good country food, learn to ride and
rope and play basketball and football and get some real muscles on you.
And nobody will be yelling at you. All you have to do is to see that your
regular work is done, go to school, obey the rules, and I mean really punch
cattle. Like the idea?"

The boy asks a few questions. "No, the ranch has no high fences or
guards or anything to keep a fellow from walking away if he decides to·
do that. Yes, you can keep your pet dog if you have one. Sure, you can
come back to town on some Saturdays to a picture show — if you do your
work and behave yourself. But you've got to do your work and carry
your share."

Does this boy want to go to Boys Ranch? Certainly.

"A sucker setup!" he is secretly thinking. "I'll even go to school for a
while — it's better than reform school. If they think they can pat a hard-
cussin', tobacco-smokin' guy like me on the head and keep me lined up
with a lotta nice little jerks they got holes in their heads, that's all. But
sure, I'll grab it. No reform school for me."

He is ready to leave for the ranch this minute. There's animation in him
now. The whole appearance of this forlorn little chunk of human drift-
wood has changed. Whatever prospect of ranch life has excited his fancy
most — the chance to ride horseback, play football, or maybe even study
the piano — it is enough to transform the pitiful little old man of a short
while ago into a boy with a face alive as a boy's face should be. It is a
triumphant moment to discover a few enthusiasms and aspirations this
boy has salvaged from his dingy existence, because of all things we seek
these are the most important. When a boy's dreams are dead, so is the boy.

I am under no delusions, however. This boy has plenty of mental reservations — particularly since he was already far on the road to real crime before he came to us. No miracle has taken place yet, to transform a wild young animal, free as a coyote and responsible to no one but himself, into a well-disciplined, socially adjusted boy.

Not by a West Texas mile.

"The secret," Cal Farley would explain patiently, time after time, to one puzzled questioner after another after another, "is the *mix*.

"Any reform school I ever knew of is geared for, and run by, the lawbreakers with seniority — the boys who have applied themselves to their trade of burglary, or marijuana pushing, or whatever, long and diligently enough to have tales to tell, exploits to embroider, expertise to pass on to the wide-eyed neophytes who come under their tutelage every time the gates open to a new consignment of lads from the juvenile courts. It's an intensive school these older experts run, and newcomers gain acceptance perhaps by telling awe-inspiring tales of imaginary felonies of their own or, more likely, by listening with rapt attention to their instructors. A reform school is one of the most efficient factories ever contrived for the manufacture of criminals, and particularly for maturing trivial offenders into cold-eyed thugs.

"At Boys Ranch we accept the challenge of the wildcats like the boy Spud, for example. Most homes for boys do not and cannot do that because they're not equipped or prepared for these youngsters. We are. But if we ever accepted too many of this type of boy at one time, we'd be in the same shape as the reform school and would need just as many bars and fences. The secret is the mix. We create an isolated, distinct little society in which it is the *good* kids who make the mold the others must conform to, good kids drawn from the hundreds of thousands whose principal problem is simply lack of a home, who haven't yet had time before they come to us to get into real trouble. They are the ones who set and pretty much enforce the rules of our ranch society, who make the wild ones realize they're better off to obey those rules than to defy them. We take a lot of punishment from the wildcats before they turn around, but with the good kids applying their own kind of day-and-night pressure, almost always they go our way."

The good kids are the mold; the wildcats, the challenge. But always there are a few swivel-tongued promoters who fit into neither of those categories and in whose redemption Cal Farley, no mean shakes as a noise-making promotional businessman himself, took always perhaps his most unalloyed delight. On a visit to Denver in the same year his Wunstop Duzzit was sold, Farley was introduced to a yellow-haired, blue-eyed prodigy to whom Cal said thereafter he would be willing to hand down whatever trophies he himself might have earned as a high-octane promoter.

Rudy, at the time he was turned over to Cal by Denver's justly famed juvenile judge at that time, Philip B. Gilliam, was only nine years old. But in those precocious years he had learned secrets of turning turmoil to his own ends that had left imprints on law-enforcement records the police and probation officers of that metropolis of half a million would scratch their disbelieving skulls over for months and years to come. Cal Farley told his tale this way:

✱ At loose ends downtown one day, the lad had decided to drive to California. He installed himself in the first automobile in which he could find an ignition key, pressed the starter button, and discovered that he could tiptoe the accelerator by sitting on the very forward edge of the seat. He edged the machine into the midtown tangle and successfully negotiated the traffic lights without interception all the way to the western edge of the city. Peering through the upper part of the steering wheel, he threaded the heavy truck traffic of a major transcontinental highway.

Thirty miles and two sizable summits were behind him before an uncomfortable odor began to cause him some concern. Black smoke was pouring from under the hood when he drove into a filling station at Idaho Springs. With suitable dignity, the boy waited in the driver's seat until the attendant arrived.

"I believe," he said with an eye as level as his insignificant stature would permit, "I'd check the oil, please."

The attendant stared gap-mouthed at his pint-sized customer, raised the hood, peered through the smoke to stare back at the boy again, then informed him gravely that the engine was burned out. The automobile had been driven the entire thirty miles in second gear.

Rudy was distressed. How on earth, he asked the station attendant soberly, could he manage to get this machine fixed quickly so as to hurry on to the bedside of his dying mother, many miles farther over the Continental Divide? Warming to his story with great, sad-eyed earnestness, he lavished many sorrowful symptoms on the astonished attendant, who restrained his generous impulses with difficulty, called the sheriff, and both automobile and boy were towed back to the city.

After that Rudy had become a steady patron of the juvenile court. Not too many visits later, an Air Force sergeant visited Judge Gilliam's chambers, wearing on his face the military version of the gas station attendant's baffled respect.

"First thing we know," he related, "comes this soprano voice through the loudspeaker in the control tower out at the field. 'One-six-oh-eight calling Lowry tower,' the voice is saying. 'One-six-oh-eight calling Lowry tower. Request takeoff instructions. Request takeoff instructions.' Just like the pilots call it in, almost. Well, 1608 is a B-29 parked down near the end of the line, and for all the tower man knows, it *is* ready to go.

"But it doesn't seem quite right to him. He doesn't know any soprano pilots. So we go down to the plane and find this towhead kid up in the cockpit all by himself with headphones on, talking away with the tower and pushing buttons right and left. We try to take him out, and he turns those big eyes on us, telling us to never mind, everything's all right, he's got permission to fly this thing, and besides he knows exactly what he's doing. He's read all about how to do it. It's all right there — in a comic book!"

In many previous long talks with this lad, Judge Gilliam had exhausted his personal salesmanship in the cause of law and order. Rudy had been always respectful, sympathetic, resilient — and always immediately forgetful of everything the judge said. This time the judge called in a psychiatrist. An hour later the interview was over, and an outmaneuvered mental-health specialist was back in the judge's chambers.

"Confidentially, Judge," he said, "now *I* need a psychiatrist! This boy analyzed himself before I had a chance to get started. He told me how his trouble must have started from a broken home and how it didn't seem that his mother had used quite the right approach to him. He told me how much he admires you, Judge, and how he wishes he could be as you want him to be. He told me that every time he goes out and does something wrong he thinks about you and he is very, very sorry. 'I just don't really know what gets into me, Doctor!' says he. And so on and on. *He* conducted the interview, I didn't."

Helplessly, the judge gave Rudy another warning and set him loose on the city once more. To Rudy it was an utterly fascinating city and all of it his for the talking. He went home only when it occurred to him to do so; there were far too many other adults besides his middle-aged foster parents who were ready and willing to part with money and services in response to the inspired persuasion of an engaging boy.

I'll spare you [Cal continues] the telling of many of Rudy's other escapades. Without access to the court records, you'd find awfully hard to believe, for example, a briefer but noisier adventure in motoring that

PICTURES ON THE WALL

occurred when Rudy wandered into a parking lot, chose a Cadillac to his taste, and dehorned seven — *seven* — other automobiles in a row en route to the street. For years to come, however, even Denver's overmatched officers of the law will be slapping their thighs over one of Rudy's adventures at the Brown Palace, the swankiest hotel in town, after escaping from Juvenile Hall for the umpteenth time.

Exploring as usual, Rudy's wayward feet led him into the quiet lobby rather late in the evening. Finding no excitement, he took an elevator and set about to prowl the upper floors. At the eighth, he opened an unlocked door and found himself in the beautifully appointed apartment of one of the hotel's permanent guests. It was unoccupied, the tenant having paused for considerable refreshment at the Ship's Tavern downstairs.

Rudy reveled in the luxury. He tried all the softest chairs, sampled the food in the refrigerator, viewed the city lights from the window — and, when he became sleepy, simply peeled off his clothes and went to bed. He was far gone in blissful slumber when the legal occupant of that bed returned to the apartment. The sight of a strange, tangled head of hair on his pillow did not help his already foggy condition. Nor did the conversation that ensued — for Rudy was fully able to assume instant control of any situation even when awakened from a sound sleep.

"Don't you remember?" he asked the irritated gentleman, righteously. "Don't you remember?"

And Rudy proceeded to improvise a spirited conversation that had *not* taken place at all between the two earlier in the evening. He reminded his host how they had met and talked at some length, how he had declared his liking for Rudy, had learned that the boy had no place to sleep, and had directed him to his apartment, telling him to make himself at home until he returned.

The man could remember no such conversation and, besides, was wanting very much to occupy that bed himself. He denied everything. Rudy insisted, fervently supplying more details. Finally, the tenant telephoned for the house detective. The controversy continued. Ultimately came the city police — but by then not only Rudy's eloquence but his tears also — were in full flood. The police listened, listened some more — then took the hapless "persecutor" of a forlorn little boy to the station, where he spent an increasingly sober hour and a half convincing the authorities that he had never seen Rudy before in his life!

I met Rudy not long thereafter in Judge Gilliam's chambers [Cal's account goes on] as a candidate for Boys Ranch. The meeting I remember as having been a bit unusual. The boy was instantly likable and shook hands quite properly. But his attention was not at all upon either the judge or myself. While the usual grown-up palaver went on, Rudy's electric eyes skittered all around the room, taking note of everything in it and everything visible through the windows—until the judge mentioned that Rudy, unless he changed his ways, was bound to go to reform school soon. That remark was enough to bring the boy's mind back to us for a moment.

"Not very soon, Judge," he corrected Phil Gilliam politely. "Remember? I'm only nine."

He proceeded quite patiently to instruct the senior judge of the Juvenile Court of the City and County of Denver in the provisions of the law, particularly the one which states that no boy could be legally committed to a Colorado correctional institution until he had passed his tenth birthday. He was quite correct.

"See what I mean?" the judge asked me in a whisper.

During his first three months at Boys Ranch, Rudy and his racing imagination ran away six times. But always he was brought back and "turned loose with the herd" again. Once he waded the Canadian River and took shelter with a road-building crew. To those men he insisted, although the ranch was barely two miles away, that he had "never heard of Boys Ranch. What kind of place is that?" Once he had hidden in the back of the ranch supply truck and escaped to Amarillo, where he walked only a few blocks to find the unusual circumstance that could be turned to his own purposes.

An automobile turning the corner opposite to where Rudy was exploring brushed past a woman pedestrian, who fell or was knocked to her knees on the pavement. Instantly Rudy was across the street, helping the woman to her feet, brushing her clothing, denouncing the carelessness of drivers in general, insisting that she should bring suit against the offending motorist. In no time at all he had installed himself firmly in the affections of the woman, who was sufficiently uninjured to go on about her errands.

This time, however, his memory of Boys Ranch at Tascosa was quite active. In answer to the woman's inquiries he spun a lurid tale of how boys at the ranch were being beaten, were made to do heavy work, and were not being given enough to eat. That was why, he said, regretfully, he had been forced to run away. As a longtime Amarillo resident who had contributed to Boys Ranch in accordance with her modest means, the good-hearted woman was skeptical. But after two days during which Rudy stayed at her home and embroidered the same story, she and her husband finally came to my office to find out whether any of these goings-on might

22 be true. We merely produced a portion of Rudy's slightly unbelievable previous record in hoodwinking his elders, and Rudy's temporary foster parents had a new topic to chuckle over at breakfast for many days to come. Rudy went back to the ranch.

After several more runaways and several more returns, we thought for a while that by patience and one timely maneuver by Superintendent Dory Funk, we had succeeded in diverting Rudy from the brilliant law-breaking career that once almost certainly had lain in front of him. That hope was strong after Superintendent Funk talked long and earnestly to Rudy, explaining that at Boys Ranch it was up to the boys themselves, and especially the leaders among the boys, to make the ranch run right.

He made Rudy a full-fledged lieutenant — and suddenly Rudy became the busiest secret operative and custodian of Boys Ranch principles the place had seen in years. For a while he was even permitted to guide visitors around the ranch, but not for long: we couldn't expose our guests to such a shakedown artist as Rudy. In his "administrative" duties, however, he was quite skillful, and his memory was amazing. One day he told me without a hitch the number of every key on Dory Funk's key ring and what lock each key fit. Only a few days after that, Dory, very busy at some task, sent Rudy with the key ring on a three-minute errand to bring something from his office. Moments thereafter the superintendent's car was seen crossing the then brand-new highway bridge across the Canadian River. Somewhere alongside the unpaved "back road" to Amarillo, Rudy lost control, rolled, and "totaled" Dory's car in a pasture, hitchhiked into Amarillo, and presented me, with a shamed face, the ignition keys he had carefully removed.

Seventeen times Rudy ran away from Tascosa, and sixteen times we brought him back. On his final departure he came under federal jurisdiction by driving a gravel truck to Oklahoma and starting a jitney service, charging town kids a quarter for a ride to a swimming hole three miles out of town. We had lost him.

Remorseful letters came from Rudy after that from four federal reformatories in succession. I answered him each time: the boy still has an endless fascination for me . . . .

In his later years, though wearing like a soft flannel shirt a respect and affection for his achievements that was truly worldwide, Cal Farley himself never dignified with the term "formula" what he called his "few notions" about the nature of the boy mechanism and the forces that make it go. This restraint reflected the fact that none of his boy projects sprang from a preconceived plan but developed instead from an amiable trial-and-error process.

He was worried. Time and again he mused to his friends in almost the same terms: "We've let our schools and our press get away from us. This country's in trouble." Always his most profound sympathy went out to the thoughtful parent faced with the mountainous task of bringing up a physically and emotionally healthy boy in an age of television, rock music, marijuana, and high-powered sports cars. Asked to reflect on the elements drained from the American family to the detriment of its young, so as to begin a search for workable substitutes, he was wont to reply:

"Well, the only boy whose shoes I have laced regularly was a restless, ornery, work-dodging country boy named Cal Farley. He was, over all, the toughest 'boy problem' I ever had to face."

Let's pursue that story as nearly as possible in Cal Farley's own terms, beginning on a not-too-prosperous farm in the Pilot Grove community near the village of Elmore in southern Minnesota.

PICTURES ON THE WALL

3

I Stole a Loaf of Bread

"The farm is an almost lyrical expression of what life means, a standard-bearer of cultural qualities linked to our historical past. Included are senses of freedom and open space, of steadfastness, of work in its most basic sense. The image has a theological flavor . . . it is a spiritual scene . . . a dream-chance many of us hold . . . a place we have fixed in our mind's eye and where, if all else fails, we can go. . . . Americans instinctively want to preserve the spiritual values of farming and the heritage of the soil . . . *we need new initiatives that will recognize farming's importance as an integral part of America's past and future."*

Justin Isherwood, who farms 1,100 acres near Plover,
Wisconsin, as quoted in the Wall Street Journal,
January 23, 1985.

RURAL AMERICA at the turn of the present century — how remote it seems, how quaint and quiet and flavorful and spacious and enviable.

It was in 1901 that a new family moved onto a 160-acre farm in the Pilot Grove District about eight miles west of the tiny village of Elmore in southern Minnesota. In due course the farmer, a tall, dour Englishman, made his appearance at the lonely Pilot Grove crossroads and let it be known that his name was Frank Farley and that he had just arrived with his family from Saxton, Iowa. Little more information could the chatty little grocer obtain; the new farmer Farley plainly was not a sociable man.

Neighbors were soon captivated, however, by the tiny, cheerful, neighborly Mrs. Farley. A mere wisp by comparison with the predominantly Scandinavian wives of the district, the quick and tireless Jenny Farley never weighed more than 105 pounds in her life. But she kept house with buzz-saw energy, and folks soon learned that she had more time than anyone else to carry comfort to the sick or an extra pie to the church social. At these affairs, when the ladies were not discussing Mr. Frederickson's beautiful new wife from the old country, like as not they were chattering about Jenny Farley, wondering how she managed with that somber husband of hers. Frank, they decided accurately, was just a natural-born silent, restless man who didn't like to farm anyhow.

Several years younger than his wife, Frank Farley was wedded in fact to the frontier and its solitary sports of hunting and fishing. His six children he regarded mainly for their value in helping with the farm chores and the fieldwork he himself cordially disliked. Companionship was not in him: he hunted and fished alone. ("I was pretty much a lost little kid, wanting my father's attention more than anything else in this world," Cal Farley was to say in later years. "But I never got it, except when I made him angry.")

As the family grew and Jenny became more insistent that Frank brace up to his responsibilities as a father and breadwinner, their acrimony only deepened. (Cal was to recall having been plunged for weeks into confusion and despair as a nine-year-old after lying awake one night overhearing a particularly bitter parental dispute in progress downstairs in the kitchen.) Eventually the parents would separate for keeps, but only after yet another move to another farm—farther north and farther west—Jenny having imparted to her brood a full quota of her own energy and unconquerable generosity.

Joe was the eldest boy—a stubby, chunky lad who even then was a size smaller than his strapping brother Dave. At fourteen, Joe ran away from home, not to return for four years; Dave followed suit some years later. Margaret and Mary were the two older girls, and finally there were the six-year-old twins, Zaida and Cal. Word-miser Frank Farley had named the latter boy Kossuth. But that was impossible, of course, and the lad was barely in school before he changed Kossuth permanently to Cal—not even the complete name Calvin—just Cal. And from the first this youngest son was a package of orneriness, a schemer with a fast, conniving tongue and little taste for work—in the eyes of a farming community a boy not much account.

In the sharply divided Farley household, Cal was hardly more than a toddler when he learned to play Jenny against Frank scandalously to his own advantage. Throughout his youth his cordial dislike for the monotony and drudgery of frontier farming never wavered; every thought he had was centered on escaping to a life remote from Pilot Grove in both miles and modern conveniences. Even in maturity he seldom spoke of his boyhood years, except to acknowledge to worried parents that the young Cal Farley had had in that farm heritage a natural discipline that was and is the best sandpaper ever known for smoothing down rebellious youth into responsible adulthood.

That discipline was inescapable on a farm. It was the discipline of rolling out of a feather tick before daylight on a winter morning and planting bare, warm feet on a floor that might have snow on it from an open window. It was pitching hay and hauling manure and the dictatorship of cows that had to be milked at home of an evening whether or not the baseball game in town would last until dark. It was walking a cultivator in the corn field, up and back, up and drearily back all day with nothing more esthetically satisfying in front of you than the south end of a pair of north-bound mules.

It was working your head off in the harvest field to keep your turn among the bundle-wagon drivers, putting on as big and as neat a load as the next man and flinging the bundles with just as wild a haste onto the canvas belt of the threshing machine.

✱ I just plain didn't like that discipline [Cal Farley would never hesitate to admit]. Hardly was I knee-high to my dad when I first made up my mind to get away from that farm—from any and all farms—as soon as I could put on long pants and leave. But meanwhile I was there, doing what work I couldn't fast-talk my way out of, and it did things for me in turn which only a few years later kept me from going sour in a big way.

When I indulged in some flagrant piece of cussedness, that control was there in other forms as well. Much to the disgust of my older brothers and sisters who had been forced into a much more stringent routine, I was quite expert in cajoling, storming, or merely disappearing to get my own way. But there always arrived a day when I went too far. In the hands of my father a six-foot willow wand had magical capabilities. He applied it with much muscle, unpleasant persistence and no noticeable concern for my psychic sensitivities. His control was perfect. He never missed a shot.

In unusually daring moments, we boys might crawl into the basement windows of Mr. Frederickson's store to snitch candy and other consumer goods which could be well disposed of and the evidence buried long before we reached home. Many years later I learned that this fine old gentleman, for whom I often plucked chickens or helped unload dray wagons in return for a few cookies, was well aware of our pilferage and had accurately guessed who the conspirators were. He had merely inserted the cost into the appropriate grocery bills—normally paid by all families twice a year—in such a manner as to keep us out of trouble. But it never faintly occurred to us to steal anything so durable as a pair of pants, for example, because all of us well knew we would quickly come by the walloping of our lives.

My boyhood at Pilot Grove is the root of my most unshakable opinion on the subject of child-raising in general. This is, briefly, that there is nothing more beneficial or necessary to the welfare of any growing child than a healthy fear of getting into trouble. Every other animal on this earth, I notice, has that fear, learned either by instinct or by painful experience. With humans this caution must be generated by the parents, especially the father. King David seemed to give priority to this kind of thinking when he said, in Psalm 1, "The fear of the Lord is the beginning of knowledge," and then when he repeated himself not too many psalms further on: "The fear of the Lord is the beginning of wisdom."

"Don't fence them in" has been the theme song of many of our "progressive" educators and family-affairs experts recently. But the fact remains that no person can make a child into a permanent human misfit more rapidly than the parent who fails to recognize the simple, fundamental restraints that hold all society together and then to cement that consciousness into the child's mind.

Now, don't get me wrong. No one insists more loudly than I do that any normal young person has the right to pick and choose his own path in life, whether that way is the parents' first choice or not. One of our early arrivals at Boys Ranch was the headstrong son of two brilliant but erratic members of a university faculty who had stubbornly demanded that their son follow a course of study he did not like. He had gone completely out of their control—stealing and finally threatening to kill his mother. At Tascosa he became the official ranch piano player. He worked endlessly with the youngsters on many special programs and caused us no trouble whatsoever.

Forcing a youngster down a narrow, preselected roadway is not what I'm talking about. I am talking about putting up a sturdy moral fence at the boundaries of decency, within which fence the child is free to roam and mature at will. Today I look at the young fellow who arrives in my office already deeply in trouble with the law and most often see in him the boy who stole the pair of pants I didn't steal and then went home to his parents — if he had any — who didn't ask too many questions. The difference between him and me is not that at his age I was a different kind of kid, one who never could have stolen those pants. The difference is that I was deathly scared of my dad's six-foot magic wand!

Necessity forced us to manufacture our own amusement. Fortunately, that section of Minnesota was true "boy country." All winter we lived on ice skates — racing, traveling to school, and playing a game very properly called shinny. That game consisted of two teams of boys in any number, one tin can, and an assortment of water-elm clubs to be swung with abandon at the can and at any unfortunate legs that might intrude upon the process of knocking that can through a goal.

Slack winter work on the farm left ample time for the absorbing commercial enterprise of trapping. Busily during the cold months we braved frostbite and missed meals to make the rounds of creeks and lakes while visions of great wealth — particularized by careful study of the Sears, Roebuck catalog — chased themselves around in our heads. The lakes were many and the results impressive: during each of several winters we three brothers came up with a total of eleven hundred to fifteen hundred muskrat skins worth seven to fifteen cents each, as well as a few prized weasel, mink, and fox. In the woods we dug out one hundred to three hundred hibernating skunks whose pelts brought good money and whose tallow was freely utilized as a chest rub for colds. (I'm sure that every neighbor within eight miles was well aware that the Farley brothers were in the lucrative but odorous skunk business!)

All of us were good skaters, living on blades as we did for several hours each winter day. The schoolhouse, for example, could have been reached by a three-quarter-mile walk across the fields, but such straightforwardness had no appeal for us. We much preferred to walk a full mile to the creek, then skate a mile and a half down its twisting channel in a nip-and-tuck race with the bell.

What went on after we got there never took on much real significance. Our three Rs, my father often commented, consisted of running, rassling, and recess. I liked history and geography fairly well, but arithmetic, and especially grammar, were beyond me. When I habitually tell my fellow Rotarians that I spent the six happiest years of my life in the third grade staring out the window and dreaming how I would some day pitch a no-hit game in the World Series, that statement is uncomfortably near the truth.

Teachers I quickly recognized as a form of authority not often to be swayed by the methods I was using at home. They had to be won over by hard work (unthinkable), or be brought to tow by an outrageous application of what I thought was charm—a policy that must have been fairly successful at that. "Book-learning" was still not my line when I finally managed to get through the eighth grade and thus end my formal schooling for good—but I'm sure that no more expert apple polisher ever attended that little school.

There was good reason for the fact that I never cared for hunting and fishing, both of which offered fine rewards in that district. These were my solitary father's sports and often he took me along with him. But my principal recollection of these outings is that of tedious hours spent guarding the team and wagon or cleaning the fish he caught. Usually I arrived home toward midnight, tired, hungry, and highly indignant because I had missed a baseball game in the village.

My love for baseball was a passion that lasted many years and died hard. The first bat I owned was a Ty Cobb model so precious that several teammates who innocently picked it up to use it found themselves suddenly with a fight on their hands. When I was barely in my teens, a Pilot Grove baseball team was organized, complete with mail-order uniforms and a ball that, with a new homemade cover sewed on now and then, could last all season.

The soul-rocking intoxication of public applause first struck me full force in a game I had organized against a team from a small town twelve miles away. A goodly crowd was on hand when we three Farley brothers and the rest of the Pilot Grovers arrived in our farm wagons.

Our opponents proceeded to hammer my brother Joe's pitches all over the pasture. We were far behind when I came in from shortstop, as a sawed-off fourteen-year-old "manager" and asked Joe to let me pitch. He did, and I managed to get the rally stopped. Even though we lost the same, the crowd was greatly intrigued by the sight of a shrimp infielder ordering full-grown men around. I was adopted as the hero of the moment and floated back to the farm on pink clouds, caring not a hoot for my older brothers' displeasure. From that day forward I knew that athletics was the life for me: no crowd cheered when I turned a team of mules around at the end of a corn row.

Baseball, to my great sorrow, had to stop when cold weather came. But wrestling could continue through the long winters. For months each year the warm hay mow in the Farley barn resounded with the grunts and protests of mortal combat. Even in harvest, when the great old steam

I STOLE A LOAF OF BREAD

engine pulling the thresher broke down or the fifty-foot belt between the two came unlaced, the waiting bundle wagons quickly shed their drivers, and assorted impromptu scuffles tore up the stubble.

It was almost always my painful fate to be the youngest and smallest contestant in these fracases. Anyone who looked closely could discover me in the very center of these proceedings, and invariably on the bottom. I learned to wrestle by the most educational route—from the bottom up. All year long my head was regularly rammed into the hay or the dirt by my older brothers. As a humiliating winter routine our muscular Swede neighbor across the road shoved my skull into a snowbank and held it there until I had had enough.

All three of us Farley boys were athletically inclined, fairly muscular, and much practiced. In the natural course of events we began to appear in town against visiting champions from neighboring villages. We were usually fairly successful. (More of that thrilling applause.) Because I practiced more incessantly I soon learned to handle my oldest brother, Joe, who was about my size. At last came the day when I first managed to flip that big bruiser Dave, too—and the great Frank Gotch himself was no more a champion than I was in my own estimation at that moment.

Those matches in town had an ever increasing fascination. They were held in the town hall above a grocery store, where a patch of canvas was tacked down over a little sawdust on the floor. There were no ropes or timekeepers; a man simply wrestled until he ran out of air. Considerable intercity betting tended to drive him to greater efforts; he knew that his neighbors didn't exactly like to lose their money.

One night during a match featuring Brother Dave, one of these neighbors strode to the mat and allowed, much to my surprise, that "Dave's hundred-forty-pound brother, Cal" (I was only sixteen then), would tackle any man in the house. A fully grown man who outweighed me by fifty pounds took off his shirt and began tossing me around. He took me on a tour of the rafters via the skylights, occasionally bouncing my knob on the mat as we passed by just to ascertain how much bounce the shrimp had left in him. (My mother had often told me that travel is educational, and I learned from that trip to pick my opponents more carefully thereafter.) The house was packed, and the crowd roared, naturally, for the kid underdog. I could do nothing damaging to this big gent, but at the same time I was on very familiar territory underneath his weight. He could do everything he wished with me except turn me on my back and pin me. After fifteen minutes of vain effort, he simply rose and stalked off the canvas. Still more applause. I was rapidly being lost forever to the corn-husking fraternity and to honest agriculture in general.

The most triumphant moment of my youthful career occurred on the day I walked down the street and saw my name actually printed on a hand-bill advertising a forthcoming wrestling match. The greatest letdown followed promptly: my opponent pinned back my ears with neatness and dispatch. I retired from formal sports competition for three full months before the lure of that applause brought me back.

Growing local prominence on the wrestling mat and the baseball diamond didn't help me much, however, in my other relations with adults. I was so bashful that during one Christmas program at school I simply could not get out of my throat the words of a well-memorized, four-line poem I was supposed to recite. Even with the teacher's help and a second try, the words wouldn't come. I sat down in a corner, and my shame and mortification lasted for weeks. I was sure that the whole neighborhood thought me abnormal. Even after I was a fully grown and a successful athlete, I remained an outlandishly green, terribly self-conscious country kid.

The restiveness of adolescence finally drove me away from home. By now my father had moved the family to a smaller farm near Hewitt, Minnesota. He was now older and less active. Brother Joe, who had run off to Canada to remain unheard from for four years, had come back to run the farm.

This meant that I sloughed off almost all home restraints and farming duties to chase the countryside at my own wild will. I now sported a motorcycle, which expanded my field of operations and enabled me to make a dashing arrival at various girls' doorsteps. My always loyal little mother, to whom nothing unfortunate ever happened but that "it could be a lot worse, son," looked upon my doings with an increasingly worried face.

A big factor in my growing reputation as the "worthless Farley boy" was my stubborn determination to make my living from athletics — baseball in summer and wrestling in winter. To the folks of that time and place, professional sports had not yet acquired their present status as a lucrative and fairly honorable occupation. Only tramps and no-goods knocked about the country in such scantily paid endeavors.

That made me a tramp, too, did it? All right, I might as well be one. I took to the freight trains.

Two of these highly educational railroad tours, the first and the last, are perhaps worth mentioning. Once a footloose cousin of mine came by from Iowa, bound for the sawmills in northern Minnesota, where his father had once spent a winter. The two of us were two hundred miles from home and without a cent in our pockets when we arrived, only to find that in the passage of so many years the sawmill had disappeared and all the available timber as well.

Soon we were achingly hungry, timidly pacing up and down the streets of the little town of Detroit Lakes, entirely too ashamed and fearful to approach any grownup with the story of our plight. Standing long in front of the enticing windows of a bakery, we knew we could much more easily find the courage to steal that food than to ask for it. And the longer we stared at that food, the more our stomachs demanded that we do exactly that. Toward evening we strolled into a little store after first making sure that the grocer was well occupied with other customers. My cousin stood as a screen while I picked up a loaf of bread and walked out.

A freight train whistled in just as my desperate accomplice joined me on the sidewalk. The depot was only a few blocks distant, but that walk seemed endless. We did manage to walk slowly with a certain guilty nonchalance, but that loaf of bread felt as conspicuous under my arm as a gold bar stamped "U.S. Mint." Every adult face we looked up at seemed suspicious if not faintly appalled. Instinctively we sidled closer together as we walked, fully expecting the whole village of Detroit Lakes to burst into a howling chase behind us.

Finally past the last of the store buildings, we lit out in a terrified run. Man, how we did run! I'm convinced that not even the whole Jesse James gang itself, taking its departure after robbing the bank at nearby Northfield many years before, surpassed the speed of our getaway. Pellmell we fell upon that fortuitous freight train, mauling the bread in the process, and put miles of fearful glances behind us before devouring that loaf.

Three friendly hoboes who were our fellow passengers informed us that the freight was heading not for Fargo, North Dakota, from where we hoped to be able to reach home quickly, but for Winnipeg, in the opposite direction. All of us stopped off at the next town, the hoboes because one place was as good as another and we in order to reverse our course. Branching out into the village, our experienced companions returned with the makings of a mulligan stew which was set to simmering in a gallon tin on a bonfire beside the tracks. We boys were asked to provide the bread, but our shattered nerves were simply not up to it. We shrank back, ready to deny ourselves a share of that heavenly stew rather than go through *that* again. Chuckling, one of the bums arose and came back in a few minutes with a loaf of bread, carefully explaining that he had bought it.

All the way back to Fargo, other hoboes enlightened us in their carefree way of life. At a hock shop there we parted with our last negotiable asset, my cousin's cheap, battered blue suit, in exchange for a pair of overalls and two impressive dollars. Thus fortified, we made it safely home.

On another occasion I ran away from home to inflict my presence for several months on Brother Joe, who by now was getting himself established as a homesteader at Fort Berthold, North Dakota, on the last Indian reservation Uncle Sam had opened for settlement.

Here occurred my last and most disastrous Halloween escapade. While a party was in progress at a neighbor's house, two of us ne'er-do-wells cast speculative eyes upon his privy out back, a structure of unusual architectural attractiveness that seemed to invite the time-honored treatment. This we proposed to execute by means of a lariat dallied tightly between the saddle-horns of two loping ponies. Silently mounted and ready, we bore down on the objective, whooping and spurring like a whole tribe of blood-mad Sioux Indians. The taut rope whanged against the outhouse, which gave way not an inch.

But my saddle-girth did!

Brother Joe's homestead was much too lonely a place for me. I set out for home again. A trainload of North Dakota's potatoes was leaving Berthold for Minneapolis. I helped with the loading upon assurance that I could ride along in one of the refrigerator cars and stoke the stove put there to keep the cargo from freezing. This was to have been an easy ride home. Unfortunately, there was no getting out of one of those cars until someone opened the doors from the outside. Unfortunately also, the railroader who was to have opened my car at Fargo neglected to do so, with the result that I stayed in that car with potatoes all the way to Minneapolis. That meant raw potatoes for breakfast, baked potatoes for dinner, more potatoes and nothing else for three full days and nights. Even when my imprisonment ended I was faced with a penniless pilgrimage of two hundred miles or more back north on the same route I had come. This time, however, I was not so proud as I had been at Detroit Lakes. I poured out my story to a railroad man who bought me a meal and gave me a dollar. After that I rode the freights no more.

For two years I managed to do fairly well playing baseball on a team sponsored by Walter Hill, the playboy son of railroad tycoon James J. Hill, who had been banished to a magnificently appointed farm in the very northwest corner of Minnesota. Here I was finally in my element and having a great time.

Baseball was not a living, though. I found myself a daytime job in a little bank owned by Edward (Ted) Florance in Humboldt. The town itself had an official population of eighty-five persons, but I'm sure the count must have been made on a Saturday night when a lot of the nearby farm folks were in town. Having time on my hands during the fall (the days that far north are so long that our summer baseball games usually began at 6:30 P.M.), I undertook to organize a football team among the little fellows eleven to fourteen years old.

What with skull sessions before the blackboard in the schoolhouse, we managed to develop a fairly classy little bunch of ballplayers. Our team was never beaten and had only one touchdown scored against it in those two seasons. I can well remember the great day when one of our youngest, only eleven, astonished everyone by placing a perfect dropkick between the uprights from thirty-two yards out. This was the son of the town drunkard, a kid who had been in trouble with every businessman in town, a kid who never got a nickel of his own at home because all the nickels had to go for another drink for papa, a kid who thereupon had started pilfering the candy and ice cream the other boys had.

In any community where all families are acquainted there is a high fence of respectability which causes every youngster to be prejudged according to the faults or virtues or economic status of his parents. This was a boy who lived outside that fence. He had been quite hard to handle when he first attempted to play football—fighting, protesting, running away from instruction. But I noticed that my hold on him increased in exactly the same ratio as his skill increased and the game got into his blood. Before long he began to listen to my suggestions as to his conduct both on and off the field, because he wanted very much to stay on the team. His football triumphs, the first of his life, were apparently all the break he needed. This boy was in no more trouble in that town after that. He went on to finish high school and married well; when I last heard of him, he was thriving on a Minnesota farm.

For preliminary bouts at my wrestling matches in those days I was training a few youngsters and taking them along on my trips. Ted Florance's big automobile again furnished the transportation, and I am still grateful for the confidence of those parents in permitting me to keep their youngsters away from home sometimes for as long as two or three days.

But suddenly the United States declared war against the Kaiser, and most of us athletes left the mat and baseball diamond in a footrace for the army recruiting offices.

Stationed for several months in Washington, D.C., my outfit found time growing heavy on its hands. Since we were not provided with traveling movie stars in those benighted days, we had to shift for our own entertainment. Promptly I was entangled again in half-nelsons and headlocks in a series of self-promoted wrestling bouts which contributed little to my mastery of the military "sciences." Entertainment, and very little of that, proved to be the only pay I received for the culminating match in that series, a bout with Joe Turner, the national middleweight champion. I lost the match. Then it developed that the promoter had creditors who immediately cabbaged every cent of the proceeds as the promoter left town.

Soon we were overseas.

Strangely, as the years have passed, I frequently wondered if that eleven-year-old son of Humboldt's town drunkard hasn't had a greater influence on my life than I had on his. In his case, without thinking much about it then or even realizing it until much later, I had come upon a simple system which has been rubbed into action like an Aladdin's lamp literally hundreds of time since, with astonishingly uniform results. Here, I think, and in these other random recollections of my own youth, is the whole skeletal framework of the system which has gained worldwide attention at our Boys Ranch.

At Boys Ranch we mince no sociology in applying the first fundamental—that of basic control. The fact that this control is supplied as much as possible by the boys themselves matters not a bit: a serious infraction of the rules by any boy gets him hours of hard extra work. (Supervisors usually, as a matter of fact, have to soften rather than increase the severity of punishments advocated by the boy's peers.)

Control, however, is only the beginning. That powerful inborn craving for the approval of one's fellows—the "applause principle"—is utilized in every manner we can contrive.

Third comes the body- and soul-building potential to be found in athletics. No lever is quite so potent in prying a boy's personality out of its shell as physical competition before spectators. I can be pardoned, I hope, if every shabby little underdog I see today who has been stuck behind the eight ball since the day he was born reminds me of the fact that my athletics, more than anything else, drew me out of a more or less comparable situation.

Athletics of course is not the only tool for this purpose; often we must try others. But essentially we merely try hard to find what a boy really wants and likes to do, whether that is playing halfback or singing soprano, then get him out in front where others can applaud him a bit. When we accomplish that, the boy will cause no more serious trouble. He'll ride his new-found hobby horse from that day forward.

A strange little drama that brought one lad to Boys Ranch illustrates this point vividly. This boy, one of seven children of a man then serving a fifty-year penitentiary sentence, had been struggling along earnestly and rather well in his schoolwork until he had been shifted to a new junior high school. There he promptly began to steal small items and to write filthy notes to girls.

One of the latter was the daughter of prominent parents who indignantly demanded that the boy be disposed of. The school principal conferred with the county judge, who was shortly to run for reelection and therefore was acutely conscious of the influence of the girl's parents. The boy was brought into court and summarily told without a formal hearing (as the law of that state permitted) that he would be sent to reform school for a year. He was warned further that if he ever came back to that town, even to see his mother, he would be sent back to reform school.

One of the boy's former teachers heard of the matter. She told an energetic young minister. Angrily the minister confronted both the school superintendent and the county judge, threatening to cause a major stir unless this injustice was corrected. I was persuaded to accept this boy at Boys Ranch, not because a move to the ranch would have been necessary to salvage this essentially good boy, but in order to save important faces all around.

The cause of this boy's deterioration had been quite plain, as had been pointed out by the teacher who championed him. In his former school the boy had acquired much skill and fame as a caller of school square dances. With that status to maintain he had been tractable and hardworking and, in spite of his shabby clothes, had been "the most popular boy in his class." In the new school he was suddenly just another nobody in tacky clothes who didn't get to call the square dances because no one took any interest in, or knew of, his talent. He did not want to be a nobody, and so had set about to distinguish himself in other channels. His stay at Tascosa was short and successful.

The final and overreaching ingredient of our system is a pinch—just a mere yeast cake—of unsentimental understanding. I doubt whether the sincerest and most highly educated guardian alive—unless he himself has been young and broke and hungry without a family shelter to go to—can fully appreciate just how fragile a barrier a plate-glass window becomes in the eyes of a hungry or resentful boy outside it.

That is why I have never yet found it in my heart to condemn any boy who started life without the training I had or, more exactly, to condemn any boy at all. Whether a juvenile wrongdoer in front of me has committed his depredations because he was hungry or simply because he has attempted to take blind revenge against a situation that makes him and keeps him a lost-dog individual, it is always a good thing for me to stop and remember the frightful piece of banditry I once perpetrated in the village of Detroit Lakes, Minnesota.

I STOLE A LOAF OF BREAD

4

Shellholes and Toeholds

I T IS COMMONLY accepted as fact in certain upstanding quarters that the American Third Division won the First World War. If they had consulted with survivors of that mighty band—particularly those of the Sixth Regiment of Engineers— our historians might not have been able to ignore the fact as they seem to have done so far.

The latter was a rather small unit of 1,500 men or so, one hundred percent volunteer troops from every state in the nation. Besides a morale that carried through seven major battles and twenty postwar years of high-spirited annual reunions, the Sixth had in its possession Rocky, the invincible mule, a beast so shrapnel-perforated that the muleskinners had to cover both his front legs when they set about on state occasions to clip his wound-chevrons onto him. In the ranks of its Company C of the Sixth Engineers the regiment also had, quite incidentally, a corporal (later a first-class sergeant) named Cal Farley. This doughfoot carried a rifle when he was not attempting to build bridges and suchlike but was chiefly known about the regiment for his energy in promoting athletics of all kinds.

Both before and after the outfit was transferred overseas early in 1918, he managed to bring about baseball and football games, boxing and wrestling matches, by busily inciting rivalry between various units and coaxing various officers to carry the necessary equipment along in their duffel bags. Then he participated vigorously in all events with indifferent success except in wrestling, where his luck was phenomenal. In later years he was prone to stick out his chest a bit and take some credit on himself for the part these many athletic contests contributed toward the regiment's unsurpassed and much-needed morale. The captain and commanding officer of Company C in those days, when he retired years later as a brigadier general after World War II, published a tribute to Sergeant Farley as follows: "The influence of Sergeant Farley's incessant energy in promoting and staging continuous sports events in the Sixth Regiment was responsible more than any other one factor for giving that unit the finest and most inspiring spirit I have ever seen in thirty-one years of army command."

✱ All this extracurricular activity of mine was not so much patriotic concern for the Armed Forces welfare, I readily admit, as it was that same primary craving for recognition and applause I had felt in the arena above the grocery store back home. The result, however, was an unbroken series of athletic events which began with a match against a sailor on the France-bound U.S.S. *George Washington* and ended at the Inter-Allied Games in Paris in 1919. Through that period I managed to come through unscathed in the wrestling department, winning a hundred and thirty-two consecutive falls.

One of my first matches on foreign soil occurred when a party of sixty of us were helping build a hospital at Neuchâteau for the Twenty-sixth Division, soon to be the first American division to go to the front lines. In their ranks was a man who had recently won the New England welterweight amateur championship, and thus a match was inevitable. The paltry numbers in our party and the fact that we hadn't been paid in weeks were acutely embarrassing to my supporters in the face of a whole division of thirty-thousand partisans basking in the paymaster's favor and clamoring for the privilege of betting on their champ. From somewhere our boys borrowed two thousand seven hundred francs, as I remember, mostly from the officers of the opposite camp. When I won the first fall, the young Irishman refused to come back for the second, actually sitting down in his corner and weeping real tears. He'd been wrestling all his life, he said, but had never lost before. Remembering some of my own earlier dumpings, I knew very well how he was feeling.

But the English were spinning back in disorder before the Kaiser's great push for the English Channel that spring of 1918. We Americans arrived on the Somme with the unhappy chore of trying to help stop him. It was at the canalside village of Villers-Bretonlux (where later an Australian national cemetery was appropriately located) that our first attack came.

SHELLHOLES AND TOEHOLDS

The breakthrough on our left was so severe that the German infantry was following the English in trucks. But here, fortunately for us, were the marvelous Aussies. I was lying beside a huge Aussie sergeant who was silently fondling a brand-new Lewis machine gun and giving me a quick education in the art of war.

"Wait," he kept saying as we saw the German charge forging across there in the trees. It was cavalry, being used ahead of the foot soldiers because of our supposedly disorganized condition. If this Aussie sergeant had been of a mind to run, I was prepared to teach him more of the technique of alternating the dogs away from the enemy than he would have dreamed possible. But this sergeant, who had seen plenty of the war, was not disorganized.

"Wait," he always told me when I prepared to pop away at long range from the railroad bridge that was our so-called line, "fire when the hosses come close; then we let 'em go on through for the boys behind. We'll work on that infantry."

Uh-huh. My stomach was as tight as if I had swallowed a French seventy-five. The charge came, and I was completely terrified. If I fired at all, I'm sure I fired into the air. Crisscrossing my mind were strange, wild flashes of farm boy sympathy for those wounded, confused, screaming horses. The Aussie calmly selected targets and mowed them down, wasting hardly any more bullets than I did with my rifle. When it was over, we were still in the same position. The charge, somehow, had been stopped. We had stayed because the Aussies had stayed.

From then on our fighting was almost continuous, with not over a few consecutive days away from the front at any one time from March until the Armistice. Worst, by far, we all agreed, was the helpless terror of being pinned tight and shelled by heavy artillery in a position which had to be maintained. That happened too often. Five years later I was finally getting rid of my stomach ulcers.

Many commentators of that half-forgotten war have remarked upon the instant comradeship that sprang up between Aussies and Yanks almost anywhere they met. Those sentiments draw a hearty second from me. I recall that, after that first afternoon of quick and bitter struggle which left hundreds of our men killed, the rest of us had finally recovered enough equilibrium to realize that we were hungry. That night, while raiding wine cellars and gardens for anything edible, we came upon a gang of these same Aussies in a tiny cafe. They were having a high old masculine time, skipping about in women's abandoned clothes, hammering the piano, and

Americans departed quickly from the scene.

It was near Château-Thierry that we acquired Rocky. The line had been stationary in that sector where a German drive had been stopped two months before, but all possible American troops were transferred from the Somme in anticipation of the attack which soon proved to be the Germans' last big push of the war. We were ready on July 4, but the enemy chose Bastille Day, the French national holiday, July 14, instead. The shelling was terrific. The worst slaughter in our company occurred when a projectile made a direct hit on a French grain binder in a little wheat field we were occupying. Steel from the shell and the shattered harvester cut down twenty or more men.

As my generation well remembers, the drive was stopped at the Marne River after about five murderous days. The Third Division held at the river, though the French were pushed back six or seven kilometers and the famous Thirty-eighth ("Rock of the Marne") Regiment was cut off. Then Marshal Foch threw in every available man to try to nip off the German wedge.

It was early in this battle that I skirted closest both to sudden death and to formal military honors, missing both by about the same margin. At the little town of Mezy, twelve kilometers downriver from Château-Thierry, we were dug in between the ties of a railroad, firing at Germans struggling across the river in boats. Our artillery could have been more accurate than it was, since for two and a half days numbers of German troops managed to cross successfully into the little grain field that separated us. Having calmed down considerably since our initiation at the Somme, we managed to cut them down and hold the railroad grade, but it was an incessant day-and-night battle.

When most of the Germans had finally retreated across the river, pinning us with a few machine-gun emplacements, a tall, straight-shooting Alabaman named Frank White pointed out the most obnoxious of the latter and said, "Let's get it." As we crawled up under cover we could see two unsuspecting Germans — one tinkering with a dismounted machine gun, the other sitting with rifle across his lap.

Each of us selected a man as a target, and White called to them in German to come out with their hands up. The rifleman fired quickly twice but missed, and by that time White had creased his skull, knocking off his helmet with a well-aimed slug. Both surrendered. Then came the problem of getting them back to our lines. It was nearly dark then, with not only the enemy but our own men firing at everything that moved. But we crawled with the two captives through a narrow ditch that led us back to the railroad bridge. Taking the two Germans from there back to the main lines, we picked up a bicycle with one of our dead runners beside it. Since White outranked me, he rode in state until a stray bullet tore off the collar of my uniform, scraping the back of my neck and wrecking the hind wheel of the vehicle.

We were sent on to headquarters to be decorated for this insignificant little sortie, but the proper officer had not returned to his billet by the time our services were called for back in the lines. We never got the decorations.

Then came the big Allied offensive. Assigned to build a bridge for artillery across the four-hundred-foot-wide Marne, we were progressing fairly well when our first real air attack caught us completely by surprise. It was an absurd little thing compared with the massive air blows these battlegrounds saw twenty-five years later, but were quite serious to us. We had plenty of captured German machine guns—much better than ours—set up for protection, and the advancing artillery had already begun to collect on the riverbank.

No one paid much attention to eight planes which came down the river at low level. The little aerial bombs started to drop, and our defenders took to a wheat field to outrun the fragments. A certain Sergeant Farley and companions, caught in the middle of the river, were bending the oars double in a tiny rowboat trying to get ashore and do likewise. Two horses and two men were killed, but there were no hits on the bridge—and I'm sure that not a shot was fired from those fine machine guns.

The German barrage became the most devastatingly precise of our entire war—and we had to go through it. Shelling alone accounted, I think, for some six hundred casualties among our regiment's fifteen hundred men. With complete command of the air, the Germans knew our positions almost before we got to them, and they could hit.

They specialized on kitchens. One tremendous direct hit on ours—while my unit luckily was a full five miles away—killed twenty-six men, the little fox terrier I had adopted at the Somme, and all our thirty mules except one. Fortunately, his tie rope was also severed, and he shambled to the top of a hill, thus escaping the gas that quickly came rolling in. He survived with more than a hundred holes in his hide.

We promptly christened him "Rock of the Marne." He became a pet who followed us all the way into Germany and back, a trophy of great and philosophical distinction. He never pulled another cartload of rations — carrying inside him such a quantity of metal that the boys insisted that they could hear him clank as he walked. For weeks we dug shrapnel out of him.

Even here the instinct for athletics was irrepressible. We played some thirteen baseball games at the front, chiefly against the Aussies. I recall one reasonably quiet afternoon while, as a few of our own airplanes were merrily knocking down German observation "sausages," our company was intent on trying to win a ball game in full view of enemy lines. Though the game ended without casualties, some of our high-ranking officers regarded our activities as an overgenerous gesture. The Germans, said they, were watching the ball game through field glasses. Thereafter we played behind a screen of trees, though we could see no reason why the Krauts should not sit in on the conflict.

Moving into the Argonne our regiment inherited a new spit-and-polish colonel, a stranger to combat. His debut was hilarious. We stood in bedraggled ranks while he made his initial speech, a carefully phrased pep talk. Near his oratorical climax came the familiar high whine of a German shell. Plainly, by the sound of it, the shell was going far overhead, so we stood fast in ranks. To a man. But not the inexperienced colonel.

In a soaring swan dive he splashed to the bottom of a convenient shellhole. Coming up at last from the waist-deep water, with slime dripping from his nose, only to see every one of his men still rooted and choking at iron-bellied attention, he scowled a moment, then roared: "Well, go ahead and laugh, you godforsaken sons of bitches!"

Thus the high repute of Colonel Edwin L. Daley was instantly established among the men of his command. Nor did he ever lose our regard. This excellent colonel spent the rest of the war ordering me to get my hands out of my pockets — betting on and supporting my wrestling bouts, roasting me royally for my unmilitary appearance, and conniving with me later to bypass an unsympathetic general in getting a football team started. It was this same Colonel Daley who was called in when the French failed to complete the construction of the stadium for the Inter-Allied Games held in Paris the next year. As the events opened the rapidly poured concrete was still dangerously "green," and all the brass in the world was in those stands: Marshal Foch, General Pershing, President Poincaré of France, King Albert of Belgium, and others. So Colonel Daley took station underneath the structure, declaring that if it collapsed he would go down with it.

There was one more costly battle — our seventh and the most utterly miserable of all. Then the Armistice: a stupefying moment which caught

After promoting and winning many challenge wrestling matches on the Western Front, sometimes watched through binoculars by the Germans, Cal Farley came home with the A.E.F. welterweight and Inter-Allied Games middleweight championships.

us lonely and unprepared. Of the two hundred fifty original troops in our company, exactly twenty-seven of us were left whole and very lucky, who had not been laid out in a cemetery or at one time or another in a hospital.

But the surge into Germany — with our mule — went on. So did the wrestling bouts, though now another kind of financial misfortune dogged our efforts. Now we had plenty of money to bet, but the information that I had not yet lost a bout made opposition money increasingly hard to come by. One night in Germany I was scheduled to twist limbs briefly for ten minutes with a good Indian wrestler from another division. According to custom, Sergeant Harry Peterson of my own company took position at the YMCA to receive bets. The flattering turnout looked like a lineup for chow. Our colonel had a bet with the other outfit's chaplain. Just before the bout, Harry climbed into the middle of the ring and dumped out two two-bushel breadsacks full of franc notes. But even with all that we coaxed only about fifty thousand francs (about thirty-five hundred dollars) out of a very large opposition crowd. My share, as usual, was twenty percent, plus five hundred francs which Colonel Daley presented me from the chaplain's hard-earned means.

Increasingly restless, like all the rest, I had a hand in what was said to be the first American football game ever played in Germany. This was simply a matter of calling down various insults upon a group of deluxe travelers (they were riding in trucks) assigned to go ahead of us to the Rhine town of Bachrach to test drinking water. Neither they nor we, until that moment, were aware of any football talent among ourselves, but one of our officers had faithfully carried a ball along in one of his Buell carts. Two impromptu teams appeared, and an energetic if highly unscientific battle was joined.

No such contest could take place in Germany — nor anywhere else in the world — without its full quota of youngster spectators. Silently they gathered from all over the city in such numbers that, before the game was well along, a young army of them were staring open-mouthed from the sidelines. I'm sure that the sight of a pack of grown men virtually murdering each other to capture a flying oval-shaped ball accounted for only a part of their astonishment. Our yells and insults, our horseplay and violence — and the fact that we usually remained quite friendly afterward — were obviously beyond their comprehension.

Here for the first time since our arrival overseas we found idle time on our hands — and there around us was the circle of quiet, unplayful youngsters' faces. Many of them were dirty and in tatters; many were

SHELLHOLES AND TOEHOLDS

plainly hungry; but all of them, it seemed to me, were most of all questioning. What made these strange Americans tick?

Drawing them into a ball game was a process which called for the utmost in diplomacy and patience. Armed with the necessary equipment, one or two of us would retire some distance from the barracks and begin idly tossing the ball around. Not many minutes would pass before the first, bolder ones would slip out from the streets and backyards to watch. Always they kept a more-than-respectful distance. Any direct attention on our part, such as an invitational motion to toss the ball to one of them, would send them shrinking away. A more successful method was to miss a catch and let the ball roll to their feet, then wait casually until some child found the courage to pick up the ball and toss it back.

Gradually more and more could be drawn into a miscellaneous ball-tossing. Then, unless some unfortunate occurrence reminded them that these were the Americans they were supposed to hate, a ball game of sorts eventually took place. After the first game there was always a great oversupply of players.

Many times this process was repeated during our several months in Germany. Scores of German youngsters made their first pathetically uncoordinated attempts to hit a baseball or tackle a runner. And many times since, in a strange town on one of my speaking trips to New Mexico or Georgia or California, I have enlivened an idle Sunday afternoon in the same way. Leaving the hotel carrying a softball and a bat in plain sight and strolling toward the nearest vacant lot, then merely tossing the ball to the first kid who comes out in the street to look, will do the trick. Within thirty minutes an uproarious game always results. I'm confident the same system would work from Alaska to Capetown.

Back in Paris the Yanks were departing homeward by shiploads every day, but we members of the athletic "beef trust" (where my hundred-forty-seven-pound weight was hardly impressive) had been elected to remain three months in training for the AEF eliminations to be followed by the postwar khaki Olympics, the Inter-Allied Games.

In spite of the solemn public embraces of General Pershing and Marshal Foch, it was no secret that we uncouth Yanks were not too welcome in Paris now that the war was over. On that fact hangs a pair of brief tales, perhaps unrecorded hitherto, about a certain studious, highly intelligent and methodical fellow in our midst who later came into considerable fame.

Gene Tunney was his name, and frequently, in those days, he was patiently trying his hand at baseball with notably small success. He was sitting with a dozen of us one fine afternoon among twenty thousand

In later years, Gene Tunney, Cal's A.E.F. teammate in the Inter-Allied Games, was a frequent visitor and Boys Ranch supporter.

spectators while a fifteen-man team of American rugby converts were engaged in titanic struggle with the French team in Columbus Stadium. With the contest at high pitch and the score tied at two, a French player bit off half a Californian's ear. (At that time I had not yet lived in Texas and had not yet learned to cheer any mayhem that might befall a Californian!)

One of the latter's loyal teammates was a Lieutenant Fish—later a famous surgeon—who let fly a foot at the Frenchman's face, accomplishing the conclusive disrepair of three of his front teeth and touching off a great unhappiness all around. Soon officials, benchwarmers, and spectators were milling all over the field in one of the more glorious riots since the fall of the Bastille.

Before long, far up in the stands, our distasteful Yankee uniforms were spotted. There was no escape. Gene Tunney, seated farther forward with several other boxers, was our outpost of defense against a whole "Brooklyn homecoming" of incensed civilians approaching from below. Precise and methodical to the last, Tunney was carefully spotting each victim in turn, studying him, then popping him unconscious back into the mob. Between swings, without turning his cool eye away from the next victim, he was delivering himself of an indignant Shakespearean lecture on the inconsiderate folly of certain wrestlers who stood behind, permitting others to shelter them against hopeless odds.

We were not exactly averse to a scramble, but there was something so excruciatingly funny about Tunney's meticulous exhibition that we were

SHELLHOLES AND TOEHOLDS

still howling helplessly in laughter when some Frenchie laid me cold on the concrete with a clout behind the ear. Johnny Fundy, a bantamweight boxer from Pittsburgh, swears that when I came to I was yelling, "Hit me again, I can still hear Tunney!" (This has been lying cold in the stadium ever since!) The papers next morning carried a front-page picture of General Pershing shaking hands with Premier Clemenceau, with a statement that these two men represented the "warm feeling" between the two countries.

What Tunney did in the light-heavyweight boxing division of the games, Charley Paddock in the sprints, and various other Americans in other events became page-one sports history back in the States. As the eliminations progressed, however, all was not well with me in the middle-weight wrestling. I was matched in the finals against Walter O'Connor of Carroll, Iowa, a member of the First Army team headed by the World Champion Heavyweight Earl Caddock, later an Omaha oilman. But a bad infection in my knee suddenly laid me low. For ten days the medics kept me in bed, fuming and discouraged as the prize I wanted about all else in my young life glimmered away toward a forfeit.

The scheduled day of the match arrived and passed, but O'Connor refused to accept the title by default. He wanted to wrestle for it, and he himself urged Colonel David Goodrich, director of the games and later my lifelong friend and business patron, to reschedule the match one week later when Tunney and the boxers were to settle their differences. That was done, and every day some of my teammates came to the hospital to wrestle with me on the bed in an attempt to keep my arms and shoulders in some sort of condition. The core was removed from my knee, and I made it, rather wobbly, into the ring.

Fortunately for me, the bout was a short one — with thirty minutes the limit, the winner to be named by decision if no actual falls developed. Most special holds were barred in a semi-amateur arrangement. For twenty-nine and one-half minutes I managed somehow to stay more frequently over than under O'Connor. Then, in true Hollywood style, O'Connor desperately turned just right for me to hook him with a head scissors and an armlock, and I managed to pin him, with some fifteen seconds left in the match.

When it was over I let go in a hurry — that head scissors was hurting my bad knee far more than it was hurting O'Connor. For the first time in my life I passed completely out. In the dressing room I woke up to discover that O'Connor and Caddock themselves had carried me from the ring and were doing a first-class job of nursing.

"Well," said O'Connor, "I wanted to win, but at least I get a chance to go home now. You'll have to stay awhile. Sure you're all right now?"

That kind of sportsmanship, in any contestant's memory scrapbook, is about as heartwarming as one could ever receive. Walter O'Connor is a barber in Ocean Park, California, these days, and we are still fast friends. For my money, then and now, he rates with the finest sportsmen who ever stepped onto the mat.

SHELLHOLES AND TOEHOLDS

5

The Cauliflower Trail

ONE LONELY wind-blown newsboy stood on the wharf when the battleship *Minnesota* slogged into Newport News, Virginia, at the end of the final voyage of her career. By then it was the fall of 1919, long after the war heroes were home and trying not to talk about war in their former civilian haunts. But that newsboy, against a cluttered backdrop of homeland, was welcoming committee enough for the 300 returning doughboys on board, most of them athletes and including Cal Farley.

Back again in drowsy little Humboldt, Minnesota, the restlessness which occurs to every American fighting man returning from overseas after any war caught up with Cal Farley quickly. Things were entirely too quiet. He stayed scarcely long enough to say a few hellos and play a baseball game or two, then set himself adrift. His military wrestling championship opened a route that offered more pay than he had ever seen before.

Soon came an opportunity to join a troupe that had come into existence to tour a ready-made circuit of homecoming celebrations then being staged by American Legion posts and by other organizations all through the Northwest. In it when he joined were the boxers Mike and Tommy Gibbons and an assortment of entertainers. (After Tommy fought Jack Dempsey at Shelby, Montana, on July 4, 1923, both he and the older Mike—in Cal's opinion one of the best middleweight fighters who ever lived—became quite noted and well-to-do citizens. Tommy was many times reelected county sheriff at St. Paul.)

So began almost a full year of meandering a colorful sawdust trail of carnivals, county fairs, and celebrations, with occasional major contests thrown in. Cal Farley was wrestling all comers, small or large, with a purse of ten dollars for any man who could stay with him twenty minutes as he vividly describes.

✳ First stop, I well remember, was the big Missouri Valley Slope Fair at Mandan, North Dakota. And one of the first opponents to present himself was a magnificent hundred-ninety-pound Indian. He was so ferocious-looking that if he had appeared with a tomahawk and in war-paint I would have called for the cavalry personally. His mate, wearing an elaborate necklace of buffalo teeth, and with what appeared to be a majority of the squaws from a large nearby reservation, waited at ringside to witness the struggle.

While the Indian and I waited in our corners, a handsome girl who traveled with our troupe as group-singing leader took the center of the ring to lead the audience in a number of wartime ballads. The crowd was a bit apathetic, but not so the mighty red man. Raptly he gazed upon this blonde angel, following her every motion with slavish eyes. In the length of a song or two he had reached a great decision. As she finished the singing he leaned out of the ring, lifted the buffalo-tooth necklace from his squaw's neck, and placed it solemnly on the shoulders of the white girl.

What followed was one bout of my career for which I had enough sense not to come out of my corner at all. Every squaw in America, by the sound of things, joined in an instant uproar. The scorned spouse took command. She sprang into the ring, ripped the necklace from the hapless white girl's neck, and set to kicking the girl's shins and clouting her errant buck merrily about his ears, all at once.

The ghost of General Custer, who had had a little Indian trouble himself, was the only one I can think of who could have enjoyed any more than I did watching those squaws pick the pin feathers out of Sitting Bull Junior as he raced frantically around the ring looking for an exit to the Dakota Bad Lands.

My own tussle with the Indian proceeded after the scattered molars were swept out of the ring. The sight of the deflated but still murderous-looking Indian threshing about the mat with the little fellow must have had its

THE CAULIFLOWER TRAIL

own hilarious aspects, for the crowd kept him there two whole days to wrestle me. He and his squaw then followed me to the next town and the next, until I could predict in advance which way his eyeballs would turn when I put on an armlock. Never again, however, did they turn and pause purposefully on the figure of the blonde singer.

Grappling miscellaneously about the country that winter and later, I made full use of whatever social advantages there were in being an erstwhile banker. Thus, instead of lying around roominghouses on the scene of a coming engagement, or killing time in endless talk with whomever happened to be around, I customarily moseyed about the streets of a town making shoptalk in the banks, decrying business conditions with the storekeepers, and looking up a large assortment of wartime acquaintances. Often as not I found myself a guest in one of the latter's homes, accepting such hospitality with alacrity because roominghouses and unfamiliar streets were rapidly becoming wearisome.

The wrestling circuit I found to be considerably changed in comparison with that of prewar days, a transition almost as great as the one to follow later when wrestling, during the thirties, was converted into the slam-bang melees of recent years. Before the sojourn in Europe, ours had been a precarious but amiable calling that required the practice of many talents totally unrelated to the ring, in a sequence approximately as follows:

Upon arrival in a strange town—always a small town—advance publicity was the first imperative. That meant a call upon the daily village "newspaper," namely the barbershop, where one would casually let it be known that a man was present who might be persuaded to test toeholds against the village champ. Use of the barbershop news bureau was a necessity; the weekly press farther down the street had its place but was no good for quick action.

Next, with as much elaborate attention-getting as possible, it was routine to begin "workouts" behind or near the same barbershop. Prospective customers for a paid bout had to be convinced in advance. Even genuine championships won elsewhere meant nothing because few had heard of them and probably wouldn't believe such reports anyway. To establish a challenger's rating it was essential to work over most of the local Samsons. But once the town's biggest butcher was informally dumped (after a satisfactorily long struggle, of course), with two dozen or more kids and a few grown-ups watching, radio itself couldn't have spread the news more rapidly over the environs. Some sort of bout quickly developed.

Then it was time for the visiting entrepreneur to coax a drayman, by means of a pair of free tickets, into the loan of a tarpaulin and a basket or two of sawdust. The same inducement usually brought from the printer a few window cards advertising the engagement. The town hall, a loft in some store building fortunate enough to have a second floor, was hired for three dollars. The sawdust was spread, the canvas tacked over it, the tickets sold at thirty-five cents ringside and two-bits general, and the battle was on. No women were present.

The invariable betting hurt the sport considerably and was largely responsible for its disrepute among the respectable — two-bit losers are always too busy shouting "double-cross!" to admit their own errors in judgment.

His bout over and won, the roving grappler pocketed three to eight dollars net profits from the gate and then quite often found it necessary to take a temporary job in order to fortify his advance into the next county. So it was — before the war.

Now the game was much more prosperous. In the day-by-day writhings of the carnivals and celebrations I was making more money than ever before, working in a special scheduled bout whenever I could do so. But now I was a specialist, a wrestler and nothing more. The promotion of the show, always half the fun, was in other hands. I missed the cracker-barrel companionship of crossroads stores and the stimulation of moving into a fresh town, sniffing out its potentialities and then packing the town hall for my wrestling bout.

Money-making special bouts with big-name wrestlers helped the bank account further. With my AEF and Inter-Allied championships, medals, and so forth, I was considered a "good card" almost anywhere, and I made the best I could of the situation. But where present-day matmen tangle two or three times a week for purses that we would have considered fantastic, we were lucky to get two of these "money bouts" in a month.

Even though my professional slate remained unscrawled by defeat, all was not buffalo-tooth comedy along the cauliflower trail. There were bruises and pulled muscles aplenty, now and then a broken bone when a body-slam or an aerial journey into the ringside seats caught a man in no position to soften the jolt with his hands or feet.

There was a daily diet of painful creaks in the cranium about the fourteenth time an opponent clamped on a headlock — a nuisance hold which never wins a match but which can be downright uncomfortable and contributes greatly to the stockpile of base medal in a wrestler's tin ears.

With every twisted joint there came the continuous fear of incurable bone bruises or other crippling injuries which terminate many a wrestler's career.

THE CAULIFLOWER TRAIL

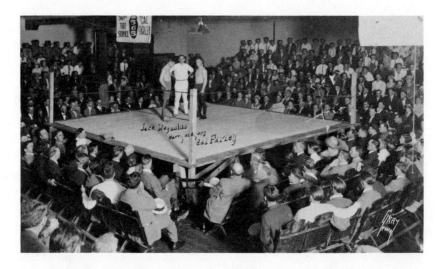

This vintage photo, annotated by Cal, shows the ring and part of the crowd of 8,000 at the rematch in Amarillo of businessman Cal Farley and world champion Jack Reynolds, which retired Cal from professional sports. Two losses to Reynolds were the climax of a period of spirited vagabondage during which wrestling and semi-pro baseball earned Cal a living.

Then as now there came eventually a great weariness with the futility of after-hours bull sessions in rented rooms. As with most men who have too much time on their hands, professional wrestlers too often talk themselves into deafening oracles on every topic from plowing corn to metaphysics — the only major fault I personally can find with wrestlers in general — a gang of very decent good fellows whom the public never could and never will understand.

It seems long since time that someone put in a good word for the men who practice the up-to-date version of the ancient wrestling craft. Crowds love mayhem and are mentally lazy. They still pay more money, for example, to watch a Babe Ruth slam baseballs over the fence than to get the thrills gained from close study of brilliant baseball finesse. For the same reason, wrestling today has become a slugging waterfront brawl that scarcely resembles the carefully controlled scientific sport we knew. As a result, the fans are many times more numerous and ecstatic and the pay is high.

The new accent on showmanship, it is true, brought all manner of freaks and "monsters" into the ring who did the genuine mat sport no good by putting every bout under suspicion of colossal fakery. The truth is, however, that even with the new trimmings added more really skillful wrestling is being done [in the 1950s] before larger audiences than ever before. States from Texas and Oklahoma and throughout the Midwest remain a citadel of "good" wrestling.

My winning streak had to come to an end sometime. It was the national middleweight champion, Walter Miller, who made a banker of me once more.

Our meeting in Los Angeles had aroused a spate of public notice on the sports pages. By that time I had been fortunate enough to compile an unbroken win-string of one hundred twenty-two falls in this country, making a respectable total of two hundred fifty-four falls in Europe, the United States, and Canada without a defeat. Miller nonetheless entered the ring a little overconfident. After a lively scramble, I managed to win the first fall by using Frank Gotch's famous stepover toehold. Several movie stars among the anti-Miller forces at the ringside, notably Charlie Chaplin and Douglas Fairbanks, passed me money and congratulations for that rare feat. But Miller's caution returned, and he pinned me the next two falls.

Swinging northward, I salved my disappointment by trimming the Canadian titleholder, Charley Olson, on a twenty-below-zero January night in 1920 when I was certain that icicles must be hanging from the ropes of that Winnipeg arena. Then Ted Florance looked over the counter of his little Minnesota bank one day to see his erstwhile clerk back in Humboldt and ready to go to work. The familiar operators of the two stores, the filling station, the post office, the blacksmith shop, and the depot, which made up the rest of the town, shrugged shoulders and wondered among themselves: "So Farley's finally decided to settle down!"

Farley hadn't, even yet. Most of the next two years I spent in the unhappy business of going about the county taking ownership of mortgaged livestock, land, and equipment then being abandoned right and left by farmers-come-lately who were caught in the severe postwar collapse of farm prices. Though all the other fifteen banks in the county closed their doors, Ted Florance managed to save his own.

But there were still those long, sparkling summer evenings, and baseball forever beckoned. While holding my job at the bank, I once again returned to part-time semiprofessional play, hiring myself out to various teams in the district.

One afternoon in the town of Brandon, Manitoba, on May 24, 1922, the queen's birthday, a remarkably keen-eyed and speedy young farmer boy named George Hugel was patrolling center field for our team. To save pitchers for a tournament later in the week, and because these opponents didn't seem too dangerous, I had decided to do the pitching. That was a mistake.

This particular set of the queen's loyal subjects took great pleasure in my offerings and spent the afternoon hammering my Sunday pitches all over the province. Most of these, it seemed, sailed out to the center pasture for George Hugel to retrieve. He did a great job of it, too, turning tail to race far out toward the barbed-wire fence to pull down the long ones or skidding in on his elbows to pick up those smoking-hot liners just over the infield. It was a superb exhibition, but by the fifth inning he was getting tired of the process. By the sixth, he was grumbling a bit.

A beefy Canuck strode up to the plate as the seventh inning opened. I threw the first ball and it came right back, screaming over second base with plenty of "fuzz" on it. My cornhusking center fielder charged in to make a wonderful diving, rolling, bruising catch, skinning his nose and chin and saving the day once more. He knocked the dust out of his pants and disgustedly threw the ball in. I climbed the mount, took a deep breath, and fired the other barrel at the second batter. This big lumberjack promptly exploded the Yankee orchid hot, high, and a far, far way — into center field.

Once more Hugel turned and outran that ball halfway to the U.S.-Canadian boundary, pulling it in with a one-handed stab that brought the crowd to its feet. But this time he didn't throw it into the infield. Enough was enough. Without slowing his pace he circled, holding the ball aloft like a Greek torchbearer, and *carried* it all the way back to the pitcher's box.

With his wind almost gone he laid the ball in my glove, panting: "For God's sake, Farley! *Walk* one — and let me get my breath!"

I sat down on the mound to laugh. The third baseman and the umpire collapsed in glee. The crowd demanded particulars from the umpire, and before the uproar subsided Hugel had plenty of time to regain his wind.

Ultimately there came a chance for me to try out as an infielder with St. Paul in the next-to-big-league American Association. No bank could hold me then for a minute.

But I couldn't make the grade. I was too musclebound, they told me, from wrestling to have a chance to make the big leagues. One day Mike Kelly, manager of the St. Paul Saints, called me in and told me plainly that I wasn't going very far in baseball. In view of my previous banking experience, he strongly advised me to cast about to get myself into business.

That news was a real blow to me. I still wanted to play baseball more than anything else on earth. I remember that I stood still for quite awhile, staring at the floor, until it soaked into my mind that what Mike had said was the truth, and that he was telling me the truth because he wanted to help me.

Finally, I managed to remark that there was a little city in North Texas, called Amarillo, that looked like a coming town. Mike soon arranged to have me transferred to the Amarillo team, in the Class D League. I arrived in Amarillo in 1923, whereupon not only the Amarillo Gassers baseball team, but the whole league, promptly went broke. Though I then still would see my name on a sports arena billboard for seven years after that, and in that time would wrestle in the two most important bouts of my career, athletics from 1923 onward was merely a means to keep me in business.

6

Patsy Saves the Tire Business

TO Cal Farley in the peg-trousered year of 1923, the Panhandle of the state of Texas was a place to earn a badly needed dollar, to take a precarious flyer into business and establish himself in one of the last remaining not-quite-conquered provinces of the westerner's West — among the free-roving, openhanded, muscularly self-assured Texas frontiersmen who twanged instantly in perfect tune with the Farley wit. He had found his home country.

The flavor of the frontier remained pure and strong over this caprock of the High Plains in the mid-1920s, and even today the people of this lately invaded grass frontier remain indeed a tribe unto themselves. They are a young people, given to many a wry boast and relishing their ability to baffle more inhibited citizens.

The spaciousness of this country is in them, some of its harshness too, and they have drawn from their spectacular origins a salty and well-weathered heartiness of temperament that makes them distinct among all Americans. Frequently they exhibit the cattle-country trait of scrapping implacably over a trader's dime with the right hand while handing off $1,000 with a whimsical left. On impulse, they may readily squander a bank clerk's competence just to pull off a practical joke.

They are fond of asserting that the flabby ones and the lovers of soft living were long ago blown away to easier climes by the unreconstructed year-round enthusiasm of the winds hereabouts. And they clearly show of tough fiber.

Even in the young West, the Texas Panhandle is a remarkably young region. So young that an immigrant outlander like Farley could see the city of Amarillo grow nearly five times in size in less than thirty years. So young that the widow of Indian Scout Billy Dixon, a participant in the last pitched battle against the Comanches at Adobe Walls, was still a patron of Cal Farley's Wunstop Duzzit when the store was sold. So young that the ageless Tom Snider, a pioneer peace officer who had seen the final gunbattle at Old Tascosa in 1889, rolled his venerable chuckwagon back to that scene on the tenth anniversary of Cal Farley's Boys Ranch in 1949 to prove himself still the incomparable master of the western barbecue.

The Fort Worth and Denver Railroad threw a span across this sea of grass in 1887. Only then, like flood debris against a bridge, did the towns begin to collect, among them a place called Ragtown which, after a few tentative changes in location, finally came to be called Amarillo. Land sales and speculation went on feverishly. Plows deployed and yellow salients of wheat speared out from the railroad deep into the grassland. These were farmers, a different breed from the wide-ranging cattlemen, but farming too was on a huge scale. Amarillo, a village of 400 in 1890, grew slowly to the proportions of a small city of 16,000 hardy souls already saddlewise to violent pitches of fortune, knowing well both the grinding poverty of frontier dugouts and the power of great wealth from afar. More important to one new arrival, Second Baseman Cal Farley, was the fact that these West Texans were a people still close enough to the massive capriciousness of their land and climate not to take anything, particularly themselves, too seriously. High-handed raillery was the sauce of their existence; they loved any sort of contest and would walk a mile for a good joke. In Cal Farley, Amarillo had acquired an uncommercial merchant who would build a business on jokes and insults—and do for the community spirit of his city exactly what he had done for the morale of the war-shattered Sixth Engineers in France.

First he had to acquire the teammate whose skills and loyalty through the rest of their lives would permit Cal to concentrate his own efforts to best effect. Her name was Mabel Fincher, the chunky, cheerful, bright-eyed daughter of a railroader who brought upon herself a lifetime of husband and family nurturing, bookkeeping, and business management by appearing regularly in a box seat near third base at every home appearance of the Amarillo Gassers.

PATSY SAVES THE TIRE BUSINESS

Mimi Fincher could play the piano; she could cook; and she could smile in an open friendliness tempered by her baseball-playing brothers to an edge fine enough even to pry open the clamshell shyness of this second baseman who, on the base paths, kept going the noisiest chatter of any member of the team. She liked that Farley fellow a lot "in spite of his thick ears," and after several weeks, when that message had finally come through to him, he approached the third-base box with heroic resolve and said hello, inviting her to be his ringside guest at his first professional wrestling bout in Amarillo then upcoming. She agreed and offered dessert at her parents' home after the match.

The bout was a bloody one against an itinerant madman named Dutch Mantell, and after only seven minutes Mimi Fincher fled white-faced home in a taxi. To her surprise, a bandaged Farley arrived later to claim his dessert and invite her to attend his return bout with Mantell two months later when, he gloated, fans by the hundreds would pay enticingly large sums to watch the bloodshed. She promised him faithfully never to attend another wrestling match in her life, and she never did. Matters developed and they planned to be married by summer, but one February morning in 1923 Cal showed up at her door, announced that he was tired of being razzed by the other ball players, and told her they were being married that afternoon in a nearby town. The Farley assets consisted of one Model-T Ford and $150. He was twenty-seven years old.

✱ The Panhandle-Pecos League was already in bad shape, and my arrival from St. Paul didn't help the situation at all. Within a few months it was bankrupt. I didn't like this manner of exit from baseball—or, for that matter, any other exit, even yet. But I did like everything about this little city of Amarillo.

What to do?

The Scott brothers, Tom and Fain, owners of the defunct baseball league, owned also a little tire shop on Fourth Street between Fillmore and Taylor. Their straits were such at the moment that they were in danger of losing the tire shop, too. An idea began to form in my mind. Undoubtedly the creditors would prefer to have the shop remain open until they could get their money out of it. The landlord would probably have a vacant building on his hands, too, if it closed. Perhaps I could sidle in, not because of my "capital," but on the strength of others' debts.

I started persuading and found a gratifying number of souls who, under the circumstances, were willing to forgive my losing the final game of the league season by stealing second with the bases loaded. By assuming five thousand six hundred dollars in accumulated obligations, I took over the shop and set about making as much municipal din about that fact as possible. Our staff consisted of Mimi, her dog Patsy, and a black philosopher named Mack, known throughout the city for his patience and trustworthiness in repairing tires.

The shop, about thirty feet wide by twice that length, was located in a building about one and one-half blocks off the main street where the rent was cheap. For sale at first I had a "Savage" tire of such miserable construction that it was available to me on credit. Trade was not exactly frantic. I installed a public wrestling mat in the rear of the shop, leaving Mack on detail in front while I busily twisted the necks of sundry mechanics and cab drivers and sometimes got my own neck warped a little. These public workouts proved quite popular about the neighborhood. I excused myself on the theory that this tactic at least let quite a few potential customers know that I was in business.

In the front window I had another stout ally. Patsy, the little brown-and-white Boston bull bitch, belonged officially to Mrs. Farley. They had been inseparable until Mimi started having a few dates with her fallen-arched second baseman, whereupon the fickle creature took to following me home and tagging at my heels everywhere I went. Mimi was irked by such faithlessness. She tried to make the best of the situation, however, by breeding her repeatedly to a bat-eared Boston.

The pups were our first commercial sensation. On display in the shop window, they sold rapidly for ten dollars to fifty dollars apiece. By uncanny coincidence, however, just about the time every transaction was completed, the rent fell due or a new can of rubber cement had to be bought. Thus, Mimi lost a second time, her just profits disappearing quickly into the large pockets of my creditors.

To our great good fortune, Patsy proved to be as fertile as she was fickle. Sixty-four fine pups in all this sexually industrious little beast contributed to the survival of the tire business. At the time that represented just enough financial adrenaline to pull us through a highly doubtful bout with the money changers.

She was an impudent and unsubordinate little femininity. At a stern command not to follow me out onto the sidewalk, she would turn dutifully enough back into the shop. But a few moments later there would be a familiar rubbing at my left calf under the stool at the ice-cream dispensary across the street. Patsy was serving summary notice upon me that she fully expected to receive some of the benefits from the business she was so energetically helping to support. Thus, one ice-cream cone invariably became two, mine being held high in the right hand and hers low enough in my left so that she could leap up for a few tongue swipes as we proceeded along the sidewalk.

It was a sorrowful day when she came in from the alley with a gimpy back, hurt in some manner we never learned. A chiropractor was impressed into duty. Again and again, he braved Patsy's bare-fanged indignation while we regretfully applied our most paralyzing wrestling holds to her on the logical assumption that a mouthful of chiropractor would have meant certain death to such an aristocratic constitution. But nothing helped. Her career was soon over.

We kept one of the best of her male pups for years after that, a sprightly little lawyer who had a more conscientious technique for obeying my stay-in-the-shop command. Planting one dutiful rear foot on the doorsill in order to observe the letter of the law, he could usually be seen stretched seemingly more than half beyond his normal length across the sidewalk while his plaintive curiosity absorbed the panorama of the downtown traffic.

Staying and expanding in business soon proved possible by use of the same attention-getting tactics I formerly had employed in wrestling behind the Minnesota barbershops. Get acquainted. Make a noise. Pay for what publicity you can afford, then steal five times as much more. Give 'em no peace.

After managing to survive for the first few months, we hired a tinsmith to build a metal replica of a small railroad locomotive on the frame of our service truck, complete with bell and smoke. (The Model-T engine produced considerable smoke anyway; we merely piped the exhaust up through the stack in front.) This was our cheapest and most successful bid for the "flat-tire-in-the-garage" trade. Amarillo's streets were mostly unpaved, a fact which made for the tinkling of the little bell in all sections of town. When little Susan and John Junior demanded that Cal Farley be called to repair a collapsed tire so that they could see the little locomotive, John Senior really had little choice in the matter.

Fixing flat tires, as my generation ruefully remembers, was a small-scale industry in those days. Split rims, thin 30- by 3.5-inch casings, inner tubes about as thick and durable as toy balloons, unpaved roads still bristling with scatterings of a generation of fence builders—all operated to create ample exercise for the repairman. It goes without saying, too, that long experience in wrestling was ideal for laboring on these refractory, finger-pinching tires and rims which sprang upon meddlers as quickly and viciously as a wolf trap. Hardly could a person walk three blocks past the automobiles parked downtown at any hour of the day without finding at least one automobile with a flat tire. To get this "flat-tire-on-the-street" business we early began inserting little white cards in the rim cordially inviting the disgruntled owner to avail himself of Cal Farley's incomparable Flying Dutchman service. Mimi, Mack, and I kept those little greetings in our pockets day and night, seven days a week, for just such purposes.

No gas-buggy driver in all history, I'm quite sure, ever coaxed a Model-T Ford engine into activitiy without applying to its throat a gentle but ominous stranglehold called the choke. Taking due account of this fact, we obtained flanged white metal caps to clamp permanently atop the choke handle bearing the numerals 565, the telephone number of the Farley tire service parlors. Once these were installed, with or without the owner's permission, on every accessible choke handle in town, we derived considerable new business and much pride from what we considered a subtle attack upon the public's unconscious.

Next, as income increased by slow stages, I overrode objections from Mimi, the comptroller in chief, to trade in my own venerable Ford coupe on a long, tall, brand-new, imposing Lincoln sedan. This baronial barouche—which sported gleaming enamel, Fifth Avenue mohair, and shiny chrome fittings never seen before—was not merely a premature conceit on the part of a supposedly rising young businessman. It was a rolling monument to the many-times-proved theory that Americans like to ride along with a winner—that while one is struggling to climb out of the ruck he'd darn well better look like a winner, even though once he's on top he'll be wise to drive the most inconspicuous automobile in town.

A little incident that happened in the neighboring college town of Canyon while my big Lincoln was still very new proved this theory, at least to my satisfaction. This was scarcely ten months after I had hung out my commercial shingle, while I was still deep in debt and still dependent on Patsy's maternal instincts and on the proceeds of my twice-monthly wrestling bouts. The Lincoln and the automobile of a wealthy oilman, it happened, were stuck side by side in the mud. The oilman, a stranger in town who had torn up a tire and was in sore need of a new one, couldn't induce the garage man to accept his personal check. Finally the dealer pointed respectfully to my mired-down chariot, suggesting that, if he would get my endorsement, all would be well. Thus it occurred that I, with proper flourish, okayed the check of a man who already had five times more money than I would ever make.

The Farley enterprise was now established and would be built with some of the most cornball foolery ever perpetrated.

On the sidewalk outside the tire shop stood a wooden bench, ostensibly there for the convenience of any idle member of the Farley corps so he could presumably leap to serve the whim of any tire-troubled customer at the very moment the latter chuffed to the curb. But this sidewalk gondola was scarcely launched before it collected a full assortment of the barnacles that have eternally attached themselves to any bench, I suppose, that ever sat on the sunny side of any street. Farley's rapid-service establishment was beginning to look from the front like the daily convocation of Village Loafers, Inc.

We wired the bench, carefully leaving sitting room at one end for a decoy's throne, giving voltage-authority to the concealed wire by means of a Ford coil operating the infernal mechanism from a switch inside the building. Much amusement resulted, including one near-fatal episode which occurred when I made the unbelievable error of flipping the switch just as Mrs. Farley collapsed wearily on the bench under the weight of a large sack of groceries. Scrambled bacon and eggs hit the curbing at virtually the same instant her furious fingernails closed on my Adam's apple. And ever after, when the annual family argument began as to whether or not I should take her to the World Series once more (an argument I never won, incidentally; she remained forever an abandoned baseball fan), some sarcastic mention of the incident tended to crop up again at a crucial moment in the debate.

Another peaceful summer afternoon was shattered when an excellent old gentleman from the creamery sat down to visit with a young friend who happened to be occupying the harmless end of the bench. The switch was flicked quickly. Without a pause in his absorbing narrative of the good old days, the elderly one casually explored the nether precincts of his faded duck trousers for the offending insect. Staff and bystanders inside the shop quickly congregated behind the window to watch.

Another flick.

The old man carefully finger-chased the electric culprit down his right inseam only to lose the trail in the vicinity of his knee.

"Naow, I was ridin' south along the fence line toward Prairie Dog Town fork. . . ." The next tick of voltage interrupted the story near its climax. There was another pursuit, then a pause as he captured the pesky bug and put an end to it by a triumphant thumb-and-forefinger squeeze against his thigh.

"So I tells off this long-eared ornery fella for fair, I says. . . ." By now grandpap, at the height of his enthusiasm, had his hand on his companion's knee. Such rare opportunities did not come every day, of course — all the force of Amarillo's city power plant struck the both of them in a blow that was well below the belt. Pants-clutching bellows from the outside and maniac howls from the interior multitude had scarcely subsided before the oldster proved his mettle by buying ice cream for the crowd.

Amusement, for a struggling young man equipped with little cash and much desire, had to come by with devious economy. Always there seemed to be many willing eggers-on who repeatedly urged me, for instance, to make sport against the wrestlers who came to town with various carnivals. Almost never were such maneuvers successful, however. Many of these yeomen recognized me on sight as a recent card holder in their own fraternity and would decline to do battle.

Sally, the donkey, was the symbol and star attraction in one of the first in a long line of storewide sales contests with which the Farley enterprises wooed the elusive customer. Now that the store had expanded into larger quarters with more types of merchandise and more employees, competitions between salesmen became regular fare. Sally participated in a sort of reverse-English handicap in which the salesman with the poorest record during a given period of time was required to mount the beast and ride several blocks at the head of a street parade.

To our own surprise, these parades grew to unpredictable proportions. Soon our second-worst salesman culprit was following the leader with a wheelbarrow and broom and dustpan; other merchants had fallen into the procession with automobiles and displays, and radio time was purchased to give the public a step-by-step description of the motley cavalcade from microphones placed along the line of march.

Results were beneficial to all except the donkey. Though she previously had grown fat on the cactus and sand-sprinkled soapweed of the Canadian River's banks, the weeks she stood on display at the tire shop during the course of each contest were her complete ruin. Apples and candy bars became her regular diet. So many delicacies were proffered by passersby, in fact, that in the latter stages she disdained even expensive alfalfa hay — and probably starved when her expensive tastes forced us finally to return her to the pasture.

At the end of our first year in the automobile tire business, Mimi told me we had made nine thousand five hundred dollars. The cattle business and the rest of the local economy picked up notably in 1924, and I managed to obtain the Goodrich tire agency from the company headed by another veteran of the Third Division, AEF, Colonel David Goodrich. The good colonel apparently saw enough progress in Sergeant Farley's Amarillo operation to give me a real break, permitting me to obtain a whole carload of tires on credit in 1925 just before the first of four price rises went into effect. That break was decisive. The Cal Farley Wunstop Duzzit Flying Dutchman service was solidly in business.

Considering the nature of our helter-skelter conspiracy in pursuit of trade, it was little wonder that boys, great numbers of boys, became a part of our daily existence in the tire shop. They were always around to view our miscellaneous attractions, clambering over the donkey, playing with the dogs, gawking at the proceedings on the public wrestling mat. No man could have ignored their eagerness if he had tried. Again, as on the regular wrestling tours of the past, it was as natural as daylight to invite them to toss each other around a bit, show them the rudiments of wrestling technique, and urge them on.

But there was a difference. Now, instead of merely seeing boys occasionally in one city and then another and wondering about them now and then, the same boys were coming back day after day. Obviously we could do extremely little for them in the way of real help. If they really wanted to wrestle, I could coax them away from smoking and swearing and make those rules stick. But scolding them for absence from school merely sent them away, not back to school. Occasionally we could arrange to put some of the more diligent ones into the wrestling preliminaries at the armory so that they could put a few dimes into their ragged pockets. We could see that they obtained a bath or a haircut now and then.

When the business expanded to include a filling station, the boys were put in charge of a soft-drink cooler in the driveway, keeping the profits for themselves. We could pay them small fees for washing customers' windshields—a job at which they proved faster and more satisfactory than the men attendants. Later on, we could begin to develop some of them into bit performers on the daily radio programs sponsored by the store. (One of the latter boys, I am happy to say, saved and studied diligently during a long tour of navy duty during World War II, later passed his bar examination and almost immediately was chosen to fill a vacancy as a county attorney in our state.)

But the best we could do was not very much. All too often we would have a boy coming along well as a wrestling prospect, for instance, by filling out his muscles, earning a little honest money, and learning at least the beginnings of clean habits. Then he would suddenly disappear, lured away by the temptations of older companions. Soon he would be just another young thug who would pass one of us on the street without speaking and with downcast eyes. We had lost another boy.

Why?

Gradually and subconsciously, without even realizing it, I began to study these kids.

7

Give 'Em No Peace

NINETEEN TWENTY-SIX was the year a great throng gathered in Philadelphia to see Gene Tunney outbox Jack Dempsey, and another throng in Los Angeles saw Aimee Semple McPherson "reincarnated" after a mysterious six-week disappearance. Cal Coolidge presumably intoned his usual penetrating prediction from the White House that "next year things will be better, or worse." Gloria Swanson and Dick Barthelmess rode Hollywood's heights. Newspapers were serializing *The Good Bad Girl.*

Here in Texas, Ma Ferguson rode back into the governor's chair after a thorny campaign directed by her cactus-haired husband, Jim, who promised everything except a reenactment of the battle of the Alamo. A famous pastor air-conditioned the diaphragm of a lumberman-parishioner with a six-shooter in the study of a big church in Fort Worth, causing no end of talk. But the biggest excitement of the year, by far, was taking place in the Panhandle to the northwest.

A drill bit changed our lives in 1926. Playing a wildcatter's hunch, two brothers, White and S. D. (Tex) McIlroy, swung the steel for the second time under their "poor-boy" rig at Dixon Creek No. 1, northeast of Amarillo in southern Hutchinson County. (Tex McIlroy had prospected awhile in Alaska with Tex Rickard during the Nome gold rush but had returned to try his hand in the Texas oil game.) Their well was already producing, having come in the previous March with a fairly small production of four hundred barrels a day. But when the McIlroys resumed drilling that January day, however, a new future took form in a matter of mere hours. The steel gouged scarcely two feet deeper into rock, and Dixon Creek No. 1 exploded suddenly into a rig-smashing gusher roaring with oil at a rate of 10,000 barrels a day. In a matter of a few days and weeks the Panhandle was roaring, too. Lines of trucks rocking under heavy equipment made their own dust-choked roads across the prairie. Other wells went down, and oil came bursting up until eventually most of the whole 125-mile curve of the Amarillo Mountains could be traced in derricks atop the ground. Pipelines, railroads, and human beings by the thousands—of lowest to highest order and from everywhere in the world—converged on the district. One of America's most spectacular oil booms was on.

Amarillo's population and its bank deposits doubled within six months. Tall new buildings quickly dwarfed the older portion of the downtown district. A listing of the city's building permits for a single ordinary week required twenty-seven inches of type in the evening paper. Wilbur Hawk and Gene Howe, who had purchased the town's leading dailies on a small margin only two years before, reportedly paid off their entire $235,000 indebtedness in eleven months of the oil boom, as Cal Farley well remembered.

★ Such was our Panhandle in one of the livelier periods of its lively history. Many of us, gaining money faster than wisdom, set about promptly to dissipate our sudden oversupply of cash. With me that was not difficult at all.

One of my more painful misadventures of that time was a final flyer into baseball, not as a player, but as a club owner. The pure love of that game was still so strong in my frame that only a real spanking would pound it out. I was spanked.

With four other oil-boomed optimists, I helped with the purchase of the St. Joseph, Missouri, baseball club in the Western league, and moved it to Amarillo. Then we dug up $44,000 to build a monument to our ignorance in the form of a new baseball park. Result: in two excruciating years we learned the vast differences between hitting foul balls and paying for them. We lost $84,000 even after managing to sell the ball-park to the Amarillo High School board for less than half its cost. Once again I was in debt and obliged to wrestle and sell more and more tires in order to bail out the financial boat.

Our store in Amarillo had reached a sufficient financial stability that it could serve as an effective base for expansion. A man could readily become the automobile tire tycoon of the Panhandle if he wished. We set up branch stores until ultimately there were seven of them but sold them one by one, neither much better nor much worse off for the experience, as we finally concluded that one large, ever expanding store was much better suited to our taste. One reason was my ever increasing preoccupation with boys. Another was the gradual realization that, to me, a store would always be a highly personal thing. A customer, whether a man or a woman, would prefer to be greeted by the proprietor in the salesroom with some sort of Texas pleasantry. Branch stores never fitted into that scheme of things, somehow.

The show had to go on. Our town was a big town now, much changed, and so the show had to change accordingly. There was paving, no less, on most of the streets. The Model-T was passing, and the tin locomotive was no more. Sally, the jackass, was back in the thistles. But there were other and bigger devices. We used grand openings, sales contests, wrestling matches, airplanes, newspaper advertising, and radio insults.

Much education in the American nature comes to a man who runs sales contests in a highly promotional business enterprise. We held contests a plenty—each one larger and more pretentious, as it necessarily must be every year to keep public interest alive.

For us, at least, it was true that, in business almost as much as in politics or in social doings, people are eternally more interested in people than in such comparatively dull matters as merchandise and mere money, even their own. Thus, when a certain crew of salesmen went into a six-week competition in the sale of radios, we didn't do much talking about radios. Instead, the salesmen themselves went on the radio program in turn, one each day, to explain how he and his wife had never been to California or New York before, how much they wanted to win that all-expense-paid trip to the Rose Bowl or the World Series, and just what he planned to do on the trip if the prize happened to come his way. The secret again, I think, was merely in offering a prize sizable enough that the richest man in town would be tempted a bit—thereby giving every purchaser the opportunity to participate vicariously in the prize-winner's good fortune.

Seven times we moved or expanded our place of business during twenty-three years, each occasion marked by a grand opening. Typical was our expansion in the depression year 1932, when the opening inducement consisted of the presentation of one ticket to a big-name wrestling match with each purchase of five or more gallons of gasoline. By then our store had branched out to include a four-lane filling station with large one-story showrooms adjacent and offering various lines of dry goods

Promotional parade, Farley style. The placard reads . . . "Us jackasses didn't sell enough Goodrich tires so here we are in this parade."

and automobile supplies. In a two-day opening, with a crew of sixteen men and boys working the gasoline pumps, windshield washing, and the oil pouring, we pumped out some thirty thousand gallons of gasoline. Lines of cars blocked traffic for four blocks in the evenings, calling for the services of several extra, unhappy patrolmen.

Earlier in the game we had well learned the rule: if you intend to give something away to build business goodwill, first provide the best quality attraction you can possibly afford and *give* it away with no strings attached. Sale price of these wrestling tickets was a dollar and ten cents, yet they were presented free with ninety cents' worth of gasoline—and the customers learned after a trial or two that they could expect to see one of the feature bouts of the whole year. Until 1931, one of the feature contestants at those bouts was usually Farley himself, the proprietor who was trying not to miss any more business bets than necessary.

Wrestling, which had predated baseball in my lifetime, lasted slightly longer. But in Amarillo it always had a highly utilitarian purpose. No regular wrestling events were being staged there on my arrival—thus, once again I had to do my own promoting by means of the back-room public mat, the newspapers, and any and all other means. By means of a number of fortunate circumstances—particularly the irresistible salesmanship of the wild man Dutch Mantell—legitimate professional wrestling became the most popular of all sports in Amarillo.

GIVE 'EM NO PEACE

Whatever the success of these labors was, my purely commercial purposes were quite plain. When Dutch Mantell and I and a few others began regular neck-bending twice a month in the National Guard armory, every three hundred to four hundred dollars I acquired from a good night's gate was carried at a fast pace from the armory to the tire shop on Fourth Street to bolster the efforts of Patsy the bulldog and help keep a fragile enterprise alive. Even more important was the fact that, excepting only the year I was out of the game with a broken leg, my photograph and my exertions on the mat occupied space in the newspapers with a regularity that must have been quite wearisome to the more respectable citizens.

Both the income and the publicity helped a lot. We burned up great quantities of energy at the store, getting and keeping a few more customers every week. Mimi developed a circus juggler's skill at keeping the books straight with one hand while restraining her financially impulsive spouse with the other. Thus, we had managed to pay off our indebtedness and even expand a bit before the big year 1926 came around. But the continuous demands for further and further expansion made that wrestling income still necessary.

I wrestled one hundred and seven bouts in Amarillo all told, losing three. It would give me a self-satisfied glow to be able to record here that I closed my long career on the professional mat with a final great triumph. My farewell appearances were pretentious enough—a pair of matches with Jack Reynolds for the world welterweight championship before the two biggest wrestling crowds in Texas's history, at least to that time. (Photo, page 54.) But I didn't win.

On June 20, 1930, in my one-hundredth Amarillo match held outdoors at the baseball stadium, Jack Reynolds showed me how much I didn't know about wrestling. Eight thousand persons were there—reportedly the largest crowd to that time ever assembled in Texas for a similar event. I had trained more determinedly for this show but Jack Reynolds merely gave me Lesson No. 2, winning this time in two consecutive falls. The final gong that night was the five o'clock whistle for me as a professional athlete.

Of the many traffic-stopping efforts employed by the Farley enterprises in pursuit of customers and a good time, I particularly enjoyed an impromptu festivity involving my former doughfoot colleagues of the First World War. The long-remembered American Legion convention in Los Angeles had just ended, leaving marks of Legionnaire enthusiasm from which that city would not recover for some time. Streams of them were driving homeward along Highway 66, the transcontinental highway which passes through Amarillo, and their high spirits were not yet spent. The opportunity was not one that an alert gas-and-oil merchant should miss.

Our highway signboards for miles west of Amarillo were quickly covered with temporary canvas placards carrying the message: "If you want to meet the guy who won the war, Stop at Cal Farley's Flying Dutchman Service, Fourth and Fillmore, Amarillo." A banner went across the full width of Fillmore Street to announce the presence of this heroic curiosity at our store and station, located on the highway.

The results were wonderful. Legionnaires by the pairs, dozens, and scores, looking for any excuse at all to pause after a long and dusty trek across the driest part of the West, followed the Flying Dutchman signs into the driveways. Out of each automobile rolled one or more belligerent ex-soldiers, demanding, "Where is this son-of-a-bitch who won the war?"

By early afternoon the traffic reached such proportions that we set up a long table on the sidewalk along Fourth Street, persuaded the kindly women of an auxiliary group to bring down tableclothes and help with the serving, and began dispensing free coffee and doughnuts. Late into the evening they lingered as more new and old friends from the convention dropped by to recapitulate their recent Marne offensive on the West Coast. Many of them found hotel rooms and stayed the night.

Next day the supply of doughboys and doughnuts reached the proportions of a junior convention. Doing our best to give them a Texas-type welcome, we borrowed the armory and put on a show complete with a highly informal parade, a singfest, a band concert, and wrestling matches. And the best reward of the whole affair, to me, was the remarkable number of real friendships that still bring me letters now and then from points all over the country.

The same impulsiveness with which we set about to entertain the Legionnaires, however, sometimes got us into trouble. Our business was personal, founded heavily on public goodwill, and these Texans have an indignation to match their enthusiasm. On the occasions of our worst mistakes we could, by making the slightest murmur of complaint, have blown our entire enterprise out of the water. But a little quirk of the public mind which an athletic champion learns the hard way served us well. This is the simple fact that the same folks who want to ride along with a winner also get tired of him when he wins too often. Then, nothing is quite so effective as a defeat for smoking a man's friends out of the willows and making them realize again suddenly that they are, after all, his friends — provided that he doesn't cry about his whipping. That was the reason why, on two or three occasions when a stunt of ours went sour and we found ourselves in a rather bad spot, our usually vociferous organization went

GIVE 'EM NO PEACE

into a period of comparative silence, except to see as many of our customers personally as possible and thereby make amends. Before too many days, affairs were usually back to normal.

Our most successful sales stunt of all—and the one on which I would have been willing to hang up my megaphone as a publicity man and call it a day—came at another time of sore commercial need. The Goodrich Company had treated me well, even to the extent of permitting me early to buy tires in several carload lots just prior to advances in price that they, but not I, knew were imminent. But my ex-commanding officer, Colonel David Goodrich, had been a little slow out of his corner in developing the heavy cord tires that put the motoring public onto safe and reasonably trouble-free rolling stock for the first time in the late 1920s. Goodyear had been on the market for months with its "Double Eagle" before the competitive casing started arriving from the Goodrich factories. And even then there had been no sales consciousness whatever in its christening. Goodrich called the tire, not the Super-Roadmaster or even Black Beauty, but merely the stodgy word Deluxe. That "Double Eagle" was still exciting the customers.

It was a crisis for the company, which launched a counteroffensive in the form of a transcontinental tour of the "Silver Fleet." This was a caravan of standard-make automobiles, driven about the country with maximum fanfare by college graduates, no less, nattily uniformed and loaded with culture, good manners, and Goodrich doctrine.

It was also a crisis for the dealers, and for one in Amarillo particularly. My salesman and I were exhausting ourselves in oratory about the virtues of the Goodrich Deluxe, only to have customer after customer come back with the suffocating inquiry, "Wal, now, how does this tire stack up against that there Double Eagle?" We were talking ourselves limp and not selling tires, either.

Driving along the highway one day full of dour thoughts on this situation, I happened to see a demolished airplane in a haystack. Two students of our pioneer skywagon driver in Amarillo, Harold English, had "frozen" onto the stick and crashed a few hours before, killing themselves in the forward cockpit while English merely catapulted unhurt into the hay. When poking about the wreckage, I noticed that the plane had been shod with Goodrich tires and that both were still inflated. That was interesting. I talked to English and discovered that, in many wrecks he had seen, the wheels had been punched entirely through the wings with no ill effect on the tires.

An idea began to form. Would an automobile tire dropped from an

Backed to the wall by the competitive Goodyear Double Eagle tire, Cal Farley risked his business future on an imaginative stunt—dropping a wheel tired by Goodrich from a plane a half mile up before a crowd of 12,000-plus at Amarillo's prairie airport. The tire stayed on the rim, still inflated, and the Farley enterprise prospered thereafter.

airplane survive? Harold thought it might, explaining to my innocent mind the principle of terminal velocity — that no matter what the height of release, any object reaches only a certain speed and no more during its fall. Secretly we experimented, using one of the brand-new, drop-center rims Ford had just produced. Results were good: the rim was bent severely, but the tire stayed on it.

For a desperate man that was enough. With all the coverage we could buy, we advertised to the Texas Panhandle that, on the arrival of the Silver Fleet, one of Cal Farley's Goodrich Deluxe tires, fully inflated, would crash to earth from the appalling altitude of half a mile. In our regular newspaper and radio advertisements we quoted letters pro and con, many of them calling us all manner of damn fools for attempting such an unheard-of trick. By all means available we kept the controversy growing until every amateur physicist in the Panhandle had sharpened his pencils and was furnishing us his own elaborate conclusion.

The big day arrived at the municipal airport, and so did twelve thousand to fifteen thousand people. I looked at the size of that crowd and was suddenly scared to death. Either that tire stayed on or Cal Farley would next be selling palm fans down in Puerto Rico! Down from two thousand

GIVE 'EM NO PEACE

seven hundred feet it came and seemed to explode in a big cloud of dust, bouncing nearly fifty feet back into the air. Finally it stopped bouncing and rolling, and the crowd converged on it at a run. The rim was badly battered, with weeds and dirt sticking in the bead. But the tire was still inflated! Back to town we went in triumph to install the rim in the front window at the store, watch the mayor sign the Silver Fleet's official scroll, and proceed to the rotunda of the city auditorium for proper ceremonies and displays. For a long time thereafter we had very little competitive sales trouble with the Goodyear tire. The stunt had plucked a lot of tail feathers from the "Double Eagle."

Busy as those years were in the store, every season found me more deeply involved with community doings. Boys and athletics—the terms are synonymous—were always involved. As early as my second year in business I had organized a young baseball team which managed to reach the semifinals in the annual regional tournament sponsored in Denver by the *Denver Post*. When the depression struck, there was already beginning to take shape the citywide youth athletics program which will be described more fully later. Boys from the streets were in the store every day and in our home on many evenings. It was a busy life for Mimi and me.

8

Hilarity in Pursuit of Trade

THE CAMPAIGN that set culture back twenty years in Texas had its beginnings, I think, in a series of newspaper advertisements our store undertook about the time of the oil boom. These ads occupied a quarter of a page twice a week, and at first only two-thirds of this space was devoted to the usual touting of our merchandise. The rest was a column of chatter under the Cal Farley byline and signature, dedicated to earnest discussion of the profound and significant topics of the day.

We discussed the advantages of Ford dealer Walter Irvin's bushy eyebrows in a rainstorm, for example, pro and con, fore and aft, in much detail. We proved scientifically that Charles A. Lindbergh could never have flown to Paris if the *Spirit of St. Louis* had been shod with anything but Goodrich tires. (This proof was a little more difficult in the case of Admiral Byrd, who dropped his Goodrich-tired landing gear in the sea off Spitzbergen on his takeoff for the Pole. But we tried.) We examined the unfortunate Oklahoma ancestry of a number of prominent citizens. We scolded Mrs. Charles Williamson, wife of one of the salesman, for the soggy pancakes that were causing her old man to arrive at the office a little slower and later every day.

In the beginning I was fairly careful to obtain the victim's consent before subjecting our local notables to such irreverent handling. But our high-spirited public responded so well that very soon we had an ample battery of volunteers who would bat back the banter as fast as we could toss it out.

But this chaff took too much time and pains which couldn't be spared from my other affairs. It had another disadvantage, too, in the mere fact that the printed word is a black-and-white, permanent thing. There was too often a chance that a victim, looking over my brilliant witticisms the next day and the day after that, might gradually begin to see some hidden gravel in them that was never intended.

Not until the day someone first put one of those shiny gadgets called a microphone in front of my twice-broken nose did my true talent for insulting the customers really begin to blossom. Here was a new blackjack that would leave no black-and-white (or blue) evidence next day, an electric prod as quick and ungraspable as the beam of a flashlight. Here was a chrome-plated challenge to a lifetime of Bronx-type noise-making, with full assurance that our citizens, who delight in public commotion, would be horsing me plenty in return. Anything for an argument. The louder the better. Dish out the raspberries unsugared and sell 'em merchandise. Never let 'em up off the canvas. Give 'em no peace.

It was fairly easy for me to begin by undertaking the job of announcing the wrestling matches. By now that sport was solidly established in Amarillo, which still remains one of the best wrestling towns in the nation. My long familiarity with these surroundings bred contempt for any dull journalistic recitals of what was actually going on in the ring.

To keep the stay-at-homes happy and give the sponsor a reasonable return on his investment, I felt it my duty to describe instead the belly-slugging, eye-gouging, body-slamming, rope-twisting, referee-belting battle these same two gladiators *might* be putting on if only they had their breath and were not troubled with a desire to wrestle again next week.

Football was another outlet. Amarillo takes the pigskin sport seriously, frequently cramming twelve thousand or more spectators into the stands for a home appearance of its high school's Golden Sandstorm team. For this reason my poetic license on the microphone had to be held in check while the game remained close. But once the score had climbed above thirty to nothing, my old deep sense of responsibility for the fans' entertainment seldom failed to gain the upper hand.

But it was only when radio moved into the sober processes of tire merchandising that poor old Marconi, dead and defenseless, began to revolve slowly in his copper coffin. What happened to radio in Amarillo was a blow below the belt that such a youthful industry was indeed lucky to survive. What happened to the cause of true culture and the rounded Harvard accent I won't attempt to describe.

We had the simple idea that radio advertising, like any other, ought

TWO THOUSAND SONS

Fresh from Elk City, Oklahoma, Cecil Hunter joined Farley as "S-s-s-stutterin' Sam" on the Wunstop Duzzit stage in "the noon radio show that set culture back 20 years in Texas." Mr. Hunter died in September 1986 at Sun City, Arizona.

to be personalized. If the purpose of a radio program was to bring customers into a store, the store was exactly the place where the program should be put on, so that the customers could come in and see it and even take part in it. We built a stage in the ground-floor salesroom at the store. We hired salesmen who could also sing or do a passable part-time job with "The Strawbery Roan," "You Are My Sunshine," and "Ten Years with the Wrong Woman" on fiddles, guitars, accordions, and pianos. We brought other salesmen off the floor to advertise merchandise from their own departments. Whether their speech was smooth, halting, or adenoidal didn't matter — we wanted the farm folks from Stratford to come into the store and ask by name for the young man with whom they already felt acquainted over the air. We invited the customers to come up on the stage and take the consequences. Finally, we contracted for a daily fifteen-minute broadcast during the lunch hour and set forth to heckle everyone the law would allow.

The carefree mechanics of that 12:45 P.M. broadcast proved baffling to Cecil Hunter, a radio-experienced Oklahoman who came to our staff in 1936 as a "S-s-stuttering Sam," a combination salesman, straight man, impersonator, accent act, woebegone Oklahoma chicken thief, and star of the show. Cecil, who in due time graduated to nationwide popularity as one of the most hilarious and original entertainers of this generation, recalls his Amarillo initiation as follows:

"At the radio station where I had been working, our entire script had

HILARITY IN PURSUIT OF TRADE

to be carefully written out, reviewed, and usually rehearsed before it went on the air, and I had been taught that such were the requirements of radio technique. During my first week I sat up nights writing out a lot of script, handing copies to Cal and to Jimmy Meeks, our bald-headed singer and occasional master of ceremonies.

"This stuff, I thought, was fine, fast continuity which I would have been right proud to hear going through the microphones. But it never did. We would begin most properly but within a maximum of sixty to ninety seconds elapsed broadcasting time all that pretty typewritten script would be on the floor and forgotten while this man Farley danced off through the sagebrush on a wild tangent toward some unknown destination. It was up to me to grab his shirttail and follow.

"After about three days of this Farley asked me, 'Why don't you go sell that typewriter?' Thereafter we would start putting that show together about 12:40 P.M. with a quick look among the dry-goods counters for a likely-looking individual to serve as a 'guest artist.' While he was being bodily escorted to the stage, the fiddler and the electric-guitar player were giving themselves a two-minute 'rehearsal,' and Farley and I held a quick confab in the office to decide who would be insulted and what merchandise would be sold today."

For some reason or other, this unlaborious static seemed to sell merchandise. Our free-wheeling commericals, I fear, would never have met present federal requirements as to length or content. We sold Phillips 66 gasoline so powerful it caused Joe Swickley's wife to sue for divorce when he stepped on the gas, shot four miles past his home farm before he could get the car stopped, and like to scared her to death. We peddled suits of clothes that would even fit the round belly on old Iron-Head Fullingim, the lawyer. We sold Vigoro endlessly, with news flashes from customers in Stinnett and Dumas who had spread the fertilizer on their lawns the day before and now were telephoning for machetes and jungle knives in order to cut their way through house-high grass to get out to work.

Many were the good citizens who served as uncomplaining fodder for this frightful microphone. First off we passed an ironclad Texas law that every individual entering our beloved Panhandle from the disgraceful state of Oklahoma had to be sheep-dipped at the state line. Poor, handicapped, Okie-defending S-s-stuttering Sam was known therefore to complain about how cold it was in that dipping vat during the wintertime. ("Well, Sam, can we help it if you wear so many layers of underwear that it takes a half-hour to soak 'em through? We know we can't take the thievin' ideas out of you Okies when you come over here, but at least we're gonna get the ticks off.")

Judge Wallace Hughes of Guymon, a state senator forever nearby in Oklahoma, stood up well under every verbal brickbat and tomato that wouldn't quite get the radio station's license suspended. We accused him of being the all-time "All-American" horse thief in a state full of 'em. We accused him of chasing off to New York after some actress or other on embezzled state funds. We charged him with the sale of defective roofing to his own state agricultural college after the roof of the college auditorium leaked rain all over a program staged by Amarillo talent. Mrs. Hughes we painted as a most wonderful woman and author of the finest potato cake in Oklahoma. About once a week we wondered aloud why on earth—with all those other distinguished Oklahoma citizens like Al Jennings, Pretty Boy Floyd, and Chief Iron Horse the Choctaw to choose from—she had to go and marry the judge. Soon both the judge and his wife each were writing us good-humored ammunition for use in further defamation of the other's character.

Uncouth?

Dear me, I suppose we were. It would be uncouth indeed for me merely to mention that, on the strength of just such goings-on, our one-room tire repair shop of 1923 had grown until it did a gross business of more than seven hundred thousand dollars in 1946, the last full year of our operations before my increasing preoccupation with Boys Ranch forced us to sell the store. More than that, this daily radio program, our newspaper advertisements, and our constant store promotions provided also a power-ful means over the years for building and holding public support for the Maverick Club; for Kids, Inc.; and for our Boys Ranch at Tascosa.

During the mid-1930s the rains never came, and the winds continued season after season to blow away crops, soil, possessions, and livelihood itself—but not the capacity of these western people to have a laugh at their own expense. The city of Amarillo itself was riding through with a com-paratively mild case of the general hard times, but as the winds finally tore loose even the toughest-rooted families from the farmlands to the north of us, thousands of them were sent rolling through Amarillo on Highway 66 toward California in the "bitterest retreat in American history."

As always, the ragged little shavers among the destitute who crowded our streets and suburbs in flight from Mother Nature's own blitzkrieg were the most pitiable and the most demanding. We had got our Maverick Club

82   in operation about this time, and in many other ways the city extended itself with its usual openhandedness to relieve the plight of these people. But everything we could do seemed so meager before that array of haunted faces that I'm sure every West Texan who had a home ate his three square meals a day with a troubled conscience in those years.

The youngsters penetrated the efforts of the Farley commercial enterprises in unusual ways. We used the radio endlessly to advertise the activities of the Maverick Club and, later, of Boys Ranch. Soon we very often called up to our showroom stage some particularly appealing and articulate urchin off the street and put him on the air—sometimes with astonishing results. Next, of course, we found ourselves coaching the little fellow with talent in the basics of vaudeville repartee or playing a harmonica or singing a cowboy song so that he could earn a few pennies and get his chin up. Those who stayed and were faithful washed windshields on the driveway or swept out the stockroom.

These performers, along with other refugees from Route 66 who had developed some athletic novelty at the Maverick Club, formed the nucleus of the Flying Dutchman Circus, a troupe which took to the road in a store-owned bus almost every Friday evening for eleven years to bring entertainment to patrons in the rural schools of the stricken farm country and to obtain for our youngsters what too often was their only full meal of the entire week.

I cannot tell that story, however, without telling first the story of the "orchestra conductor" of the circus, who was also the most riotous citizen Amarillo ever had. He was noisy, unlettered, ill-mannered, tough-talking, and great-hearted. He was monumentally ugly and enormously popular. He labored sixteen hours a day at buffoonery so outlandish that the plainest recital of it too often gets a man called a liar. For twenty-five years he kept the Texas Panhandle alternately howling with glee or yelling for his blood. To him one brand of public noise was as dulcet as the other: public tranquillity was the one thing he could not endure. He was eternally at the right elbow of any man or any organization attempting to help Amarillo's boys.

His name was Dutch Mantell.

9

A Dutchman Amuck

THE FUNERAL was oddly successful. For the occasion the
Great Dutch Mantell wore his
red-and-green cowboy boots furiously polished, and his huge white
Stetson was lying on his chest. The dark blue suit he lay in was one of
Cal's. A desperate search of the man's erratic wardrobe had turned up no
reasonable facsimile of conventional costume.

The kids from the Maverick Club for underprivileged boys were there,
a downcast lot of them, finding the whole business a little hard to
comprehend. Most of the big shots of the city were there, too, and the
wrestling arena crowd, and a sunburned assortment of other Texans from
a hundred miles around. The quality of their silence was proof that their
presence was individually a personal matter. For himself, the Dutchman
no doubt was pleased to note that he had pulled the usual standing-room-
only house for his last appearance.

The *Amarillo Daily Globe* had memorialized the event over most of its
front page that morning. The Dutchman's dismaying face, photographed
in some rare former instant of mutinous repose, grinned a tin-eared
goodbye to his customers from a cut four columns wide and a foot long.
The story beneath carried the byline of sports editor Jerry Malin, who
was also a pallbearer. It was a warm story and a long one, but it could
sketch only thinly Mantell's outlandish excursions about this planet.

As if there were nothing strange at all in the sight of this Luxenbourgian
apostle of pandemonium lying front and center in all this quiet, the

solemnities proceeded satisfactorily to their normal conclusion. No earthquake brought the church down; no trapdoor opened under the pulpit during the short sermon; no mob howled down the street behind the hearse; and to date no oil well has spouted from his grave. Any such phenomena could have been small surprise to those who knew what manner of man was here being buried.

By trade Dutch Mantell was a wrestler; by self-appointment he held public office as Amarillo's municipal jester, commissioner of homicide, expediter of anarchy — spending in those unpaid duties a far greater portion of his time. By lifetime concentration he was, most of all, an actor.

In the ritual of the ancient fraternity of showmanship, Alfred Albert Joe de re L'Guardier (he had possesed such a name once) was a high priest. That brotherhood is about as impenetrable and forbidding to the uninitiated as any secret order ever known. Its passwords are occult. Its Templars hold themselves remote from the substantial humans of the race, who exist for the sole purpose of showing themselves amused, impressed, and incidentally generative of enough contemptible cash to keep the actor alive. But there are also fiercely guarded caste lines within the order. However well paid they are, actors who shuck their stage personalities on and off for working hours, like a plasterer's white overalls, cannot so much as carry incense to the higher incantations. There, in a jealously hidden professional retreat, pace the great pretenders, who have worn their antic dispositions so long that they have really no other nature. Dutch Mantell walked in the murkiest, loftiest sanctum of all.

Alfred Albert was born in turmoil to a Roman Catholic mother and a Masonic father in the year, we believe, of 1880. Not many years thereafter his father died, presumably between shouts in a marathon family argument, and his mother eventually made the mistake of putting her lad out as a butcher's apprentice. But that was a peasant craft indeed for a boy whose thespian zodiac was already pulling him in another direction.

Promptly he ran away to England, en route, so he thought, to the United States. A schooner skipper needed a cabin boy and he signed on, only to learn at sea that the ship was bound, not for New York, but for Australia. To Alfred Albert the error was inconsequential. He departed the vessel at Melbourne and blithely patrolled the subcontinent behind a pair of explosive fists that earned his living for a while.

Soon, however, he abandoned boxing in favor of another proficiency acquired in Contusion College along the waterfront. Wrestling plainly demanded a less earnest concentration upon the carnage of the moment while at the same time offering a far wider opportunity for irrelevant

hamming and ferocious insult. Already this young de re L'Guardier was 85
a performer to whom wrestling was another name for massacre staged
Cecil B. DeMille style, and whose greatest delight was the sound of a
crowd bellowing frantically for his own blood.

America was still his goal. He shipped out and landed in Africa. Again,
he reached Calais and London. A fourth time, the rusty steamer actually
anchored within sight of the towers of lower Manhattan. But the captain
passed down the stern word: no liberty ashore under any circumstances.
No jumping ship here. Thus the ship, and Alfred Albert, went on—to
Brazil, around the Horn to Chile, and back to Melbourne.

Now it was bigger events, with the name L'Guardier sitting high on
the placards in tall type. His rhapsodic manslaughter had made him a "good
card," and among his faithful following was one man who most certainly
could recognize a stage performer when he saw one. For weeks the great
Shakespearian actor Robert B. Mantell was never absent from the ringside
during his favorite's matches, shouting his partisanship in resonant
Elizabethan syllables. To perpetuate such a portentous meeting of great
minds in mummery, Alfred Albert Joe promptly dropped the whole de
re L'Guardier business and took upon himself the only name he ever used
thereafter—Dutch Mantell.

At last he reached America, on a windjammer which beat around the
Horn to Liverpool, back to Chile, and finally to New York. Staying around
the metropolis for a year or two, Mantell wrestled miscellaneously against
any and all opponents of as much as half a hundredweight more than his
own wiry hundred and forty-five pounds. Then, on another merrily aimless
impulse, he went back to sea as a U.S. Navy tar.

"Twenty-four of us on a leaky old can," he later reminisced. "Dat vass
fine stuff! Den dey got 'em destroyers 'th speed. Paint on 'em. Keep
dungarees clean, mate. Lots more men. Dat vass not for me. I got out."

The year was 1906 and Mantell was already a naturalized American
citizen. He assailed Amarillo briefly for the first time that same year and
instantly preempted it as his hometown. For many years thereafter, his
travels seldom if ever brought him this way, and the remote little frontier
city remained unaware that it had been adopted totally into a capacious
and sanguinary heart. But sidewalk pedestrians from Toronto to San Diego
to Seattle were being treated constantly, nevertheless, to the sight of a
bouncing sweatshirt and nondescript trousers with the legend, "The Flying
Dutchman of Amarillo, Texas," lettered prominently on the back and the
seat thereof, respectively.

Those years continued to be more carefree than the ones before, if that were possible. Life was an uncomplicated saunter down an open road to anywhere, with nothing but a little honest wrestling and a lot of high-handed foolishness in one town and then another. Always childishly chesty about his full-blown and official American citizenship, he undertook as a matter of principle to hand out a little extra punishment to any "tam lousy foreigner" who climbed into a ring with him. From the vigor he applied to all these activities a considerable number of dollars customarily shook down into his pockets, to stay there momentarily if at all. The Flying Dutchman of Amarillo could spend money almost as rapidly as he could give it away to any and all takers, and his latter talent was prodigious.

If there chanced to be enough cash left to permit him to ride first-class to the next town, well and good. If not, no matter. Some train would be coming through soon, heading one way or the other—and in either direction there was another town.

∗ Dead broke in a strange locality, Mantell frequently put into motion a campaign of financial recovery that did full justice to his many-sided imagination. Carefully choosing the favored town's leading Greek restaurant, he began by ordering the biggest and rawest steak in the house. In such surroundings, he well knew that he was wearing two meal tickets, in the form of his gorgeously cauliflowered ears, which were far more satisfactory for such purposes than mere money. The Hellenic innkeeper never lived who could ignore such prominent badges of his ancient national sport. Within minutes the proprietor himself would be standing beside the Dutchman's table, ordering out the best possible service, beaming under his guest's artful compliments about the food, and reviewing the prowess of Jim Londos or some other leading Greek wrestler of the day.

Before the last forkful of steak disappeared a great and admiring friendship would be accomplished. Arm in arm, Mantell and his host would stroll toward the cashier, where would occur a furious slapping of the money pocket, searching of the clothes, and a flood of apologies as disarming as only Mantell could make them.

"Jeezchrist," he would confide, totally embarrassed, "I musta been rolled down at a roomin' house!"

The proprietor, still glowing from the sunbath in his hero's reflected glory, would invariably insist that the mighty Mantell depart in peace, accepting the steak dinner as a paltry token of esteem.

But this was no elaborate mooch. Not with Mantell, who would owe no man. Shouting down any suggestion of a free meal, the Dutchman always demanded so stubbornly to be permitted to wash dishes or mop floors that he was soon doing just that.

At this point the rest of his plan began to unfold. Within two hours after Mantell invaded any kitchen as a dishwasher he had inevitably taken over the place in fee simple — as a cook. His preoccupation with good food around the globe had not been as a large-scale consumer only. His skull was full of culinary tricks with fine recipes — which, along with his jovial ability to make the regular chef his ally, brought customers and new fame to the cafe.

There followed two or three weeks, let us say, which the delighted Greek would never forget. There would be endless experimenting and swapping of recipes, endless hours of confab that set the Dutchman digging deep into his warehouse of wrestling lore. The cookery and clowning, along with the Dutchman's frightful face, were more than enough to keep the restaurant in a joyous and profitable uproar. The customers, of course, would promptly scatter to all points bearing the news that mighty Mantell, "the world's greatest rassler, by Gott," was in town and ready to meet all comers. A match, a hundred bucks in the Mantell jeans, and his departure for the next town could take the appearance of a procession. The Greek was happy, the town was happy, Mantell was happy — and his opponent was, very possibly, in the infirmary.

Mantell, incidentally, was an expert wrestler by legitimate standards whenever he chose to be. He was double-jointed and as flexible as steel cable. These were days long before freaks and phonies had brought the sport under the scorn of polite citizens, and a large share of the fans were likely to be technically critical of the performance. An outclassed opponent might get off lightly if the Dutchman's spirits happened to be below par, in which event the antagonist would serve as a mere stage property for a nonchalant display of Mantell skill.

But serious wrestling had a tendency to become entirely too businesslike for Mantell, whose principal concern was always that neither he nor the customers should suffer boredom. And he had learned before his time that more violence and show, as a general policy, sold more tickets. Thus, a tough and capable opponent, particularly a larger man, too often became nothing more than a man-sized sack of oats to be slugged, gouged, stomped upon, flung into the furniture, booted jackasswise, and otherwise flamboyantly assaulted by every method known to the waterfront. And, if he came unprepared to hand back the same kind of treatment, he could take what comfort he could from the fact that, when Mantell sent him to the

A DUTCHMAN AMUCK

hospital, the Dutchman would probably be there ahead of the ambulance to pay his bill.

Sports writers thus customarily ran up the storm warnings whenever Mantell hit town. ("This match will need a referee, of course, able to look out for himself as well as Dutch and Joe Kopecky, as Heavyweight Sapulveda managed to do two weeks ago.") And the crowds came.

Spectators? They were present, it seemed, to be lampooned, defied, and outraged in the sensibilities if not in the person, particularly if events on the canvas were becoming dull. In a routine bout with Basanta Singh of Singapore, who prayed orientally on the mat before the contest, it soon developed that either Singh was not in the Dutchman's league or, as one reporter commented, "had got the wrong set of prayers."

Dutch tired quickly of flipping this 'tam lousy foreigner" around the ring at will, and his stern sense of showman's duty demanded that other measures be employed. Whereupon he took vast offense at the remarks of certain ringsiders and spent the rest of the evening shuttling back and forth, into the ring just long enough to plant the Burmese bone-crusher momentarily, then out to bruise and bellow at and push over the chairs of a score of offenders. It was a lovely melee which, to his great disappointment, stopped a little short of a full-dress riot. On other, similar occasions when the blue coats did have to move in on the proceedings, his ecstasy was that of a conductor who has just led a masterly performance of Tschaikovsky's Fourth.

At certain times, however, paying customers were known to save his life. Vagabonding into Nebraska once, he paused in the bailiwick ruled by Farmer John Pesek, a great wrestler and a mighty man. Rashly he put out his entire stake of ready cash in bets before taking a precautionary look at his opponent. When Farmer John rolled into town to meet the challenge, Dutch looked, but too late. "Dutch, y' tam fool!" the invader was muttering to himself before Farmer John had time to disembark from his brass-radiatored Ford roadster. "Y' purple-pantzed tam fool. Y' sure got no tam business in *this* town!"

Mantell's two hundred dollars was as well as on its way to feed Pesek's chickens. Plainly it would never do to scrimmage politely with this muscular Pole. And in this case the opposite tactic of playing rough would be nothing but a shortcut to a broken back. What to do? Fight the crowd, of course.

Fortunately the match was a short one, scheduled for one fall or twenty minutes. Mantell put one gingerly foot on the canvas before assaulting a vocal local at the ringside for his comments. Pesek was too mannerly to follow; by his rules, a match was supposed to be conducted on the canvas. The full twenty minutes thereafter the Dutchman expanded in magnificent indignation on one side of the mat and then another, skirting Pesek at all times but loudly offering to whip anyone who dared to call him yellow. Anyone but Pesek. Finally the proceedings were declared "no contest." Mantell was given back his two hundred and sent on his way, happily fingering just that much more money than he would have had if the battle had been joined.

Discretion is a precious asset. More for laughs than anything else, Dutch and I once arranged a match with a semiretired and out-of-condition heavyweight named Ignatz Guthrie, who outweighed the Dutchman by nearly seventy pounds.

"I'll moërder dat blubber," quoth Mantell.

Guthrie's wind was bad, but he had enough strength and weight to keep the Dutchman under him for many minutes. Finding the crushing sensation decidedly unpleasant, Dutch wriggled free and sank a powerful foot into Guthrie's outsized stomach. The referee swarmed over him in protest. Mantell felled him with a right hook to the jaw, piled him thoughtfully on top of the prostrate Guthrie, and stalked with rapid dignity to the dressing room. Scolded to the effect that he ought to return and finish the match, facing the displeasure of the slowly rising gentlemen in the ring, he disappeared into the shower with the studious remark: "Old Papa Mantell didn't raise no foolish children."

But it was a rare day indeed that found Mantell retreating from combat. His handling of an explosive situation that occurred during Borger's wildest days always remains vividly in my mind. Under martial law the Rangers ruled so freely over the boomtown that we were sure they could shoot at will, telegraph Governor Ma Ferguson that they had "got another one," and rest assured that little more would be said. And the Rangers, as well as most of the rest of the town partisans, unfortunately were betting heavily on Yaqui Joe, Mantell's opponent and a very tough wrestler. For a good-sized fee I had been reluctantly persuaded to act as referee, on the presumption that only the incorrigible Dutchman's best friend might be able to keep him from getting too far out of line.

But as usual, after a few uneventful minutes, the fray moved out into the seats where Mantell was joyously bouncing the Indian's skull on the steel bottom of a collapsed chair.

The crowd reared in a tone I didn't like at all. Not the least emphatic were a line of eight pistol-heavy Rangers seated in the front row. Heaving Dutch off the Indian by the Adam's apple, I yelled in his ear that he was going to get us both killed in just about ten seconds.

"Ya, ya, ya," he choked, purple-faced in my stranglehold, "I be good. I be good."

Like a shot he was back on the canvas to meet Yaqui Joe, who had crawled completely under the ring to come up on the opposite side. But by now a fourth party was joining the Indian Wars on the redskin side. A tall and very angry young Ranger, hand on gun, was climbing between the ropes and shouting threats at the Dutchman's back.

The crowd's uproar of a moment before flicked off as with a switch. In deadly silence not even a popcorn sack rustled. Every spectator present knew too well that, in a town which was then consistently averaging three to five murders a week, Dutch Mantell might very well finish this bout not bruised but perforated. But Mantell had sensed the intrusion. Quick as a tree cat he was across the ring to meet it, standing so close that when the Ranger pulled himself erect inside the ring the Dutchman's shapeless nose was a defiant two inches from the officer's wagging chin. Motionless and unspeakably ugly, Mantell tiptoed tight against the uniformed chest while the hotheaded ranger, beginning to waver, finished his speech. For long seconds they stood, the Ranger's fingers tapping his holster a moment, and then uncomfortably dropping to his side. Then the little Dutchman spoke, not loudly for once, but with menace that carried to the bleachers:

"Get t' hell out of this ring!"

Hearing no vocal support from the ringside, the young Ranger got. A much-subdued crowd then watched Mantell proceed, without breaking another rule, to take Yaqui Joe apart.

Such a man was Mantell while plying his trade. For his more important "public" duties, his first concern was to arrange himself in proper jester's costume. In summer, his daily tour of Amarillo's streets might be conducted in black homburg, white duck gym shorts, Mexican huaraches, and nothing else. A typical winter getup might well consist of opera hat, scarlet earmuffs, tuxedo coat, dungarees, and high-laced lumberman's boots. Daily the assortment changed according to the dictates of the man's abandoned imagination. Today's boots, sweat pants, and Stetson above a bare chest would certainly be switched tomorrow for a sweatshirt lettered like a sandwich board ("Dutch Mantell, World's Greatest Wrestler—From Amarillo, Tex., Oil Capital of the World") atop the sloppiest of plus fours, bare legs, and the same old huaraches. For a while Gene Howe's daily

Farley, flanked by Dutch Mantell and Mike Rodrigues, at a boisterous training camp in New Mexico in the 1920s.

column plugged jovially for Mantell's appointment as the nation's only postmaster-in-shorts.

Insanity, indeed. But, like everything else the Dutchman ever did, his sartorial excesses were a studied design for attracting attention. All his life the food to satisfy his enormous appetite had depended on titillating John Public's curiosity to the point where J. P. would pay his dollar at the arena box office merely to see what the wild man would do next.

As professional clowns go, Mantell's face alone was enough to upstage any competitior before the show began. It was a sour person indeed who could so much as look at his egghead with its blond hair cropped to quarter-inch bristles, his roseate ears slapped on like two careless blobs of putty among the wrinkles of ten thousand headlocks, without coming apart in a belly laugh.

The sidewalks, coffee counters, pool halls, filling stations, and clothing stores were this clown's tanbark. With him it was always a riot or a snore, with no milder graduations between. He rose late in the mornings, thus giving his citywide patronage a chance to eat breakfast, recuperate in peace from the antics of the day before, and perhaps even conduct an hour or two of honest business before the next foolishness struck. But from 10:30

A DUTCHMAN AMUCK

A.M. until the wee hours of the next morning he labored incessantly at his real vocation, which was disorder.

Friends quickly learned the hazards of walking down the street with the Dutchman. Progress was always slow. The most casual greeting by a passerby (and he knew everyone in Texas) would be taken as a high insult to his character that called for a long harangue and a physical mauling. But the Dutchman's companion, not the greeter, would get the hammering. Next there would be a few unscheduled stops and a practical joke or two in some unfortunate business establishment. Then more greetings and more horseplay, with knots of onlookers gathering from up and down the thoroughfare. By the time a lineal distance of two or three blocks had been covered in this way the Dutchman had insured the presence of at least a dozen more paying fans at his next wrestling bout—and his companion had wasted an entertaining one to two hours from the middle of the day.

Such journeys could also be embarrassing. Let two or three unwary friends walk abreast with the Dutchman bouncing as always two paces in front, and a disturbing fate awaited the first really handsome young woman they met. Wavering this way and that to find a passage through this forbidding wave of masculinity, she would swing innocently toward the Dutchman, who was making extravagantly courteous motions toward getting out of her way. That was her error. At the crucial moment the Dutchman would always stumble, a marvelously genuine stumble. Falling against her, he would scramble up the length of her like an orangutan seeking equilibrium, finally clasping her in an outrageous double brassiere-lock such as no other wrestler ever dared to display in public. Nor was this a momentary grapple in any sense. While his companions blushed in a helpless huddle, cursing themselves and wishing for an open manhole to drop into, Mantell continued to clamp the astonished young woman tightly about the bosom for the full duration of his eloquent apologies. Only when he could think of no more to say would he release her to proceed, flustered but invariably laughing, on her way. To Mantell the whole performance was for the sole purpose of a full-throated bellow at the expense of his humiliated associates.

With a true vaudevillian's passion he hated the movies. Now and then, however, some host in a strange town might persuade him to attend. But that host would never make the mistake a second time. At the first moment of real dramatic tension on the screen there would arise an outburst of demented laughter that shook the walls of the place. Ushers would scurry.

A love climax—and more pathological hysteria from the audience. That would bring the manager. To him the Dutchman would protest lavishly how much he was enjoying the show.

"Best tam show I ever seen, sir." With words of warning the manager would depart. Then there would be more laughter and more protests, until the place was a shambles. Finally the manager would demand that the Dutchman take his leave. Deeply hurt, the Dutchman would be always willing to comply.

"But I got to have my money back, sir!"

"Call at the box office. You'll get it!"

"Bring it here!"

"Just come out, please. I'll take you to my office and pay you back. Just leave the theater!"

"Brink ta money here! All I want is my money, but dis is a sure fine show, *sir*!"

When the manager finally complied, the Dutchman, still profuse and complimentary, would make his usual noticeable exit.

The man had two remarkable aversions regarding money. A debt of any kind was intolerable; he gave himself no rest until it was paid in full. But, on the other hand, the presence of any amount of money in his pocket beyond the needs of the next twenty-four hours was equally unpleasant. Not only was he the world's softest touch among his colleagues of more flexible philosophy; also it seemed that he would practically give chase to bums of all sorts to urge them to relieve him of his cash.

Too much liquor (which he never touched) and too much money, he frequently remarked, got a man into trouble. Though he earned over a half-million dollars in thirty years of wrestling, he was well past forty with nothing more tangible to show for it than a crop of unsalable cauliflower before Mimi decided to take matters into her own hands.

Thereafter, each time Mantell returned from a wrestling trip Mimi and her friend Gertrude Doche at the store set upon him bodily with better results than I had ever managed against him in the ring. (Early in his Amarillo days I had met him in two matches. Both ended in ugly brawls, with a cracked skull for the Dutchman and enough free-flowing blood from the pair of us to establish the sport solidly in the city's favor from that time forward. After the second meeting, we agreed it was better to be friends.)

Those were plaintive scenes as the two determined women tamed the terror of the Panhandle, flushing nondescript wads of greenbacks from all parts of his clothing, and doling back living expenses five dollars at a time. The rest of the money they invested in cottage apartments, which provided him with a place to live and offered prospects of a steady income after his departure from the ring. He suffered loudly at each robbery, but he never had a chance against Mimi.

"Chee, Mimi, Harvey Southworth's got the purtiest red car he wants to sell. I gotta have a car, doncha think? Kin I please have eight hundred dollars?"

"No."

The end result of these proceedings was signaled one day in the store only a few years later, when Mimi was able to present a docile, grateful Mantell with a paid-up mortgage on his own cottage and six rental apartments. Embarrassed himself for the one and only time in his life, he concealed the tears in his eyes by giving forth with his "Alaska nosewipe" (a complicated vulgarity involving the use of an entire sleeve and forefinger, followed by various finger-wipings about his own and others' persons). Then he kissed her solemnly and stalked out.

The Dutchman's radio career was short and notably unsuccessful. Once in awhile during my own broadcasts of the wrestling matches I brought in Dutch as a visiting expert. While a technician stood guard at the station to throw a switch at all outbursts of profanity, his commentary quickly resolved itself into a deluge of wrestling instructions to his favorite:

"Clamp dat headlock! Now flip da tramp! Ya, dat's it! Ya! No! No! Y' tam fool, y' dumbunny, doncha know he's gonna throw ya a scissors? Here he comes. Ow...."

His bull-elephant lungs were too much for the little station. His announcing career ended the night he blew out a tube and put the station off the air. Later, on one of the store broadcasts, on a day when I was out of town, S-s-stuttering Sam made the unhappy tactical error of baiting Mantell about a wrestling match.

"Why, y' stutter'n' ape!" roared the Dutchman, charging. In a second Sam had been hoisted by his bushy hair and tossed from the stage into the showcases, the microphone still with him. "I'll show ya who was under who...."

This incapacity for moderation was again in evidence the night the sheriff called me to come down and bail Dutch out of the Potter County Jail. Earlier in the evening Matty Matsuda, who had been reluctantly persuaded to risk his jeweled championship belt against Mantell, had spent the entire miserable bout keeping out of danger's way. Mantell had proceeded downtown and either climbed or talked his way into the drug store where the belt was on display and was now refusing to give the thing back to the Japanese, claiming he had won it. Matsuda had called the law. When we found Mantell in the lockup, he was gleefully instructing several other prisoners in the art of wrestling while conversing learnedly with a guard about the quality of his accommodations.

Of the other endless tales about the Dutchman still being regularly served across Texas coffee counters, one hears frequently about his match with a four hundred and fifty-pound bear. Fifty-year-old Mantell grew weary of lying on the canvas under all that weight and rubbed the bear's nose with red pepper he had brought along in a bologna skin packet stuffed inside his trunks. The bear soared over the top rope of the ring, and what had been a crowded carnival tent was suddenly empty and sagging.

Another scene which would have delighted Mack Sennett involved the electric sweatsuit, tailored along the lines of a straitjacket, which Mantell borrowed when he was "down in the back." (Jack Reynolds had once thrown him out of an Iowa ring, chipping a vertebra.) Lulled to sleep by the warmth, he reached the perspiration point, shorted the circuit, and demolished a considerable portion of the roominghouse before his room-mate could manage to pull the plug.

What we called relaxation from our regular duties usually meant an invasion of nearby New Mexico. Then the party often included, besides Mantell and myself, S-s-stuttering Sam and Rufe Davis, the rubber-faced bird- and animal-imitator from Hollywood. The customary excuse was a visit to the hot springs baths near Roswell, but what happened must have taxed even the patience of easygoing New Mexico. A guide in the depths of the Carlsbad Caverns one afternoon tried several times to restrain those three irrepressibles from disrupting the progress of a party of a hundred or more tourists by trying out their trick speech in the echoing darkness. But it was no use — he finally interrupted the tour and invited the trio to put on a half-hour of professional entertainment, which they proceeded with great relish to deliver.

During years of foolishness which merited action by the state troopers, the only person who managed to stop this invasion cold was a waitress in a Roswell cafe. Rufe Davis, a big, forbidding fellow, had squeaked his order at her in Donald Duckese, "I-wants-steak. I-wants-steak." Mystified, she had turned to S-s-Sam, only to receive a hearttending, unintelligible flood of stuttering. Then Dutch, hammering the table and bellowing in his cheese-thick accent: "Vat t' hell's d' matter, Agnes? D'man says he wantsa steak!"

She fled, but met me returning from the washroom and froze me to the floor with, "Now let's hear *you* talk!" We ate our steak in another cafe.

A DUTCHMAN AMUCK

Putt Powell, sports "biographer" of both Mantell and Farley, at his desk at the *Amarillo News* in 1986.

Mantell and the great Jack Dempsey, on the latter's frequent visits to Amarillo in later years, seemed to spend most of their time slapping each other around like a pair of amiable grizzly bears. Jack, however, never did manage to win my private twenty-five-dollar bet with him that he could never get behind that old sailor.

He was utterly fascinated with the first colored sheets Mimi installed in our house. ("Oh, dem passionate sheets!") Promptly he bought white sheets, had them dyed scarlet, then installed impudent red light globes on the front porch of his flat.

It was a murderous game of golf he played, running at a high lope every step between strokes.

A pet squirrel rode his shoulder into many a strange hotel, carefully trained to leap past the astonished room clerk and make a shambles of the key boxes. Regardless of his momentary prosperity, he consistently refused to stay in any hotel fancy enough to have an elevator.

"You'n Cal should come down with me, Mimi," he would often plead as we took our separate ways. "It's good people in dem little hotels."

The credit man at the Farley store learned by experience to give weight to Mantell's uncanny judgment of human beings. An offhand "He's all right" or "Don't give dat guy nut'n, he's no tam good" never failed to be confirmed by subsequent events. And many a companion was surprised to hear coming from this fountain of irreverence, now and then, Bible quotations that displayed a considerable knowledge of the Scriptures.

At fifty-two, Mantell played rough once too often in the ring. A young wrestler named Sailor Moran kicked out an assortment of his Teutonic teeth, and the mat career of the great Mantell was over. He could never find store teeth which would stay in his violent head. By now he didn't really care a great deal. The wrestling arena had grown dull by comparison with other activities, such as the immense triumph he scored in his own eyes when he was chosen, by popular demand, to lead the annual football day parade.

Thereafter he was free to spend his full time piling up shocks of conversation fodder for his hometown to harvest long after he was gone — to devote himself to his public and to the small regiment of kids which habitually dogged his course about the streets. Those kids were the climax of Dutch Mantell's life. Through the depths of the Great Depression and after, there was ample work for him to do and a vehicle for doing it.

The latter was the theatrical nonesuch we called the Flying Dutchman Circus. This home-talent jamboree began as a small-scale "program" put on by half a dozen child performers before parent-teacher associations of the Panhandle, and grew eventually to a troupe of thirty or more whose bookings included some rather important audiences across the country. Every Friday night for eleven school terms the show went on somewhere, and only the Second World War stopped it.

The circus — it was nothing but a circus in which the clowns had taken full command — drew its name from a coincidence. It had Flying Dutchman Mantell as its orchestra leader, and the so-called Flying Dutchman wrestling hold had been so much publicized as my own specialty in the ring that I was using it as a business trademark.

Amarillo's Maverick Club had just started, providing a worthy but inadequate haven for a few of the homeless horde of boys the depression had released to the streets. It was our purpose to advertise our store while making performers of a number of these hungry lads for the good of their souls and their bodies as well. At least there was no shortage of food out on the farms.

At its full strength the troupe numbered thirty persons staging a full two-hour show of song and dance, wrestling, boxing, tumbling, and corn-fed comedy. It was quite a procession which left the store Friday evenings in a bus or several cars to try to unravel its way through blizzards of snow or dust in accordance with some farm lady's elaborate instructions

A DUTCHMAN AMUCK

for reaching a certain country schoolhouse. Normally we'd find it, after getting lost two or three times, and discover a crowd that in better weather overflowed into the schoolyard, lining the outside of every windowsill with faces.

As one of their noneducational activities the PTA ladies had always spread a magnificent supper of chicken, roast beef, ham, gravies, salads, milk, cakes, and pies by the score. Flouting all the laws of the theater, our performers would fall upon that mountain of food and make a small knoll of it before the show went on. Kids who in all likelihood never enjoyed another square meal during the entire week could look forward to tall feasting on Friday nights. I frequently wondered, in fact, whether this sterling performance at the dinner table was not more responsible for the success of the show than anything that came after. The joy of those hearty farm women rose higher with every ravenous mouthful the kids devoured.

Hungry as our street urchins were, however, it was the Dutchman himself who set the pace. Here was eating that challenged him to the quick, and he really leveled off on that food. Having stowed away enough for three harvest hands, he was then all over the place, praising the cooks, looking after his kids, forcing more food onto surfeited youngsters' plates, and then thumping their skulls merrily if they could not put it away.

"Polish dat plate, young' un!" was his often-shouted command.

These tasks accomplished, he was ready to take the stage—if he didn't fall asleep first. Weary of sending a flying wedge of youngsters to roust him out of the parked automobile for his cue, we let him snore one night straight through the show, then piled the troupe into the other cars and drove home.

"Cancha poot a blanket over a man?" he grumbled in town the next morning. "Don't leave him out t' ere t' freeze."

Besides all the athletic events we could stage in restricted quarters, there were some specialties in the show of a nature seldom perpetrated since. S-s-stuttering Sam Hunter evoked sympathy and doubled on the saxophone. Our daughter, Gene Farley, and her friend, Marilyn Cornelius, did tap- and toe-dances and sang in a trio with Vesta O'Dell. A limber lad named Vilas ("Lady Esther") Newby presented a surefire soft-shoe dance in bloomers and evening gown that brought about ardent lovemaking by the Dutchman and ended when Mantell booted Lady Esther out into the audience. A boy named Gib Howard and his sister, Floy, proved to be audience killers when they sang the raucous "Friendship" or flooded "The Old Apple Tree" with real, lugubrious tears.

It was a fixed rule that each youngster would take his turn at the microphone announcing the acts. Beginners would be coached in one single wisecrack, and we never ceased to be amazed at how much this little maneuver would do for a boy's soul. However sorry the joke might be, an appealing youngster was sure to put it across with the crowd in a big way. And that applause—to a boy who possibly had never heard a dozen decent words from grownups in his life, to say nothing of real handclapping—did him even more good than all that marvelous food. It was enough to bring tears to a man's eyes to stand offstage and watch that boy swell about a foot taller and swing into his act. Two Caterpillar tractors couldn't have pulled that kid out of his place in our troupe after that first burst of applause.

Came the Dutchman's lecture on physical culture. No one in the audience could understand more than an occasional word of his ear-shattering brogue. But his fists pumped madly back and forth to illustrate, I suppose, some of the delicate personality benefits to be derived from regular exercise. When his suspenders came unbuttoned and flew over his head, the shouting and arm-waving went on with his pants at his ankles. That was my cue to seize the corrugated washboard used in the orchestra, dash on stage, hammer him over the head with it while pulling him off by the shirttails. This portion of the act was dropped, however, after I became a little too enthusiastic one night and made a necktie of the frame of the washboard.

Final disintegration took place with the orchestral finale. Mantell, as dynamic a conductor as ever took the podium, used also a three-foot baton in the manner of a blacksnake whip.

"Sount yer A!" he would bellow, and Newby would respond with a taradiddle from the washboard and thimbles. The Dutchman's face would collapse into a transport of musical delight. Bounding about sprucing up his other players (including a somewhat unprotected Farley at the piano ready to play the only set of chords he knew, with a harmonica strapped about his neck), he would announce the "Sextette from Lucia," and the aggregation would blare forth "Turkey in the Straw."

"Request yer favor-ite melody, pleeze!" the conductor would roar at the audience.

"Nobody Loves Me."

"Yar' n a hell of a shape! Request *numbers*, I said!"

"Home on the Range!"

"Hokay. We got it. 'Home on the Range'!"

Again it was "Turkey in the Straw." Without too much more of this,

A DUTCHMAN AMUCK

we let the battered audience escape for some fresh air.

As time went on and the kids polished up a fairly fast-moving show that warranted a wider field of operations, we wandered rather far from Texas. There were appearances, for example, at Yellowstone Park, at the Chicago World's Fair, at Rotary clubs in Denver and Washington, D.C., and at many other places. But my pleasantest memory from the whole irresponsible enterprise arose from an incident on the way to a performance in Toronto. The troupe had been at some pains to learn the French to the old song, "Alouette," in honor of the occasion. On a bus headed downtown they suddenly burst into the song, and it was wonderful. That unpremeditated outburst from two dozen young voices, ringing through the quaint, sunny streets from a crowded bus as pedestrians turned to stare and then to smile, came about as near to expressing a pure and spontaneous joy of living as any sound these ears will ever listen to.

The crazy Dutchman was not with us on that trip. He was not at all well. Only a short while remained for him to set the Maverick Club gymnasium into a furore by merely dropping in to "coach his poys," or to drive the other coaches to despair by buying ice cream for lads momentarily in disfavor for infractions of the rules. No more summers were left for him to herd his usual troop of alley "tough guys" out to his camp in the scenic Palo Duro Canyon near Amarillo, where the lot of them would chop wood, build fences, hunt rabbits, and romp the red-and-yellow arroyos for days on end.

Driving back together one night from Lubbock, where a doctor friend had told him the cancer was all through his system, Mantell and I spent a little longer than usual calling each other unmentionable names and thanking the gods that neither of us had been so unfortunate as to fall into the tender mercies of the other.

He lived about four months more. His will, when it was opened, contained no surprises. His house and all his property went to the homeless kids at Boys Ranch.

10

The Mavericks are Corraled

THE BEGINNING was small, but the need could not be ignored. The year 1934, the third year of the Great Depression, was also the first year of dust and mass-scale tragedy in the Wheat Belt. Amarillo itself had been somewhat sheltered against the big blow by discovery of another major oil field the year before, even though bad times and federal restrictions had prevented anything resembling another boom. But the farms faced disaster.

Already the first streams of homeless, hopeless, wind-scourged thousands were flowing through the city. They had their children, and Amarillo had its own — ragged and hungry kids by the hundreds prowling the streets and alleys, stealing to eat or, for lack of anything else to do, learning crime instead of arithmetic, pushing still higher the rising wave of wasted human lives.

Mrs. Lee Bivins, widow of the cattle-and-oil man, and her son, Julian, had made available to a minister named Emmett Galloway a small building on West Fourth Street to house a small youth center. It did not have much room, but a tiny ring was set up for wrestling and boxing and a handball court was contrived. A reading room was stocked with magazines, checkerboards, and a few parlor games. Forty to fifty boys a day sought harbor there.

This was the start of the Maverick Club. Its purpose was as unpretentious as its facilities, being principally the idea that, if the club managed to draw a few boys off the street and get their tongues hanging out from two hours of strenuous exercise, they would have just that much less energy left with which to cause trouble.

✷ Our thinking had not progressed much farther than that. We figured that it would be cheap insurance at twice the cost of the club if we could curtail the pilferage of merchandise off our shelves and forestall some big tax increases that would be necessary to control the flood of refugees from the Dust Bowl so that we could survive ourselves.

By the time the Reverend Galloway left the city the following spring, several businessmen, including Mayor Lawrence Hagy, cattleman Chanslor Weymouth, druggist Roy Pool, and I had become convinced that maintaining and expanding the Maverick Club would be a civic necessity. A good supervisor was needed. On a hunch one evening I telphoned Ralph Dykeman, a husky, friendly, easygoing young insurance man from California who was then the popular leader of a Boy Scout troop and had already lent us some assistance in our initial work with boys. He agreed to spend four hours each evening, from five to nine, at the Maverick Club.

That move proved to be one of the most fortunate breaks the kids of Amarillo ever had. Before long, Dykeman's fascination with his multiplying "family" of boys shoved the insurance business out of the picture. With the unceasing assistance of his attractive and energetic young wife, he was soon devoting full-time, often sixteen hours a day and seven days a week, to his boys. As this is written sixteen years later, the same calm Ralph Dykeman remains the central figure in an effort now grown to such size and success that it is frequently termed "easily the outstanding municipal youth program in the United States."

The Maverick Club was less than two years old when its first major expansion was arranged. The tax-supported city junior college was moving to new quarters, leaving a large frame gymnasium to be disposed of to make way for new construction. Though the Maverick Club had exactly sixty dollars in its treasury, a sympathetic school board sold the building to the club complete for five hundred dollars, "pay-when-you-can." Again the Bivinses provided the site, donating several lots not more than four blocks from the downtown district. Then the work of tearing down and rebuilding began.

There was no money, but Amarillo believed in the Maverick Club. Unavoidable costs were guaranteed by a few of us businessmen. The *Globe-News* lent strong support. Aroused by some of their own members, the plumbers' and electricians' unions furnished necessary work free of charge. Volunteer carpenters swung their hammers at the direction of paid foremen, and the building went up.

The Mavericks themselves set out to do their share by delivering telephone directories about the city and by selling programs at the city's annual Tri-State Fair. These proceeds plus occasional cash donations amounting to about two thousand dollars paid off the entire six thousand five hundred dollars expense of the venture in three years. The result was a building worth at least fifteen thousand dollars at depression prices, containing basketball, wrestling, tumbling, handball, and shower facilities — and the opportunity to serve, not a few dozen, but several hundred boys. Old but sturdy, the building has seen as much actual use during the succeeding years, I venture, as any gymnasium in America.

The organized sports program began with basketball. Youngsters swarmed in at the announcement, seeming to drop from trees and spring out of curbstones in order to join the club and to play. Then came football, Dykeman's personal favorite among the sports. (Though he had once played a good tackle in high school at San Diego, California, it had never before occurred to him to use his fine natural coaching talent.)

To start the junior football league Dykeman first made a tour of high schools in Amarillo and neighboring towns, begging discarded equipment. Hundreds of suits, jerseys, and shoes still in usable shape piled in locker rooms were "borrowed" — again with the connivance of friendly coaches and school boards — with the provision that the goods be marked and returned to the schools in the event they were needed again. They never were, and the Maverick Club had plenty of equipment. This search, moreover, stimulated similar action roundabout until at least a dozen nearby towns had formed teams of their own.

Then Dykeman moved into an Amarillo tent-and-awning shop, sat down at a sewing machine, and quickly devised a method whereby a few swift seams would reduce high school football pants to little-shaver size. Shoes he patched, cleated, and mated from his sizable pile. Soon the shouts, struggles, and strategy of more than a dozen teams of young gridsters was filling the crisp autumn air on sandlots all over the city. And the total equipment cost, as Dykeman says, was "not more than five dollars in actual cash for the first two whole seasons."

Softball was next — a summer-long sport that instantly attracted enough boys for several dozen teams. But team athletics was by no means the whole program. The basic idea, which fortunately has never been forgotten at the Maverick Club, was to take boys off the streets who never had had a chance to play or grow within the heritage of normal childhood and use their innate human *desire to excel* as a lever for teaching them self-discipline. We wanted to employ any and all legitimate means to get a boy's chin up. We wanted to take the wary, cornered-animal look out of his eyes and show him that grownups are something more than the objects of spiteful mischief. We wanted to give him some personal achievement to be proud of and put into him, perhaps for the first time in his life, the idea that it is, after all, a fairly simple matter to be just as decent and respectable as anyone else. To give every possible lad the chance to put his "name in lights," therefore, the fullest possible sort of athletic program was instituted. And the results have ranged from excellent to astonishing.

Tumbling is a Maverick specialty. Within a few months after instruction began, the boys' professional-caliber performances were drawing enthusiastic applause from various public audiences. Other boys take to the trampoline as if it were a candy-counter, and are compensated for their efforts by staging exhibitions between events at school gymnasiums or the city sports arena.

Wrestling has its devotees as well, shepherded by professionals who delight in making the Maverick gymnasium their headquarters during stopovers in the city. Handball courts see almost as much activity during evenings and weekends as do the basketball courts, where as many as fourteen league games are run off on a single Saturday.

As important as anything is the big Maverick record board. On it are posted, as advertisement of its champions and a challenge to its newcomers, the club's top official marks for most conventional events as well as a score or so of others rarely seen elsewhere. Beside each record is the holder's name and the date of his achievement. By this means many youngsters who may never be outstanding in the team sports still have a chance to "be a champ," and our endless search is always to find something every single boy can do, and do well, if he tries. Something he can be proud of.

Something to bring his chin up.

A number of phenomenal records are lettered on the Maverick Club board as evidence of the kids' enthusiasm. In "muscle grinds," for instance, the record stands at barely less than a hundred. This is a strenuous maneuver, involving coordinated kicks to keep the entire body rotating from the elbows around a stationary bar across the back. Interest in it rose suddenly when a professional circus acrobat set a new "world's record" of 106 revolutions while his show was in town. Many a Maverick youngster tried ardently but vainly to exceed this figure over a period of weeks, and nearly did. In failing, they took a little consolation from the

Wrestling, tumbling, rope-skipping, freethrow shooting... anything to get a boy's chin up!

fact that the circus professional used a gleaming bar set on ball bearings while the Maverick gymnasium had only a bolted steel rod that did not even turn!

Most surprising to outsiders is an unusual maneuver that has become another Maverick specialty: skipping rope while lying flat on the floor. With an arched back and a rhythmic rocking from heels to the back of the neck, this seemingly impossible form of exercise can go on as long as the back muscles hold out. To post a new record on the board a boy named LeRoy Boyter lay down in the gym one day and started skipping, nonchalantly crossing the rope at will, and was still going strong thirty-five and one-half minutes later when the official timers had to call the performance to a halt and go to a meeting. For a crowd-pleasing show stunt, as many as ten sturdy Mavericks have sometimes lain side by side on the floor and skipped a single rope, swung by two "outsiders," in perfect unison for several minutes.

One day a visiting wrestler who called himself the Masked Marvel dropped into the gymnasium where several boys were occupied at the moment doing "deep-knee bends"—squatting to their heels, then rising erect with arms extended. He looked at the record board and expressed

THE MAVERICKS ARE CORRALED

great surprise to see that one Maverick had performed something more than 1,000 consecutive deep-knee bends without stopping.

"Never saw that beaten but once," he remarked to Dykeman. "Once in Bombay, India, I saw a man do one thousand two hundred fifty."

Donny Sharp, a wiry, perfectly formed little seventy-five pounder, overheard the statement. Two evenings later he approached the supervisor and said, "Mr. Dykeman, don't you think we ought to best that record? Do you have time to count them?"

He stopped at three thousand. Johnnie Ward promptly topped that with three thousand twenty. But Donny Sharp came in early after school a short while later and kept Dykeman and a helper counting steadily for three full hours before he stopped his regular squatting and rising. Then he skipped rope a few minutes "to limber up his legs" and raced home for a late supper. The record of four thousand three consecutive deep-knee bends he set that day, as far as Dykeman has been able to learn, has never since been approached either in Amarillo or anywhere else. The same Donny Sharp also executed one hundred and seven left-arm pushups and then turned immediately to do fifty-three with his right arm, and hung up ten other Maverick records that still stand. He is now grown, married, a war veteran, and still as fine a specimen of physical and mental health as one is likely to find.

Success and a new spirit found among the Mavericks were also important factors in the later life of Donny's competitor Johnnie. Of a family of eleven children who were habitually pulled from school at an early age to work during cotton-picking time, he became the only one to finish high school. At last report he was proceeding happily as a high-ranking journalism student in a large Texas university.

These are outstanding but quite typical examples. I could readily cite hundreds more, for the Maverick Club grew until it reached a peak membership of 717 boys. By then the kids from the *right* side of the railroad tracks were jealously wondering why they had no such program! It was time to give them one.

World War II was on. Fathers and older brothers were away in the armed services. Mothers were working in the local shell-loading plant or in other industries. Other youth activities were necessarily curtailed. Schools as usual still had room for no more than a small percentage of their students on regular basketball and football teams. This meant that the younger brothers and sisters were running loose, keyed up to high nervous tension but with even fewer normal outlets than usual for all that energy. War or no war, it seemed to us that our investment in these youngsters was entirely too heavy to be allowed to deteriorate.

We called the year-round, citywide program Kids, Inc. It began with a softball league in the summer of 1944. The announcement was barely made before enough boys between nine and fourteen showed up to make more than fifty squads. And the eight-year-olds, barred in our initial announcement, were swarming around us in protest faster that we could comb them out of our hair. When sixty teams were organized, we called a halt for that first season and then set about the more difficult task of obtaining coaches and playing diamonds. Our businessmen were as much overworked as any during that period, and it was not easy, at first, to persuade one hundred twenty of them to give their time to a softball team two evenings a week. But a series of appeals to the city's luncheon clubs did the trick.

Ralph Dykeman is in the habit of explaining these beginnings with the statement that "that guy Farley is a hard man to say no to when he gets to talking about boys," but that is unfair to a large number of willing, community-minded men. Many of these coaches scarcely knew third base from second when they began, but they could keep order and discipline, and they soon learned the game. All over Amarillo the spirit was there, waiting only for something specific to transform it into action.

After that first season, in spite of its mushrooming size, Kids, Inc., seldom has had difficulty in recruiting enough enthusiastic adults to keep the program in high gear. (Even a coach who wants to quit seldom can, short of leaving the city. Before the new season opens a clamoring regiment of youngsters takes position on his front porch to beseech him to go on — and what else can he do?")

Lumber yards volunteered wire and materials for backstops, and softball diamonds sprang up all over the city. During the fifth summer of kid softball, 111 teams participated in season-long competition, each on its own diamond. We had learned that an area as little as one-fourth of a block was enough for softball in the ten-year-old and younger groups; older boys required a little more room. But hundreds of vacant lots large enough were available.

After the softball season closes, an idle period of thirty days or more is allowed. By the end of this period the small fry are becoming restless again, and anticipation is high. (Moreover, the same mother who occasionally complained during the summer that athletics kept her boy away from home too much is again not only willing but eager to have him taken out from underfoot.) Then the football squads—twenty-two of them—go into action. After football the same strategic waiting period occurs before the forty-odd basketball teams start their competition. Another comes in the spring before softball begins again.

[Cal Farley continues, speaking as of the year 1951]:

Two hundred eighty grownups serve as coaches, referees, and team managers, usually discovering to their surprise that they, themselves, benefit as much from the fun and exercise as their charges do. A number of women have proved highly successful as coaches, one of them, Mrs. J. O. Hutto, gaining the distinction of bringing her team of ten-year-old boys to a city basketball championship. The comment of this energetic young mother is revealing of the spirit that prevails among these loyal adults.

"I simply had too much time on my hands around the house," she says. "Several of us housewives were playing bridge relentlessly two or three times a week. But I felt useless. One of the neighborhood youngsters begged me to take a team that was about to be disbanded for lack of a coach. I didn't think I could coach them very well, but at the same time it seemed like a shame for all those little fellows to be left out in the cold because no man would take an interest in them.

"I was scared but I tried, and soon found out I could handle this team by giving up only my bridge games, which I didn't really like too much anyway. Once I started, there has been a different thrill every day to watch how eager the boys are to play, and how easy it is to teach them good manners, good citizenship, and just about everything else beneficial they need to know, on the basketball court. I'm having more fun that I ever had in my life."

Discipline in all the leagues is simple but strict. Sassing a referee or any other serious infraction of the rules suspends a player's membership card and makes him ineligible to play on any other team in the city until reinstated by his own coach. Any team which uses an ineligible player in a game, knowingly or otherwise, must forfeit the game. This rule is never broken.

Each player signs a contract which is countersigned by his parents before he becomes a member. It is a "parents' permission clause" and an injury waiver. Doctors contribute their services free on request of the managers, but injuries have been negligible.

Both the Maverick Club and the Boys Ranch enter their own teams on an equal basis with the others in all competitions, almost invariably developing strong championship contenders.

To continue its ardent editorial support of the program, and to serve as well what is now a citywide readership demand, the *Globe-News*, as well as the *Amarillo Times*, assigned top-flight sports reporters to cover nothing but news of Kids, Inc., during most of the year. Frequently during the height of a softball season, for example, both the daily summaries and the full-dress stories about the feature games occupied as much as a crowded half page.

"And woe unto us," moaned a sports editor, "if the slightest error appears in one of the box scores. Players of eight and fans of eighty-five ring this telephone off the desk in protest."

In addition to what financial support the city can arrange to give to the youth program, the astonishingly low budget is made up without difficulty in cash donations and incidental income. When Ralph Dykeman, for example, was debating whether or not an extra eighteen hundred dollars could be found to buy T-shirts bearing the Kids, Inc., insignia which the small fry wanted so badly to wear on the streets, he sampled the public by telephoning, in order, the first ten names appearing under the letter *A* in the classified telephone directory. Nine responded, offering a total of a hundred ten dollars. He bought the shirts.

Championship ceremonies are a pretentious occasion. Both the winning teams and the runner-ups in each of five age brackets are entertained at banquets by the various luncheon clubs. There each boy is personally presented a small gold or silver ball as his name is announced, the presentation usually being made by a famous athlete brought in for the occasion.

After the third year, the public demand for crossing the sex line was so strong that a girls' softball program was launched as well. It quickly rolled up an active participation list of more than eight hundred girls.

The results?
Besides those eight hundred girls, the Maverick Club and Kids, Inc., by 1950 were keeping an active membership of more than twenty-four hundred boys in organized play during most of the year. That number constitutes more than seventy percent of all boys between eight and fourteen years of age in the city. In most respects, too, these athletics supplement those of the schools, so that perhaps eighty percent of the boys in our city have the advantages of organized play. Yet Kids, Inc., was being run in 1950 on an annual cash budget of ten thousand dollars—a sum which included the salary of Ralph Dykeman, the only paid supervisor in the entire program!

These phenomenal figures represent, proportionately, the most comprehensive municipal youth program in the nation, and the ordinary Amarillo citizen is tremendously proud of that fact. But still we have never yet seen the bottom of the boy barrel. There are boys yet who are clamoring for a chance to fill vacancies on the teams and many others who may not have much initial desire but would quickly become enthusiastic once their friends persuaded them to join. The number of boys who fall into this latter group are a constant source of surprise to Ralph Dykeman. Our next big problem will be to secure new gymnasiums for expanded basketball and other winter activities. It is during the "indoors" months when idle hours hang heaviest and mischief multiplies.

What makes the program go?

The formula is not complicated at all. It is nothing more nor less than a single-minded community devotion to the idea of *keeping the greatest possible number of boys and girls playing—and playing hard to win—against other boys and girls of comparable age and skill.* Certain simple policies are necessary to avoid channels which would carry the program away from that basic purpose.

First there is the matter of team organization. A youngster, like a grown-up, quickly shies off from any activity in which he appears to poor advantage. A third-string basketball player from Hillville High School would feel foolish indeed if he were forced to appear on the same court with professionals. He would quit at the first opportunity. But, if the same player is permitted to compete with teammates of his own caliber against other teams of about the same skill, he will play his heart out indefinitely. And the most famous basketball player in the country will have no more fun or enthusiasm for the game than he.

In Kids, Inc., these facts of athletic life are recognized in the following way:

Suppose, for example, that a call has been issued in suburban San Jacinto for prospective basketball players to meet at the new $290,000 youth center built there by the Kiwanis Club. Fifty-odd boys appear and try out. The first coach picks his squad from the best players and enters them, let us say, in the "Prairie" league. The second coach chooses the best remaining boys for his team in the "Southern" league, and so on until every possible boy gets his chance to play on some team and can regard himself on a par with the other boys.

All over the city the same procedure is being followed. Needless to say, the names given the various leagues are strictly noncommittal as to the quality of play expected, but the championship playoffs seldom fail to bring some startling surprises.

Next: incentive.

Besides the wonderful kid-glory of seeing one's name in the paper or listening to the applause of one's elders at a championship banquet, we use an unusual play-off system to keep competition white-hot to the finish.

Winners of regular season play in each of the eight different softball leagues of eight teams each, for instance, pass automatically into a "world series" at the close of the season. But the next four highest teams in the standings at the close of league play have a chance to participate in an intraleague playoff from which the winner also goes into the "world series." This arrangement keeps not only the leading five teams in each league scrambling for the top, but the sixth-, seventh-, and eighth-ranking teams fighting hotly for a place among the first five. And it is not at all unusual for a second-, third-, or fourth-place team to catch fire and win the citywide championship. This method sometimes draws criticism from ardent adult fans whose sons happened to play on a team which won the league and lost out later—but it keeps hundreds of kids playing their hardest.

Finally: the "iron curtain" against commercialization of any sort.

This policy is the most vital of all. Every request that would permit individual business firms to sponsor individual teams in any league, as is customary in most other cities, has been firmly denied for many good reasons.

A commercial sponsor wants his team, first and foremost, to look pretty and to win. Soon he is engaged in an expensive competition with other businessmen to see which can provide his chosen players with the fanciest uniforms—thereby injuring the pride of all other boys who cannot dress as flashily. More important than that, the commercial sponsor naturally wants his team to recruit the best players, to whip every other team in sight, and to get the most publicity for themselves and the firm. That is the reason he sponsors a team.

Clearly, such an emphasis defeats the whole basic purpose of a youth program conceived along the lines of Kids, Inc. There is a vast difference between putting boys on a field or a court to find out by elimination which boys happen to be most proficient in any particular sport, and putting them there *to play* in the greatest possible numbers for the good of their bodies and souls.

In this manner Amarillo gives its youngsters something more than jalopies, ice cream, and picture shows to occupy their leisure time. It is an utterly simple and inexpensive program which deserves the attention, I sincerely believe, of every community-conscious businessman in America. Those who have supported other efforts of this general nature only to become discouraged when their money and time appeared to be dissipated

THE MAVERICKS ARE CORRALED

short of the goal could do well to renew their confidence. A large cash budget and formalized administrative organization have been proved unnecessary — where the community itself has been made fully aware of the problem and shows willingness to meet it. Where that willingness has not been developed, *no amount of money will do the job.*

Let other authorities argue that athletics is not the whole answer — that our kids must have a variety of physical, artistic, and spiritual activities for complete training. I do not disagree.

But I do know that something on a huge scale must be done which is not yet being done. I know that a shamefully large percentage of our young men are being found physically or mentally unfit for military service. I know that there exists an enormous hunger among our children for clean, hard physical exercise and the soul-stirring excitement of competition.

I know that we will never go back as a nation to the rural, outdoors sort of living that built bodies and responsibility in the days of my own boyhood. But I have also seen conclusive proof of mass-scale miracles which can be accomplished in building good bodies and in teaching cooperation and self-discipline — in one word, citizenship — to our boys by simply giving them the chance to play regularly in properly supervised games. This was done at a cost — in Amarillo — of about three dollars a player a year, plus the time and effort of adult volunteers who sometimes form on the playing field their first really happy, rewarding friendship with their own children.

Let no one say the same thing cannot be done in any community in America where one, two, or twenty well-known and trusted citizens are willing to light and tend the fire.

11

Americans We Don't Know

ONE HOT AUGUST afternoon Ralph Dykeman and I happened to meet on Polk Steet, dodging under the same awning to escape the sun for a few steps.

"Ralph," I asked him, "do you remember that tough little redhead named Tommy we sent down from the office to the Maverick Club last week? How's he getting along?"

"He's not there," Dykeman said. "I spent a lot of my time with him the first two days, but we haven't seen him since."

"What was the matter?"

"Too much a roughneck. He spits on the floor. He smokes whenever he wants to, even inside the building. Put him into a pair of basketball trunks and he's bashful about going onto the court—says he feels naked. He can't catch or throw a ball as well as an eight-year-old girl, so he takes out his spite by rabbit-punching another player. Put him to wrestling and he rams his knee into the other boy's back after the bell rings."

This information was particularly disappointing to me. I could not help but like the fiery little fellow.

Tommy had given the policemen fits. Among his other depredations about the city was a racket which began with an innocent-faced appeal for money from motorists seated in parked cars. Those who refused or offered unsatisfactory donations were treated to a shower of upholstery tacks tossed under the tires of their automobiles at the moment they pulled away from the curb, plus a nose-thumbing from Tommy as he took to his heels. Just for spite, he had flattened the tires of a police car in this way.

In the jail one day, according to the officer who had brought him to us, Tommy had been prayed over by a woman evangelist of one of the louder persuasions. This lady—and I do not snicker at her, since she at least had the interest to visit the boy in jail—was rousing heaven and the rest of the cell block on behalf of Tommy's sin-splattered soul. While her eyes were closed and the policeman watched, the boy had calmly reached into her open purse and stolen a pack of cigarettes!

"We had an awful time getting Tommy into the shower room," Ralph Dykeman was saying. "He acted as if he had never taken a bath before. He's an intelligent little fellow, but he won't or can't get along with anybody. He's just plain disagreeable."

On the way back to the store I started thinking—hard. Tommy was neither the first nor the sixth nor the sixteenth boy we had sent to the Maverick Club with these unsuccessful results. The club was progressing splendidly, we thought. Only two years old at that time, it already had an active membership of five hundred boys. And already its young athletes had gained a good name among the ordinary Amarillo citizens for their skill, their enthusiasm, and their newfound sportsmanship.

But we were losing a certain kind of boy. Frequently, I knew very well, Ralph Dykeman and others had neglected important tasks in their sixteen-hour daily schedule to talk and devote individual attention to any boy who proved especially difficult. In every way we knew—even to the extent of neglecting some of the other boys a little—we had tried to make the Maverick Club program attractive to these "tough ones," because they needed it most.

But they didn't come back.

It had occurred to us that perhaps a lad like Tommy was simply show-ing the usual American resistance to vested authority—that perhaps another boy his own age might get him interested in the games and straighten him out where no amount of urging by a supervisor would be listened to. We had long talks with a number of our outstanding Mavericks who had been fairly tough themselves at the outset, explaining how much we wanted to help other boys like themselves and why we couldn't do that without their help. Then we had assigned one of these boys to act as a companion to each of the new lads who appeared to have the greatest adjustment prob-lem and help him over his first hurdles. Our Mavericks had worked earnestly and well at their task. With many boys they had succeeded wonderfully well. When they failed, it was usually with boys like Tommy.

Tommy simply didn't come back.

Cal Farley arrived at Yankee Stadium not in a second baseman's uniform as he had so fervently hoped, but as a successful businessman enlisting Babe Ruth's help in reclaiming errant boys.

Something plainly was wrong with our thinking. Progress of the Maverick Club had given us more confidence than ever in the body-building and character-building benefits of properly run athletics with ninety-five percent of all boys. But here was Tommy, a boy who did not know how to play games at all and did not want to learn. Nothing we had to offer, in fact, seemed to interest him in the slightest. He did not fit anywhere else in the "respectable" world, and he didn't fit here.

Yet Tommy was the boy we had originally set out to reach—the kid at the bottom of the social barrel. Among all the underprivileged or delinquent youngsters in the city, it was a boy like this wild, smart, incorrigible redhead who was clearly the best bet to grow into a big-time criminal. He had the intelligence and the energy—"the stuff" to do almost anything well.

Fumbling for an answer, I did not stop at the store that afternoon. Instead, I took my automobile and drove off in search of the policeman who had brought Tommy to us in the first place. By following his directions, I finally found the boy's mother. She was sitting in front of a homemade automobile trailer near one of Amarillo's huge grain elevators. The wheels of the trailer had been replaced by wooden blocks, evidence that Tommy and his family had made this their home for a considerable

AMERICANS WE DON'T KNOW

time. There was no evidence of running water, toilet, or electric facilities nearby. Trash and filth were ankle-deep all about the trailer.

A bitter-faced, slatternly woman she was, idly peeling four wrinkled potatoes and kicking sticks at a sniffing dog. To all appearances her dirty dress, made from a flour sack, had never been removed from her person for two weeks. She hadn't had a bath since the last rain.

I introduced myself, telling her what we had tried and failed to do for Tommy. She made no motion to stop peeling potatoes nor to move from the wooden box on which she was sitting. I found a chunk of wood and sat down on it. The police, I told her, were sure that Tommy was rapidly going bad. Could she suggest how we might be able to appeal to her boy and help him? Her answer was an old, familiar tale.

Tommy had been a good boy, she said, in a whining voice, until he had just got too big for his britches. Wouldn't listen to his mother no more at all. He was just running around with the wrong bunch, that was all. These older boys had been learnin' him to snitch candy and cigarettes and finally bigger things. He was getting into trouble and was going to wind up in the reform school for sure.

All this she had told him many times, she said, but it didn't seem to do no good. Tommy'd come sneakin' home late at night with his pockets full of stuff, and she'd scold him and beg him and bawl a little, but the next day it would be the same thing all over again.

Squirming in spite of myself in these unsavory surroundings, I suggested to Tommy's mother that he might stay at home more often if the place were cleaned up a bit. She simply stared at me and said nothing.

Gradually the cold facts of this situation began to fall into place in my mind. *This woman, I began to realize, had no particular consciousness of being dirty, nor of being anything less than she should be as a wife and mother.* She herself had been brought up under similar conditions, and had never seen or learned of any others. Her husband, Tommy's father, was shuttling between his WPA job and the liquor stores. *Both were living the only way they knew how to live.*

Talking to this woman was obviously going to do little good. Ten full years of conscientious, sincere effort by social workers probably would not change the pattern of these parents' lives a great deal. Any long-range improvement would have to come with a younger, more pliable generation—with Tommy himself. Tommy at least had energy enough to be as ornery as sin.

And orneriness, in ninety-nine of every hundred boys I have known, is simply another name for ambition. This his parents no longer had.

TWO THOUSAND SONS

After awhile I took my leave and went immediately to find Tommy.
His mother told me the usual alley hangout of the "bad crowd," and there
I found him, squatted on his haunches with two other boys.

As I drove up the three boys started to run. I stepped out of the machine
and called to Tommy. He recognized me, and all three of the lads stopped
a safe distance away.

"You know I'm not a policeman, don't you, Tommy?" I asked.

"Yeah, but you're gonna take me back to the Maverick Club, or to jail,"
he said, and I winced to hear him put the two in the same class.

"No, I'm not," I assured him. "But I would certainly appreciate talking
to you and your friends for a few minutes."

More talking was required to convince them that my visit was peaceful
and that I merely wanted to ask them some questions. Finally they came
back with me to the car and sat down. I explained to them as carefully
as I could the purpose of the Maverick Club and said that kind people
all over the city were giving money to me and Mr. Dykeman so that boys
who needed it could have a place to play.

"But it looks as if Mr. Dykeman and I are falling down on the job,"
I said, turning to Tommy. "There must be something wrong with the place
or you would be back there playing instead of hiding here in an alley."

The boys shrugged.

"All I want you to tell me, Tommy," I went on, "is what we're doing
wrong. Why is it you didn't want to go back to the Maverick Club? We
want to make it a better place. Just tell me how we can do it, and I won't
bother you boys any longer."

Before Tommy could answer, the largest of the three spoke up—
obviously a ringleader trying to keep his ranks intact.

"Aw, he don't wanna hang around down there with a bunch o' sissies!"
he said. Obviously, the older boys were telling Tommy that "nobody but
pansies" went to the Maverick Club, and he was believing it.

Lamely trying to head off that one, I said, "That's exactly why we want
Tommy down there. We'd like to have all three of you. We don't want
a club full of sissies. Tommy's got the stuff, and that's the kind of boys
we want."

Cool silence. These mavericks were rope-wise. My loop was not even
close to their heels; they scorned it.

On my way back to the store some more cold facts began to appear
in the picture. No matter how cautiously I approached boys like these,
I remained the well-dressed big shot from the other side of town—the
camp of the enemy. I was trying to interfere with that candy-and-cigarette

route set up by their own leaders. One way or another, they knew I wanted to take away their freedom to prowl and steal whenever they jolly well pleased.

These boys needed help worse than any others, but I would be plain silly to assume that they would stand obligingly still long enough for me to help them. They liked their coyote freedom, and they didn't like me. To them I was merely a snooper, intruding uninvited into the only way of living they knew. And I was getting the same reception usually given to busybodies.

Here was the Maverick Club, doing a wonderful job for a lot of boys. With the Kids, Inc., program, it would soon expand into the upper social levels so that nearly all the boys in Amarillo who wanted to play games could do so. But what about the boys who *didn't* want to play? Could not some way be found to draw these boys in with the others and gradually teach them to *like* to play normal games?

More and more, as I thought about this problem during the days that followed, I realized that it could not be done. The Maverick Club, built and maintained primarily for the welfare of underprivileged boys, could reach only some of them. Rarely could it arouse the interest of a member of Tommy's little gang, and then usually not for long. Here was another demonstration of a fact we were learning by experience: boys from the different levels of our society do not mix readily and never will, any more than their elders do.

We had built the Maverick Club on the fine, broad theory that "any boy in town who wants to play" might join and play his head off. Officially that is still true. But it had not worked that way. As the club became popular, attracting more and more of the city's youth from the higher economic brackets, the poorer kids had just as rapidly dropped out. When we had seen that happening and quietly changed our emphasis to bring back the boys from poorer surroundings who had less opportunity to play elsewhere, the youngsters with more money had disappeared from the roster. At first, this action cost some money and support from adults who did not understand, but it was necessary to keep the Maverick Club true to its original purpose. At that point, the broader Kids, Inc., program had become a necessity.

Earnest sociology students in our colleges may bewail this "caste system" of ours. I see no purpose in refusing to recognize what, to me, appears to be a basic fact about human society that has prevailed through all history. It is enough to protect the channels by which, in our American society, a man can climb from level to level by his own efforts, and to extend whatever help we can to those who have that desire. But the social divisions are still there.

I know, for example, that if I were to intrude myself into a pitch game at the rear of an ordinary poolhall, I would probably be treated with as much courtesy as elsewhere. But the cronies who play there regularly would be just as uncomfortable as I until I returned to my own house and my own crowd across town. And it would represent no "lack of democracy" on my part or theirs that we had no common ground for friendly relations outside regular business.

I know just as well that boys from good homes, with enough money in their pockets to attend the uptown shows, are equally unfamiliar with the existence of the corner newsboy who goes to a two-bit theater to see a horse opera.

We had noticed that it was not wise policy to mix boys from two sharply different social levels on the same team — though each boy would play his hardest on a team composed of his own fellows against another team from the other side of the tracks. With the same rules of sportsmanship rigidly imposed upon both sides, "caste" had proved no great problem, down to a certain level. Now we had encountered Tommy and his gang, who did not want to play at all.

After months during which he had worked as persistently as he could with a few of these most difficult little individuals, one by one, Ralph Dykeman had been forced to an inevitable conclusion.

"What can I do?" he asked. "With time and patience I am sure we could bring many of these tough ones around in good shape. Others we can never reach with the athletic program. But I have five hundred boys to take care of, and one boy like Tommy requires as much of my personal attention as a hundred of the others. Can I let the five hundred go unattended while I try to straighten out one?"

The answer was too plain. To a certain degree the Maverick Club, too, would have to operate on a policy of "the greatest good for the greatest number."

This is a capsule history of nine in ten of all the youth programs launched in the past in sincere efforts to help the youngsters who need help most. Once the organization is established and the program a "success" in the public eye, it becomes by easy stages more and more respectable. The white-collar youngsters appear in greater numbers, and the ragamuffins retire to the alleys again. There are never enough dollars or enough workers to serve both. It is therefore the most natural course possible to spread the available money and effort among the greatest number — meaning,

Among big names in the sports world who worked with Cal to salvage lost kids, none was more helpful or a more frequent visitor than Jack Dempsey, shown here roping a calf at the ranch.

simply, among the most cooperative youngsters. Big numbers tend to make a far better impression on those who contribute their money in a public campaign. Besides, there are few individuals indeed who are willing to undergo the shin-kicking and the risk of failure which the real troublemakers will certainly provide.

(Not in the slightest sense are these remarks a reflection upon the fine and necessary work being accomplished in our country by various "boy" organizations and youth programs. On the contrary, there is a place in America for any honest *working* effort to improve the welfare of our children of whatever class — and the sum total of support and attention devoted to all of them at present is entirely too small.)

Though I never saw Tommy again, the cocky little rascal refused to be absent from my mind. Gradually it became clear that "the greatest good for the greatest number" was no real answer to the problem at all.

Was it not this exact rule which had operated against Tommy all his life to help make him a potentially dangerous enemy of our society? In school, an overworked teacher could not devote the time necessary to work out his individual problem because there was little time enough to do justice by the other, more tractable youngsters. At home his dirty old mother, to her credit, at least had tried to keep him straight but had finally given him up. The same process had been repeated in the courts, welfare agencies, or any other chance charity which from time to time may have attempted to give Tommy or his family a lift. Now the Maverick Club, reluctantly, was giving him up, too.

Yet there was every powerful reason why Tommy and his kind should be receiving, not the least, but the most attention of all. As a businessman paying heavy taxes, I had never been able to pass lightly over newspaper items which stated that the total cost of crime in the United States— enforcement, courts, penal institutions, and all the rest—stood in the neighborhood of ten billion dollars a year and was growing always higher. It made me somewhat unhappy to read that more and more of the money I worked for was going to provide board and room for habitual criminals, just one of whom might easily cost the taxpayers forty thousand or a hundred thousand dollars in the course of his criminal career. The questions I was asking myself in the mid 1930s are even more valid in the '50s.

Who are these criminals? What kind of boys were they? What sort of families furnish the raw material for our reform schools and penitentiaries? What group of our citizens is responsible for the bulk of that huge annual crime bill as well as the further loss to society in wasted time, money, and lives?

With only occasional spectacular exceptions, the boys at the top of the economic ladder hardly enter into the picture.

This is not to minimize the growth of mischief, vandalism, and real delinquency among boys of more well-to-do families in the turmoil of these recent years. A regrettable situation definitely does exist, as juvenile authorities in almost any city can testify. Very recently, for example, the Denver courts had to deal with an adolescent "club" of at least twenty-one members from as many wealthy families of the city—consisting of only boys who had qualified for membership by stealing an automobile!

It has been also my observation that some of our most pathetically neglected youngsters are those who have been physically pampered and emotionally starved in prosperous homes.

But suppose little Johnny Uptown gets into trouble with the law. Father, mother, relatives, and influential friends are in an uproar immediately. Emergency conferences begin in the family library and continue in the office of Papa's lawyer. Tears flow. Influence is brought to bear. Most important of all, the alarmed parents come suddenly face to face with their negligence and settle down to be *parents* to the boy again, at least for a few weeks.

Except for the most flagrant offense, it is not likely that this boy will ever come to trial and even less likely that he will see the inside of a penal institution for any length of time. Papa pulls too powerful a stroke about the town; political officials automatically exercise caution and leniency in dealing with his case. In any event, this boy does not become a significant burden on the taxpayer.

Examination of reform schools and penitentiaries discloses only a negligible percentage of inmates who came from homes in the upper thirty percent of the economic scale.

Look next to the large "steady-income" group of our citizens, encompassing, let us say, another sixty percent of our boy population. These are the families ranging downward in income from that of smaller merchants and subordinate executives to that of regularly employed day laborers. They are, in other words, the great majority of our citizens—neither rich nor poor, the great "responsible" group which contains, I sometimes think, the most stable families in America. It is the good fortune of children in most of these families to have had a lifelong familiarity with decent living standards and the irreplaceable security of a genuine home.

Criminals do not grow well in this environment. In proportion to its great numbers, this group furnishes only a small part of the prison parade.

The conclusion, then, is one that is universally recognized by those familiar with these matters. It is, namely, that the real bulk of our criminals—and therefore the heavy share of cost to our society—arises from the families in the bottom ten percent of the social scale.

These American citizens—technically endowed with as many privileges of free democracy as you and I—live next door to us in every city and town in the nation. But the life they lead is as foreign to what we consider normal American living as that of the peoples of other continents, frequently more so. In squalid instability and ignorance they are born, shuffle through an existence which gathers only an odd assortment of crumbs from the table of American plenty, and die with no material improvement in their mental or physical condition.

These are the facts that prevail, as they appear in excerpts taken at random from the files in our office:

"George and Bobby F— —are two of fourteen children, eight of whom are under age fifteen and are living at home. The father has been a steady

though uneducated day laborer in the past, but seems to have been gradually defeated by the mere growth in size of his family. More in despair over
his own ineffectiveness than anything else, he took increasingly to alcohol,
and finally, disgusted with himself, simply ran away. Mother is ailing and
has had a recent serious operation. The only support available for the entire
family is what can be provided by two daughters working as waitresses
and two married sons. Recently the ancient family automobile broke down
beyond repair, eliminating the only transportation available to the grown
daughters between their work and the little house three miles out of town.
Living conditions are generally as poor as might be expected. . . .

"This boy, now ten years old, has spent much of the past three years
alone in a hotel room while his mother, a good worker, spends long hours,
sometimes far into the night, working as a waitress for their support. This
boy is in no sense malicious, but has lost interest in everything, finally
dropping out entirely from school. Extremely listless, though not mentally handicapped. . . .

"Linton lived with his mother in an apartment house in Kansas City's
foreign neighborhood. Father's whereabouts unknown. With lack of adequate supervision, particularly by a father, he began stealing, not from
need, but apparently as an outlet for his great energy. He has a long court
record which began with the theft of one hundred baby chickens from
a Montgomery Ward warehouse. Will go to reform school with current
offense unless other placement is feasible. . . .

"From a family of ten children. Billy's intelligence is far above average.
Has had much abuse. Declares quite sincerely that 'the nicest time I ever
had was during those four months in the reform school. . . .'

"Walter and his father are constantly at odds. Lives with his mother,
who is of morally abandoned character and increasingly untidy about her
person. The sheriff says she's hopeless. Boy has intelligence enough to be
dangerous, and has threatened to kill his mother. . . ."

"Father killed in automobile accident. Mother overworked to support
her family. Home facilities very poor. . . ."

"Parents of high mentality but both have become habitual drunkards.
John has been living with his grandmother whose person and two-room
apartment are equally filthy. . . ."

"Harrison lived with his mother through three marriages and three
divorces, two of the latter within the past two years. Father married again,
took the boy with his wife's consent, but she changed her mind and decided
she didn't want Harrison in the house. Stayed only at father's insistence,

but started stealing...."

"Father is thirty years older than mother. Neither has any real control...."

"Bertie's new stepfather didn't want someone else's kids around...."

"Elmer and Sam, twins, were picked up while soliciting for donations about the town. The mother is a known prostitute...."

"No yard whatever to play in; sanitary conditions miserable; mother has no control. Boy stole neighbor woman's purse containing $20...."

"Father has tuberculosis, having spent most of the time during the past five years in bed while his family tried to carry on his job of hauling trash for the city. Alfred's trouble has been minor, mostly attributable to his craving for attention...."

These are Americans we don't know.

12

A Place in the Country

WITHIN A MERE two or three years the Maverick Club had enrolled a membership of 750 underprivileged boys in a year-round program of athletics and had captured the city's loyalty as a major deterrent to youth crime and delinquency. With the great further success of the Kids, Inc., program, the city could, and rather noisily did, pridefully claim to have established the most comprehensive citywide youth program in the nation. Cal Farley's personal fame already was bringing him before enthusiastic audiences from coast to coast, and his business had prospered to a degree permitting him freedom to carry his gospel of youth athletics wherever he wished. In any "normal" pattern, Cal Farley was now more than ready to step onto a broader stage and expand still further his already held status as one of the most popular and deeply respected citizens of Texas. A goodly share of his closest friends were already vigorously nudging him to enter politics and carry his message to the nation in the halls of Congress. His election was considered a cinch. But the *Globe-News* announced his contrary decision in a front-page headline: "THE KIDS WIN AGAIN."

Cal could not yet see his job finished, his formula complete. He simply could not shake off his preoccupation with the lads even the Maverick Club could not reach—the boy Spud or Tommy, the redhead—the extremely neglected, forlorn little toughies who steal to eat and who "don't know whether to bite a softball or throw it" because never in their lives have they played the games of a normal boy.

Sooner or later, after all halfway measures were found wanting, Cal and his friends came to accept the formidable conclusion that nothing less than a real home, providing not only adequate food and shelter but also intelligent supervision and affection twenty-four hours a day, could hope to solve the problems of this kind of boy. This was clearly a major undertaking — one not likely even to be understood, let alone acclaimed, by the passing throng. Clearly also, he would not have time to earn the second, "easy" half of the fortune required for membership in the millionaire's club.

Later, close friends could recall no backward glance by Cal Farley toward the earned rewards left by the wayside as he turned up the rocky climb toward his ultimate goal. Instead, his concentration focused intensely on what kind of full-time home he could build — and first of all where it should be.

Common sense pointed immediately to a location away from the city, preferably a genuine farm or ranch well out in the country. Such a location, he thought, would assure a sharp break from the environment these boys must forget. If it were far enough off the beaten path that only those adults sincerely interested in the project would come, he further reasoned, the boys could continue to feel that they were living in a home, not a zoo for idle sightseers. Furthermore, to be quite practical about it, a degree of remoteness would discourage runaways from the home without fences he had in mind. A boy would think twice before setting off to walk twenty dry miles to a main highway.

Historic Old Tascosa was near Amarillo and seemed almost ideal for this purpose. This fact found its way into the conversation one afternoon when Cal and Julian Bivins happened to meet on the street in the fall of 1938. Tall, quiet, thoughtful Julian Bivins, a big-time cattle rancher and member of one of the most prominent pioneer families of the Texas Panhandle, owned the huge tract of oil-rich prairie which surrounded the ancient water hole of Spanish and Indian days. He and his mother had warmly supported Cal's previous efforts, making available, for example, the Maverick Club's first gymnasium. As they met, Julian told Cal later, he was still thinking about the "boy problem" as it had only recently touched his own family. A wandering lad of fourteen whom he had befriended and taken into his home as a helper had suddenly departed with a quantity of the family's most precious table silver.

At that time the Bivins family was still living in the renovated Old Tascosa courthouse. Julian's attractive and lively wife, Berneta, had never permitted the family's wealth to dull her own great zest for the open life

"forty miles from nowhere." She had insisted that, as genuine ranch folks,
her sons should ride and swim and grow as much of their childhood as
possible under the big cottonwoods by the Canadian River. They had done
so, enjoying the fine summers and making out well even when the blizzards
blew in on the Panhandle's famous "blue northers" in winter.

But the children, Julian now reflected, were at an age when a move
to town for school purposes was almost a necessity. Why shouldn't Tascosa
live on to a new destiny as a home for cowboys from the alleys?

"A ranch like that could be a great thing, Cal," he said. "I might have
something there at Tascosa you could use. Why don't you drive out and
take a look?"

Following directions, the next Sunday afternoon, Cal and Mimi Farley
and their daughter, Gene, drove out the "back road" as far as Turner Creek
but concluded, upon inspecting the quicksand in that wet creekbed, that
they might lose the family automobile if they attempted to cross. On
another trip shortly thereafter, however, with Julian Bivins, Chanslor
Weymouth, and Ralph Dykeman in the party, the proposition was approved all around.

"How much land do you think you'll need, Cal?" asked Julian.

"You're doing the giving," Cal replied. "Suit yourself."

With that, an area of approximately 120 acres, including two lakes and
the whole townsite of Old Tascosa, was stepped off for later surveying.
Later that winter Julian Bivins signed over a deed to this property and
moved his family into the city.

The fatherless ones began to arrive at Tascosa, and the scrawniness of
their bodies was as nothing compared with the undernourishment of their
souls.

The stout ones came in pitiful belligerence, the weak ones in pitiful
listlessness and defeat—all of them more ravenous for adult love and
attention than for food. Superintendent Alton Weeks and the motherly
Maud Thompson, who would be matron of the "courthouse gang" through
its first eventful decades, could only do their best, knowing that not a
thousand gulps of that affection could fill the vacancy left inside any boy
whose own blood father had let him down.

Five boys in the beginning, all from the alleys of Amarillo, put down
their puny bundles of clothes and boy gadgets behind the stone railing
of the courthouse and began their groping pursuit of manhood on that
chilly first day of March, 1939.

Fortunately, at Tascosa, elements other than human ingenuity were pres-

A PLACE IN THE COUNTRY

ent in abundance to aid that quest. To these five boys, and the hundreds who would follow them, the spell of the open country has been instantaneous and everlasting. The booming wind, the quiet, the thick and pregnant brush where dark animals could hide, the knolls strewn with pebbles for throwing, the sailing hawks and vaguely glimpsed coyotes, the wet sod that sinks under a boy's bare feet before he steps into the coolness of the creeks: these were mysteries requiring endless summer exploration that could be interrupted only by the dinner bell.

But cautiously at first. Hazards of this utterly strange new world were not the known perils of streets and railroad yards and traffic; rather, they were obscure things like rattlesnakes, cacti, beasts, ghosts. Mightiest and most challenging marvel of all was the Canadian River. Enough fascination to last a lifetime was contained in its flats of red sand stretching away to the ends of the earth in both directions, its rippled dunes bearing the tracks of all manner of wild things, its beds of jellylike quicksand ringed with red froth and unknown danger, its cattail thickets, and its infinitely intriguing debris washed down by high water.

Cal Farley's Boys Ranch had opened for business with an initial endowment that included the stone courthouse and the cottonwoods, the many springs welling up through thick watercress and bubbling down into a sizable lake for swimming and fishing, a cemetery atop a nearby knoll where twenty-seven men who had come out second best in six-shooter conversations lie buried, an assortment of crumbling 'dobe shacks, and twenty surrounding acres of pebbly pasture.

Of the Old Town there remained a vestigial population of one. Legendary Frenchy McCormick, toast of Old Tascosa's dance halls during the 1880s, had married the last of the gamblers who had ruled this raucous crossroads during the cattle drives, and had never departed. The first Boys Ranch hands chasing cattle across the creek could see the ancient widow on any sunny afternoon, drowsing between the crooked tree and the front door of her shack, a hunched and somnolent figure whose meager wants were supplied by neighboring ranchers while she drifted toward her own fast-approaching death.

✱ Within that first Boys Ranch was the pattern of the hundreds of boys who were to come later: the fighters, the inert spirits, and the boys in between, destitute and homeless, but with reasonably normal reactions that needed only a stable home in which to blossom. There was the unforgettable boy Spud, whose vengeance burned bold against everything alive and was not quenched until he discovered in the pigpens the miracle of

In sharp contrast was a boy named Ralph, who drifted in a muffling lethargy we did not penetrate for months. Long ago deserted by his father, Ralph had been left with grandparents when his mother moved from town. He had been missing school consistently to plod aimlessly about the streets, and at ten years of age he was still regularly wetting his bed.

Living, to Ralph, was the dull trance of an automaton who could not complain or fight or steal to get even the essentials of survival. He created the impression of one who would eat if food were shoved within reach of his hands but, if it were not, would go quietly off and lie down under a tree.

Ralph caused us none of the usual boy trouble at all, a fact that became a worry in itself. Nearly a year passed before we were able to break his infantile habit. Shaming him seemed to do little good. Like so many boys of his kind, Ralph lacked the training that would permit him to be embarrassed to good advantage; wetting the bed was normal procedure. Finally, gradually, through a combination of the efforts of other boys and a growing interest in healthful outdoor pursuits, Ralph's improvement began to be permanent. As his bodily health and strength increased, he began to take serious interest in his schoolwork as well.

Ralph left the ranch after four years to return to his mother, who had remarried under happier circumstances and then was living in an eastern city. The moment his age permitted, he joined the navy, spent three years with the Seabees, and returned to finish high school and go on to college in Texas. Now personable and self-confident, he married the bright blonde daughter of a solid family. With her earnings as a typist and his own out-of-school clerking for a trucking company which has promised him a job upon graduation, the pair, as this is written [in 1951] are saving and building for a future that certainly was not in sight for Ralph the day he arrived at Tascosa.

His transformation was not spectacular or newsworthy. Instead, it was a slow growth to health and dignity and good citizenship. His career, probably, will never rise higher than that of a junior executive who owns a small white house on a middle-class street. But our satisfaction will remain as great as if he were to become president of General Motors. Here the downward flow of one family's bloodline was halted and turned upward into usefulness and responsibility, with benefits to our community and our country that will multiply in Ralph's children and his children's children.

A PLACE IN THE COUNTRY

The joys of endless summer exploration on horse or afoot is mirrored in these grinning faces. . .

When Boys Ranch opened, we had little foreknowledge of the large number of our new boys who would arrive in a condition similar to Ralph's, boys for whom life had stopped almost before it started. In many respects, the problem of these bed-wetters is the most difficult of all and by far the most demanding of sympathy and patience. For them, kindness or abuse, cleanliness or filth, candy or castor oil, feasts or starvation — all are almost equal to them. This suffocation of a boy's vital forces stems more often, I think, from his father's absence than from any other single cause. A boy is the branch of his father's tree, and almost any ineffective, part-time male parent is better than one who completely abdicates his fatherhood. Often a struggling boy spirit can draw enough strength to survive through a mere splinter of sound wood in an otherwise rotten trunk. But when the father is lacking entirely — through absence, alcohol, abuse, or plain neglect — something is gone from his boy which I question is ever fully replaced. Certainly the most devoted father alive would be thereafter an even more attentive and understanding parent after spending a day or two studying the boys at Tascosa. The craving for the demonstrated love of their elders which shows so openly and poignantly here, he will realize, is different only in degree from that of his own children.

Between the apathetic and rebellious extremes, a third type of boy serves a vital function at Tascosa. This is the homeless and neglected lad of no particularly violent tendencies who probably would have "gone bad" if

... and in winter cold young cowhands learn the tough faithfulness that care of livestock demands.

not rescued but had not done so, who may be utterly filthy but has no insuperable objections to taking a shower once a day, who has seen a glimmer of decent living but never before had an opportunity to practice it. This is the "essentially good kid" who heavily predominates in nearly all the publicly and privately supported boys homes in America. Always, in the Boys Ranch family, it is these "good kids" who have accomplished about as much toward the salvation of themselves and the others as all we adults can do.

It is they who form the core of "public opinion" that exerts such powerful force in swinging transgressors toward the common goal. They assume responsibility, captain the work crews, entertain visitors, keep close watch on the livestock, and in many instances exert the most effective informal discipline.

George and Gene, brothers who came to live at Tascosa when Boys Ranch was still new, and who were "adventurous," are good examples. Their parents had separated, and the mother found herself increasingly unable to keep the pace with two lively boys of twelve and thirteen.

Gene, the older brother, was a quiet, intelligent, agreeable lad who promptly became one of Tascosa's most conscientious citizens, never resenting the fact that his fireball brother, George, considered it his duty to direct their mutual traffic. Seldom since has Boys Ranch acquired a boy politician with the irresistible manner of the round-faced, handsome George.

A PLACE IN THE COUNTRY

132   It was George's firm policy to determine the individuals from whom most benefits could be derived and take action accordingly. From the moment his mother first approached us to ask that we take care of her boys for at least a year or two, he turned upon me a flood of beguiling personality that would have undermined the Sphinx itself. On his arrival at Tascosa these ardent affections were immediately transferred to the cook and the superintendent, especially the cook. There was never a moment of doubt that George would get along very well indeed.

At that time the ranch boys were still attending a one-room public school located on the property, and Adolf Hitler had become the subject of outspoken disfavor among young Americans. One evening some of the other lads, always sensitive of their collective reputation, reported to the superintendent that George had slapped a girl pupil at the school and urged some public punishment for the sake of the common welfare.

Investigation showed that the incident had resulted primarily from exuberance. On the school grounds that afternoon, George had been loudly insisting that that fellow Hitler was a nasty individual in all respects. Finding one girl uncommonly perverse in resisting his persuasive powers, he had slapped her by way of emphasis.

The superintendent restrained an injudicious smile and handed over the contrite and apologetic culprit—unwisely, as was soon learned—to the boys themselves, who spent a busy evening with their wild-West storybooks contriving a proper chastisement for his crime.

Next day they pressed into service a certain venerable gander which, by his success in battle against human, canine, and coyote antagonists that had disposed of all the other geese on the ranch, had earned the deference due one of Tascosa's most lordly residents. "Prisoner" George was stripped to the waist and spread-eagled Indian fashion on the ground, his wrists and ankles tied with cords attached to stakes. Over his bare chest the boys sprinkled a generous layer of corn which the gander plucked off, kernel by kernel.

(Boy punishments, we quickly learned, should not be allowed to proceed without supervision. One summer afternoon several months later, the superintendent, sensing an unusual silence about the place, arrived in the dining hall just in time to halt a "hanging" in the Old Tascosa style. Having caught one of their number mistreating one of the riding ponies, the boys were angrily determined that he should learn never to do so again. A rope had been tied to an open cross beam, and the tall young offender was already hanging by the neck, his flailing feet several inches off the floor and his hands gripping the rope above the "noose" as best they could.

Although no slipknot had been used and although one of the older boys stood on a chair close by, ready to cut the rope with a sharp kitchen knife when the victim's face became satisfactorily purple, the alarmed superintendent considered such proceedings hazardous and put some stern new regulations into effect then and there.)

No momentary setback, however, could long retard young George's salesmanship, which was soon being displayed beyond the bounds of the ranch. Because of his fearless delight in front of an audience of any sort, I began to take George with me on some of the numerous speech-making trips I was taking as the then district governor of Rotary International.

His first four-minute public address, which we had carefully rehearsed along the highway, so thoroughly captivated the Fort Worth Rotarians that our departure was delayed several hours while George was fitted in fancy western clothes and showered with enough other presents to fill the back seat of my automobile.

Without warning, during the long drive home, I asked my grinning and happy little orator what he thought should be done with the gifts he had acquired in cash, amounting nearly to fifty dollars.

To his great credit, George immediately recalled the money jar on the refrigerator back in Tascosa and replied, "I guess this'll buy a lot of ice cream for everybody."

"But," I pointed out, "the money was given to you because you made a good speech."

"Yeah," said George quickly, "but if one of the other boys, like Tubby, for instance, had been there, he'd have given a good speech too, and he'd put the money in the pot. I know he would."

We finally agreed that George should have two dollars for his own, three-fourths of which sum went to buy a bar of candy for a fourteen-year-old girl singer he had met at a radio station during a Boys Ranch program. The labored correspondence between the two for months thereafter brought him much raucous teasing and also increased his fame about the ranch.

After several years at the ranch and several more profitable years in the navy, George came back to Fort Worth with the homing instinct most of us humans possess toward the locality which gave us our first major triumph. In his present job with a large business firm, he is prospering and rising as rapidly as we had originally expected.

Maintaining an adequate nucleus of sound and "good" boys is a matter of constant concern at Tascosa. A ranch family composed principally of the so-called wildcats probably would remain nothing but a family of

134 wildcats in spite of the best efforts of all the "boy trainers" obtainable. Without a good mixture of boys who have had the home training of George and brother Gene, and many others of their stamp, the ability of the ranch to accomplish real reclamation would be little better than that of the ordinary state reform school, which must accept all boys sent to it.

As the Tascosa courthouse rapidly filled to overflowing with new boys, an honor system and a student government went into operation. Alton Weeks, the sincere and capable young first superintendent of the ranch, and his equally capable wife, Veva, set in motion the initial election campaign, a full-dress affair that included speeches, parties, printed ballot forms, and an election commission. After a week of unusual commotion about the place, five officials were installed: a foreman; first, second, and third wranglers; and a Texas Ranger.

Although nothing at the ranch, personal possessions or otherwise, was under lock and key, disappearances were extremely rare from the start. Every night for more than three years the fruit jar on the refrigerator, which held the boys' "recreation fund," derived principally from proceeds of the sale of soda pop to visitors, matched exactly the count of empty bottles. Then came a day when twenty-five cents was missing, and a general assembly convened immediately. The superintendent reviewed the remarkable record of the honor system to that date, and the culprit, a new boy, arose with little hesitation to confess the theft. The Boys Ranch hands respected and rewarded his courage: in his second year this same boy was elected ranch foreman.

Payday brought a long queue past the table of the bespectacled boy who held the position of ranch banker. Thirty dollars a month, the going rate for regular cowhands in the Panhandle at that time, was payable to each hand in bills of "one-buck" and five-buck" denominations printed with official BR brand and the drawing of a bucking horse. Of this sum an extremely modest spending allowance, gifts to the church, and savings put out at interest were redeemable in United States currency. The rest the boy paid to the ranch authorities at specified rates for his keep, thus being constantly reminded that his living would never come free and, at the same time, learning the responsible feeling of a man who pays his way.

More boys came.

Though Boys Ranch may have been always short of adequate quarters, supervisors, and supplies, never yet has it encountered a shortage of boys desperately in need of a home. Heartfelt appeals began to pour in from every state in the Union as the fame of the Tascosa ranch spread, and we came gradually to realize how deeply and painfully nationwide the prob-

"Nobody ever found much glamour in milking a cow, but it's a good way to make sure you eat breakfast." (Cal Farley)

lem was. An always greater portion of our time in the downtown office was spent in trying to make other satisfactory arrangements for boys not quite so direly in need, usually by initiating contacts in their home communities from coast to coast. But always there are so many in really critical circumstances, and it is very hard to keep on saying no day by day and week by week in the full knowledge that each refusal is almost tantamount to sentencing another potentially productive citizen to reform school and, eventually, to prison.

Thus, the enrollment of Boys Ranch always grew at a pace just a little faster than that of its theoretical capacity. Boys arrived who fell upon their first platefuls of food in the dining hall with dirt-encrusted bare hands but often became, within a few months, the severest sticklers for good table manners. So many came with a violent aversion to bathing that our older boys served regularly on "scrub crews," scouring down recalcitrants with stiff brushes until they succumbed to gentler self-application of soap and water. Others came in a number of instances from well-educated and even wealthy homes, drank in the health-giving personality tonic of open country living, and departed with past troubles forgotten and a fresh grip on their expanding young lives.

The grandson of a British diplomat, who had married into one of the ruling families of Peru, gave us one of our more interesting tussles during the early days of the ranch. This dark-complexioned, handsome, precocious

A PLACE IN THE COUNTRY

lad of ten had acquired considerable local fame by attaching himself, apparently for permanent "duty," to the air base near Amarillo. As a sassy little mascot who seemed to live in carefree disregard of whatever home he might have, Rod had been enthusiastically adopted by the officers and airmen.

They found him a bunk and fed him scandalously rich rations. They conspired with a tailor to provide him with a uniform, toured airplanes with him, made him stand inspection, and taught him to bark orders to ranks of grinning airmen at muster. Each new accomplishment was rewarded with a "promotion," and neglect of his so-called duties periodi- cally brought him a "busting" to a lower grade. Finally, a resplendent pair of pinks and a diminutive officer's blouse arrived from the tailor complete with what later came to be described as a fifty-mission cap, and Rod was "commissioned" a second lieutenant with ample military ceremony.

In comparison to this seventh boy heaven, which existed for him at the air base, it was not at all surprising that Rod found his school and home duties intolerably dull. Eventually his mother, a tiny woman of obviously good breeding and education, appealed with many tears to Boys Ranch to try to rescue not only Rod but his nine-year-old brother, who was rapidly following the same course. Rod, she said, would come home "only long enough to get clean underwear now and then."

We learned the family story only much later and by accident. Although she was a cousin of the then president of Peru, Rod's mother had been a citizen of the United States and a resident of Detroit most of her life. Her second husband, a man of French extraction, had proved so jealous and intolerant of her two sons that she had finally left him to come west and attempt the unfamiliar task of making her living alone.

Boys Ranch, as usual, was overflowing with boys, but we could not turn our backs on this unusually devoted mother. We agreed to try to bring Rod around if she would cooperate to the fullest in a purposeful masquerade we have staged many times since with the understanding assistance of the Amarillo sheriff.

By prearrangement, the boy was arrested by the provost marshal at the air base and turned over to the sheriff, who conducted him to jail with many stern remarks about his misdeeds and the punishments to come. As if by afterthought, the sheriff then "relented" a little and brought the young offender to me, telling him that he would try to keep the judge from sending him to reform school under the Texas truancy law if I could be persuaded to accept him at Boys Ranch.

Listening gravely to the sheriff's recital of Rod's wrongdoing, I shook my head. Repeated pleas by the sheriff and the boy's mother brought from me only the same negative answer.

"This boy," I said, pointing a finger at him, "has been having the most fun you can imagine at the air base. He thinks he has the world by the tail and no one is going to tell him what he must do at all. How could we do anything for him at the ranch, where he'd have to live with a lot of other boys, go to school, obey rules, and do his work every day? Cows have to be milked night and morning, you know, whether the boy assigned to milk them wants to do it or not."

"But, Cal," the sheriff picked up his cue. "I hate to send this boy off to reform school. He has a fine mother, and I think he's really a good boy underneath . . . ."

"No, I'm afraid not. We're so overcrowded."

After a good deal of this sort of talk considered sufficient to impress some genuine concern for his fate upon the boy's mind, I agreed, as a "favor" to the sheriff and the boy's mother, to give Rod a trial, making a stipulation that he would be returned to the hands of the law at the first sign of rebellion. The boy departed to pick up his clothing at home, supposedly to return to my office at two o'clock that afternoon.

Late in the day no Rod had reappeared. Our performance had been in vain.

Again the provost marshal picked up the lad, who was making another joyful round of his familiar haunts. It was evening when the sheriff ushered in a still not-quite-repentant boy for another talk with me.

This time our playacting was more convincing—perhaps because by this time both of us were late for dinner and beginning to mean exactly what we were saying. The sheriff made an admirably long, eloquent, and really tough speech to the boy, and when he had finished Rod was thoroughly scared for probably the first time in his carefree young life.

That scare saved that boy. (Unless any boy has a healthy fear of something or someone, nothing will stop him short of violence: Adolf Hitler was afraid of nothing.)

At Boys Ranch, Rod showed never an inclination toward running away. He applied himself quickly to his work and his studies, and his exceptional intelligence earned him favor with the teachers. He was prone to keep himself in disrepute among the other boys, however, by asking for special favors—and being refused—within their hearing. Soon his younger brother, a lad of comparatively tractable and popular disposition, joined the ranch family (much to Rod's disgust), and their mother promptly returned east to remarry her husband.

A PLACE IN THE COUNTRY

Personal difficulties dogged Rod for many months, in spite of his obedience of the rules. His good-looking face wore a built-in sneer that seemed always implying to every boy he met, "If you knew anything at all I'd take time to talk to you, but really I don't think it worthwhile."

We assumed that this mannerism derived from his unfamiliarity with ranch life and from the memory of his former lofty mode of living as a "commissioned officer." Our general principle of public applause, we hoped, would work as well in tempering Rod's arrogance as it had in fortifying the weak self-confidence of other boys, and we waited for a chance to apply it.

Rod proved to be quite talented as a cartoonist. With encouragement, his cartoons soon became of such quality that one of the Amarillo newspapers agreed to print them regularly in conjunction with its regular weekly column on Boys Ranch. This new distinction, earned with his own hands, did a great deal to solve Rod's problem. Time and companionship did the rest.

Occasionally we have had cause to realize that more cautious and experienced persons might have regarded our whole idea of a ranch a foolish one at the very onset, merely from the standpoint of physical dangers involved. If the pressures of establishing a town and providing for such a rapidly expanding family of "sons" had permitted us time for reflection, we might indeed have dredged up fears that would have greatly hampered our progress.

Boys whose entire lives have been spent in the light of neon signs and in the human and vehicular traffic of city pavements theoretically should encounter serious if not fatal hazards when suddenly transplanted, under supervision that never could be termed "adequate," to such a remote spot as Tascosa. Skittish ponies and high-strung registered livestock; a dangerous river; guns and hunting knives; a deep swimming hole; tractors and other farm equipment; lonesome hills covered with loose rock, cactus, and a plenitude of rattlesnakes a full hour's drive from the nearest doctor — none of these could make Tascosa a "safe" place for city boys.

Fortunately, however, before we had time to think a great deal about the subject, the assurances of actual practice forestalled the greatest of our worries. As the years passed we saw in operation the heavenly guardianship my friend Fred Gipson once detailed in a delightful story of boy escapades he entitled "Angels Work Overtime." The new Tascosa has proved that boys still can survive and thrive under conditions scarcely more clinical and scientific than those endured by the families who settled the plains of West Texas two generations ago.

It is true that angels of the interceptor patrol assigned to hover over Tascosa have inscribed an enormous amount of flight time in their celestial logbooks, but thus far they have achieved a near-perfect record in their dogfights against raiding evil spirits. There have been many emergencies large and small: falls from horses, broken arms and legs, fevers and poison oak rash, now and then a more serious mishap. One youthful duck hunter lost a toe in the accidental discharge of a shotgun; our top horse wrangler had his head cracked by a rearing albino stallion. Once or more each month, after the ranch grew to accommodate a hundred and more boys, an automobile has sped off to one of the always considerate Amarillo hospitals carrying a sick or banged-up boy. But in the first fifteen years of Boys Ranch no boy died of sickness or accident or was permanently injured.

This fact is due in part to the tough animal wariness bred into these boys by the hard knocks of their young lives. Supervisors are continually being surprised to see how many lumps their charges will absorb without personal complaint, often recalling as typical an incident that occurred during the first year of the ranch operation.

A certain ragged and beaten youngster who never in his life had had a brand-new pair of shoes to call his own had been provided flashy, two-colored cowboy boots. For a week thereafter he strode about the place with his eyes more often fixed proudly upon those new boots than upon his path ahead. While chopping wood for the kitchen, however, he swung a glancing blow of the ax which cut, not only through a boot, but deeply into his foot. After a long minute of silent, heartbroken inspection of the damage, he turned, with a pair of unheeded tears sliding alongside of his nose, to plead with another boy nearby:

"I've ruined the boot. Don't tell Mr. Weeks I've ruined one of my new boots!"

To speed his recovery, a new pair of boots arrived at the doctor's office almost as soon as the boy did.

Among a number of hairbreadth escapes through the years, the worst occurred, not at the ranch, but in a highway collision at the edge of the city in which the ranch truck overturned with its usual cargo of boys and supplies. Our most prolonged scare, however, was entirely a false alarm.

Big Herman, a crashing right tackle on the Boys Ranch football team and the kind of cowhand one would almost expect to see wrestling any bull he could not drive, succumbed to wanderlust one summer afternoon. Staging his departure with dramatic elaboration, he hid spare clothing and a sandwich or two in the brush before splashing with the crowd throughout the regular swimming period. When the other boys were out

The near-perfect safety record compiled by the guardian angels assigned to the Tascosa interceptor patrol confirms the ancient law that the open spaces, by birthright, are the natural habitat of a boy.

of sight but not out of hearing, he heaved a big stone into the water with a mighty yell, then hid in the weeds while would-be rescuers, finding his pants and shirt still on the bank, swarmed the entire lake looking for him.

For the next two days crews dragged the lake bottom. But, because of our suspicions, we luckily delayed notifying the boy's relatives that he had disappeared. Two weeks later the lure of the forthcoming football season overpowered Big Herman's aversion to the punishment he knew would be awaiting him; he came home and put himself in "condition," as I remember, by standing many days of heavy duty cracking rocks for a new retaining wall.

Eventually, that phenomenal safety record was marred. [Editor's note: see Chapter 14.] But after twelve years it seems reasonable, and refreshing, to conclude that the same ancient natural law which applied when Samuel Clemens and Tom Sawyer were patrolling the Mississippi never has been repealed. The gist of this law, as the guardian angels of Tascosa well know, is that boys by birthright alone are in their true natural habitat out-of-doors. This companionship with nature, which most quietly and surely develops a man from a male child, is a deeply instinctive thing, far transcending the comprehension of more timorous adults. Otherwise, how could eleven years of daily prowlings of the Tascosa prairie have passed before any Boys Ranch resident was first even bitten by a rattlesnake — and then with no serious results?

Any special safety dispensations, human or divine, are needed to the utmost by the fatherless boys of Tascosa in their gropings for manhood, a process which also could utilize individual study of, and affection for, each boy in far greater quantities than any home like Boys Ranch has ever been able to provide. Women of the ranch staff always have been of incalculable value and assistance. Mrs. Maud Thompson, for example, who came to the ranch as a grandmother, over two decades expended her apparently bottomless fund of motherhood to the huge benefit of the smaller boys of the "courthouse gang."

But because so many of these boys have never known their fathers and have long since defied their mothers' control, much can be accomplished only by a direct masculine influence.

Several thoughts I had expressed on this topic during a speech before one of the large Los Angeles luncheon clubs brought an immediate challenge from a member who came to see me after the meeting. The son of a former friend of his, a Los Angeles doctor who had died when the boy was ten years old, was awaiting his third appearance in juvenile court for automobile theft and was almost certain to go to reform school.

A PLACE IN THE COUNTRY

"Robert's mother," the man related, "has devoted her best efforts to the upbringing of her son and his three older sisters, but this boy has driven her frantic. He is a very intelligent boy, though his health has not been too good, and it has seemed to me that his stealing and troublemaking are primarily just his way of proving to the world that he is a he-man. I believe Tascosa would do wonders for him."

His analysis proved quite correct. This mother had been entirely too solicitous in sheltering her only son. A slender boy at best, he had contracted malaria on a family vacation trip into Mexico, whereupon a dozen kinds of medicine had been forced upon him as a permanent part of his daily diet. His string-bean physique prevented participation in school athletics. Although scorned or disregarded by most other boys because of his sickly frame and the trace of stuttering he had developed, Robert nonetheless showed good breeding and, on the whole, quite a pleasant personality.

Of recent months, however, he had fallen into the company of three boys whose attitude was different from that he encountered at school. They needed him; they treated him as an equal and even with a bit of deference. Robert, after all, habitually had plenty of spare money in his pockets, and whenever they needed an automobile he could borrow his mother's. Soon Robert learned that these boys were stealing automobiles, two of the gang having had reform school training in this occupation, and his vanity was stimulated. If he could prove himself a man no other way, perhaps he could do so by stealing automobiles he did not need.

The Los Angeles judge welcomed an opportunity to send Robert to Boys Ranch, and in due time he arrived with a case full of ointments, tonics, pills, and elaborate written instructions for the regular dosage of each. The superintendent studied the situation carefully for several days, then approached the boy on the playground.

"Bob," he said, "I don't believe you will need all that medicine here. We'll have you looked over regularly by a doctor downtown and let him prescribe for you. Right now I'd like to suggest that you gather up every bit of that medicine and chuck it in the river."

Robert stared at his mentor in great surprise. Finally he grinned broadly and ran off to make quite a private ceremony of flinging those bottles and pillboxes as far as he could into the Canadian. As long as he stayed at Boys Ranch thereafter, he never had to take another pill.

Instead, he learned to ride horseback and practiced long hours with a lariat. His stuttering disappeared. When his muscles developed a bit, we started him in softball—as a pitcher! He was terribly clumsy, but in the daily games around the ranch this was a matter of little consequence. And how hard he tried! Scarcely anywhere else in the United States, I suppose, could this gangling boy have occupied the important pitcher's box without being jeered off the playing field for his almost hopeless awkwardness. At Boys Ranch, however, where the crowd is habitually quick to award an A for any kind of earnest effort, he was encouraged and cheered on whenever he managed to throw a ball in the vicinity of home plate.

Robert's difficulties simply evaporated. Within only a few months he was ready to return home the happy and well-adjusted young man he has remained ever since.

These were the beginning years of the new Tascosa. Boys Ranch hummed with ever increasing activity, and we realized almost from the very first that it must grow big but that it never could grow big enough. Expanded a hundred times, and remaining true to its original aims and philosophy, it still could never meet the demands of all the boys whose parents and patrons would be pleading for their chance at just such a home.

Ours was always a miscellaneously interesting family of the fatherless. Quick-witted or slow, genial or quarrelsome, quiet or noisy, studious or reluctant—each boy was an individual fascination that sometimes required months of study and tinkering before we managed to forge a key to his personality. But with hardly one in a hundred did we ultimately fail.

The smaller fellows, taken to the ranch because their former path to destruction was plain and inescapable, came with a physical hunger for affection that would twist the heart of the most world-weary onlooker. Familiar adults could not move out-of-doors without a clinging swarm of six- to ten-year-olds about them, hanging to their clothing, crawling upon their laps, using any excuse or none at all in mute appeal for the bodily gestures of affection so painfully absent from their little lives.

The elder boys usually maintained a surprisingly distant dignity, but the same hunger was theirs. Five hundred times a day members of the ranch staff would answer questions or receive inconsequential intelligence. Boys would race half a mile to report to the first available adult the discovery of a rabbit warren or the appearance of a Coca-Cola truck on the far side of the river. Any minute event or personal adventure was enough to send them running in a flagrant plea for adult attention.

Supervisors and teachers, carefully selected for their durable patience and genuine love of children, could hardly have survived except for the natural diversions offered by the ranch itself. A boy's unassisted discovery of the pecan tree around the hill by the cowbarns might keep him occupied for a morning or a day; others seemed never able to exhaust the marvels of the red bluff that rises from the river half a mile downstream. One boy from an eastern city who had never before seen a calf, actually lay alone and motionless throughout a full afternoon merely watching a Hereford yearling pick at the bunch grass. Another caused historic excitement by discovering a crumbling human skeleton in a shallow pasture grave that probably dated from Indian days.

For the more ardent wooers of cow-country adventure there came into existence a fraternity known as the Boot Hill Club. Initiation required a boy to pack his own bedroll, climb alone to the cemetery of Old Tascosa, and spend a full night among the gravestones. Escorted rambles provided each candidate some prior indoctrination in the night calls of coyotes, hoot owls, and the chuckwill's widow. Even so, this sojourn among the restless spirits of suddenly departed gunmen was not an experience that permitted a great deal of sleep on the part of either the boy or the superintendent. The rewards in public esteem, however, and the right to regale bunkhouse assemblies on many subsequent evenings with dramatically gestured accounts of the night's events, were rich indeed.

The aim then, as it is now, was to provide for these boys a home as nearly normal as we could possibly contrive. Besides school and the vocational and outdoors training of the ranch, this new life included regular trips to town for movies and restaurant meals. It included athletic contests with the smaller high schools of the district. It included dozens of "programs" at the ranch and elsewhere, spook-parties at Hallowe'en, turkey at Thanksgiving, gifts at Christmas, and the scrupulous observance of birthdays. It included regular church attendance on Sunday mornings, with the boys conducting their own services on occasions when no minister could be present.

For one very special party when the ranch was three years old, the boys had depleted Amarillo's supply of violently perfumed hair oil in preparation for the arrival of the girls of a Sunday School in a nearby town. To do justice to the occasion Alton and Mrs. Weeks put together a jingle and a tune as a "Boys' Ranch song" to be sung for the fair feminine guests.

The party was a success warmly remembered yet today by boys grown men and possessing families of their own. But I am sure that any adult, listening in the darkness just outside the courthouse while those strong young voices clambered over that tune with much vigor and occasional harmony, would have found most unforgettable the two lines of the song which ran: *"The summers are hot. The winters are cold. I am too young to be feeling so old . . ."*

They *are* so young, these fatherless ones, to be feeling so old.

13

Boys Ranch Gets a Water Tower

WE BUSINESSMEN had started our boys ranch in a very "un-businesslike" manner. No preliminary campaign had "awakened" the community. No fund-raising speeches, accompanied by the outspreading of blueprints, had occurred before the luncheon clubs. (Most of us already had become weary of buying blueprints that seemed always awfully slow to materialize into brick and mortar.) No parades had been staged and no slogans coined. We merely had obtained a place in the country and started our ranch.

It was simply impossible for me as an active businessman to solicit support for the ranch. I well knew that in a reverse situation, if my own best friend had come with his hat extended, telling me that he "sure would like to start a ranch and take care of those kids," my impulse would have been to reply, "Well, run along and start one, dreamer, and let me hear from you later. I'm busy making a living."

For me in particular it would have been absurd to think that I could succeed in selling a man an automobile tire with one hand while holding out the other for money for my pet charity. The only way Boys Ranch could be built was to get something started, try to let everyone know what was going on, and after that, hope. Ask no man for a nickel but keep on talking about boys. People may be tired of organizations and campaigns, but they are never tired of hearing about individual boys. Show everyone in every possible way what was being done and try to not ask for help in such a way as to make it easy for anyone to help who really wished to do so. Then hope some more.

The help came.

Most important of all was the warm and wise support of publisher Gene Howe and editor Wes Izzard at the *Amarillo Globe-News*, who already had helped lift my business out of the tire-shop stage by consistently finding my doings and my joshing chatter worthy of being printed. Through the years to come the assistance of the press and radio in Amarillo and throughout Texas—soon that of nearly all the national magazines as well—never ceased to grow, creating the public interest that enabled Boys Ranch to progress.

Within a few months after the ranch opened, the courthouse was bulging with boy population, even though it seemed we spent half our days refusing admittance to others in desperate circumstances. Then, for the first and just about the last time we ever permitted any indebtedness to be incurred at Boys Ranch, druggist Roy Pool, rancher Chanslor Weymouth, and I put our names on a note for fourteen thousand dollars to build a gymnasium and school. This time, in contrast to my venture in building a baseball stadium some years before, the "fans" were not long in gathering around to help.

The framework of the big gymnasium, with a stage in front of the playing floor and wings on either side to accommodate schoolrooms, recreation hall, dispensary, and showers, started to go up on the former site of the "county building" on McMasters Street just east of the courthouse. After one series of pictures appeared in the newspapers showing construction actually under way, there was never much question thereafter whether the help would be forthcoming to rebuild Tascosa.

Confronted with this plain evidence that we meant business in our crazy idea of a Boys Ranch, the people of the Texas Panhandle were told simply that the gymnasium would enable us to take twenty more boys out of the alleys and give them a home in the country. On that basis the lumbermen were ready and eager to contribute materials without being asked. The furniture dealers' association, on its own initiative, collected and delivered the necessary furnishings. The carpenters' and plumbers' unions telephoned to notify us that necessary labor would be available free of charge on weekends. Truckers offered to haul men and material to the scene. Cash contributions came in one-dollar bills and hundred-dollar checks.

The gymnasium was finished and paid for in a matter of weeks.

The dining hall, the next major structure to go up, was proposed and

20th anniversary celebration at the ranch. Rancher Julian Bivins brought new life to a ghost town by donating the courthouse and townsite of Old Tascosa as a home for boys from the streets. A few months later merchant Cal Farley, cattleman Chanslor Weymouth, and druggist Roy Pool signed a $14,000 note to build the frame gymnasium-school building shown at the right—the first new construction since frontier days.

paid for during a single weekly meeting of the Amarillo Rotary Club, shortly after Father Edward Flanagan, builder of the great Boys Town at Omaha, had visited Tascosa and returned to make a speech in Amarillo on our behalf. This building, large enough to seat one hundred fifty persons, family-style, at tables of six, with a large kitchen and a walk-in refrigerator, had a fifteen-thousand-dollar price tag that represented a lot of money in that spring of 1941. But the Rotarians had seen enough of Boys Ranch to require no further convincing. Without a "plea" or even a speech from me, the club took up the subject and promptly voted to build the dining hall.

Then the chairman, considerably to the surprise of the membership, spoke up against a solicitation, saying, "I suggest we settle this matter before we get up from the table."

Fifteen Amarillo businessmen put themselves down for a thousand dollars apiece then and there.

A well was needed. The Roundup Club of Amarillo, a riding group,

BOYS RANCH GETS A WATER TOWER

found a driller, begged a tank, and piped the water into courthouse and gymnasium, drawing most of the labor from its own membership on weekends.

World War II was in full pitch, and as always Boys Ranch was bursting with boys made homeless before and during that war. In spite of severe shortages, the Amarillo area Bell Telephone superintendent and employees scrounged the materials and strung a difficult sixteen-hundred-foot span of telephone wire across the Canadian River to Boys Ranch, and we were called upon not so often thereafter to rearrange oh-so-cleverly the "script" of our noon radio show in the store downtown to alert the ranch superintendent to meet a supply truck at the river crossing.

The Allis Chalmers Company donated a used tractor, and it was then possible to retire into pasture the span of mules Alton Weeks had declared, with forgivable exasperation, "must have been broke to work in World War I" and whose prime duty in the first years had seemed to be pulling stalled automobiles out of that quicksand river crossing. When this tractor was in turn retired many years later, ranch supervisors ascribed over five hundred such quicksand rescues to its credit.

Fuel was a terrible problem. Expensive butane donated in quantity by Lyle Blanton of Hereford, and wood chopped and sawed along the river, could not be hauled in by truckload fast enough to keep the boys warm during the coldest part of the winter, and the nearest natural-gas line was seven miles away. Harold Dunn—president of the independent Shamrock Oil Company, gin-rummy fanatic, and a determined member of our Boys Ranch board—mentioned the problem to his friend Boots Adams, an ex-basketball player for Frank Phillips's Sixty-Sixers team and who had succeeded to the presidency of Phillips Petroleum Company.

"Get me seven miles of that used pipe you've got lying around somewhere," Harold Dunn said, "and Shamrock will lay that line."

The line was finished in 1945, and it leaked. As soon as new pipe became available after the war, the two companies relaid the line at their own expense, and for years thereafter their accountants—greedy capitalists all but frightfully negligent—omitted ever sending us a bill for all the gas we could use.

For years thereafter, help for our boys in a hundred ways from the Phillips Petroleum Company, through Thomas C. Craig and its vice-chairman, Paul Endacott, was only a telephone call away.

Farm women's groups from two hundred miles around dispatched thousands of quarts of canned fruits and vegetables every fall for the first decade or more, and hardly a week went by when some farmer or cattle-

The Boys Ranch Board of Directors in 1952. From left: Lyle Blanton, C.F. Robertson, Superintendent John Nickles, Cal Farley, J. Harold Dunn, Bob Lindsey, Virgil Patterson, and Dr. John Vaughn.

man or merchant we had never heard of did not offer by telephone, or merely drive into the ranch with, a load of potatoes or livestock feed or hay or durable goods of some kind. In Amarillo, Doctors B. M. Puckett and John Vaughn, early members of the ranch board, devoted much of their professional time to providing medical services for our boys. Dentists, optometrists, and other professionals volunteered free services.

The furniture dealers association put furnishings into our new buildings as fast as we could put them up. The carpenters', plumbers', electricians' and other labor unions were always ready when they heard a job needed to be done; often they would make their working trip to Tascosa a family weekend outing.

The list goes on and on, adding up to a demonstration of spontaneous and continued generosity which stands as convincing evidence that Americans are still as warmheartedly responsive to the needs of their fellow human beings as they ever were, provided only that they are shown real results for their money.

I was as preoccupied as always with the promotion of the ranch. As district governor in 1941, it was my duty to pay a formal visit focusing on the health and welfare of each Rotary club in my sprawling district. During that year, I confess, Rotary's organizational well-being received precious little attention. Often on these visits I would take along my lively

BOYS RANCH GETS A WATER TOWER

daughter, Genie, and her song-and-dance trio, or some other performer from the ranch or the Maverick Club who had graduated from the Flying Dutchman Circus. When the time came for me to unload my gubernatorial wisdom upon the local membership, my usual opening was; "I'm sure you fellows know much more about running an effective club in your city than I do, so this year we'll skip that lecture. I'm going to talk on something I do know about—what's going on at Boys Ranch."

Rotary International survived.

A ranch, we decided, should have a rodeo, and a boys ranch should have an all-boys rodeo. We decided to stage one on Labor Day, 1944, at the ranch, and the results were unforgettable, not to say disastrous. After much puzzling, we took a wild guess that, at the outside, maybe one thousand people would make the long trip to Tascosa, and we arranged a barbecue to feed that many. Labor Day came, a beautiful day, but the cantankerous Canadian River was up, and traffic to the ranch had to be directed northwest along the highway to Channing, then southward along a twelve-mile dirt trail to the ranch—a formidable trip totalling seventy miles.

Even so, more than two thousand visitors had descended upon the ranch before noon, consuming all our food before the rodeo could begin—and our troubles were just beginning. Not far from the ranch the automobile trail from Channing descended into a gully to a ford in a small creek. By midday the fragile track through the creek had broken down, and automobile after automobile became hopelessly stalled in the sand. Our faithful ranch tractor was pulling them out as fast as it could, but other impatient drivers compounded the disaster by attempting without success to ford the creek elsewhere.

While the rodeo events went on, I commandeered S-s-stuttering Sam and his light plane—as I often did in those days, Sam having been a flight instructor during the war. We flew northward along a seemingly endless line of stalled motorists nine long miles before we spotted what seemed to be the last rodeobound Texas family. Finding a half-smooth open spot in the mesquite, Sam landed. I spent the afternoon walking those nine miles back to the ranch, objectly apologizing to each driver for the fact that, if he did manage to reach the creek he couldn't cross, and if he did manage to cross, the rodeo would be over and we couldn't feed him so much as a hot dog.

By the time I had waded back across the creek, the crowd had been fed every bite of food in Maude Thompson's pantry, the ranch's whole flock of chickens had been killed and eaten, and the boys had not a crust

News service photo of Cal and his daughter Genie taken during a promotional visit to Washington, D.C. Sudden national recognition of the ranch in the 1940s set Cal to work harder than ever to raise money for expansion.

of bread left to eat for supper. The superintendent set off on horseback to Channing to get breakfast rations. By the time the last car had been pulled from the creek and its occupants had been sent back hungry toward Amarillo about 1:00 A.M., S-S-stuttering Sam spoke to me and to a circle of bone-weary sheriff's deputies: "Now, Cal, wouldn't you say you might have overpromoted this deal just a little bit?"

A story by Neil Clark in the *Saturday Evening Post* that same year, 1944, the first coverage of the ranch by a national magazine, brought in a flood of three thousand one hundred letters, almost all of them pleading with us to accept boys, the rest expressing genuine interest in, and support of, our effort.

This new national exposure, plus perhaps a speech or two of mine in Los Angeles, no doubt helped bring MGM Producer Robert Sisk and his troupe of eighty-three actors and technicians to the ranch in 1945 to shoot a feature-length film in which the pranks of our capricious Canadian River and the stories of our ranch and some of our boys were portrayed. The premiere showing of the film *Boys Ranch* was a major event in Amarillo. Our new mayor, my friend Lawrence Hagy, was vigorously shaping the progress of the city in the heady days after release of wartime restrictions. In doing so, he had signaled a new era for Amarillo's youngsters by

BOYS RANCH GETS A WATER TOWER

Cowboy singing stars Roy Rogers and his wife Dale Evans were loyal patrons and frequent visitors during the formative years. Roy and some of his troupe are shown here at the 20th anniversary celebration in 1959.

removing "keep-off-the-grass" signs from the city parks; by persuading the Junior League to undertake a strenuous program of games, storybook sessions, and other summer diversions in the parks by those of our little ones not involved in the Kids, Inc., athletic schedules; and, by maintaining, as a ranch director, an ardent interest in all our doings at Tascosa.

The jovial mayor was in his element at the premiere, for which we rented and sold out two theaters at ten dollars a seat, netting the—for us—unprecedented sum of twenty-eight-thousand dollars. With this money we purchased and moved to Tascosa several surplus buildings from the disbanded Dalhart Air Force Base, including the white chapel, and three barracks which we converted into dormitories.

Other Hollywood stars began to come to help the ranch, of whom none were so faithful as Roy Rogers and Dale Evans. When they agreed to headline our annual rodeo in 1949, we shifted the event to Amarillo for that year only to accommodate the crowds. After that, Roy and Dale continued to help us in many ways; beginning in 1952 and for several Christmases thereafter they presented every boy resident of the ranch a pair of resplendent cowboy boots emblazoned with the BR brand.

In 1955, Roy and Dale were lavish hosts at their California ranch to our by then nearly two hundred boys, all transported to California for five days on a special train by the Santa Fe Railroad and various Los Angeles civic clubs in the most elaborate of several ranchwide summer outings that had begun in 1953.

On these trips—to Colorado Springs as the guest of the Jaycees; to the Cheyenne Frontier Days rodeo as guests of the *Denver Post*; to Freeport, Texas, for deep-sea fishing as guest of the Jaycees—our boys proved to be themselves the best possible salesmen for the ranch, creating what can only be described as uniform public astonishment at their appreciativeness and irreproachable good manners. It was a matter of immense satisfaction to me and the rest of the ranch staff that all these logistically formidable trips were carried off without misbehavior or a single public relations "incident" significant enough to remember.

So the building went on. A hundred lively tales could be told, but perhaps I can typify all and summarize the process by telling just one: the fairly elaborate promotion which brought Boys Ranch its sorely needed water system. It was done through a chain reaction of good feeling that extended from Pittsburgh to Pasadena and involved at least eighty individual givers, some of whom had never heard of the ranch before, capped finally when Bob Hope and Jerry Colonna broadcast their national radio show from Amarillo in a benefit for the ranch.

The best price quoted in 1946 for the erection of a fifty-thousand-gallon water tower was fourteen thousand five hundred dollars. Months went by, and as usual we did not have that amount of money to spare. Then a convention of water engineers from four states took place in Amarillo, with the salesmen from the pipe- and steel-companies in full attendance. The water situation at the ranch was becoming desperate: I stretched one of my personal rules and asked the Amarillo city manager, who was also our city engineer, to arrange for me to speak at the noon banquet, which was to close the convention. For ten minutes I sketched the growth of the ranch and the nature of the work we were trying to do, mentioning the generous and unusual manner in which our village had obtained its other utilities along with our present need for a new well and water tower. Then I went back to the office, a block away, and waited.

Later that afternoon a salesman from the Pittsburgh-Des Moines Steel Company came in to tell me that he had happened to remember that the president of that company, back in Pittsburgh, always had been interested in poor and delinquent children. Probably, my caller believed, this interest would lead him to give us a lift toward acquiring a new water tower. I

154 provided the salesman with copies of the *Saturday Evening Post* and *Reader's Digest* articles about the work of Boys Ranch to be mailed to his home office.

The president of the steel company did not wait to write a letter. He telephoned the manager of his Dallas district to congratulate him for his commendable alertness and community interest, sending word to us that he would like to "figure awhile" to see what he could do. Evidently, he figured long and expertly, and he notified us later that the company was willing to provide and erect the tower, freight included, for only six thousand two hundred dollars.

Mayor Hagy went to work on a friend who was president of the Rock Island Railroad and saved us five hundred dollars more by obtaining free transportation of the tower from Chicago. A driller named Jamison came down from the town of Dumas to drive test holes until the right source of water was located, by which time the D. R. McDonald Drilling Company was standing by to put down the thirty-six-inch well and contribute the steel lining free of charge in the process. Three machine shops in Pampa kept bits sharp and threaded the pipe.

Nearly a mile of pipe was needed to bring the water from the well and distribute it among the buildings, and pipe was scarce. Because of its standing as a heavy purchaser, the city of Amarillo secured delivery of the pipe, then consented to postpone some of its own less pressing projects in order to let Boys Ranch have what it needed at cost. A big bulldozer was brought more than a hundred miles for use on a Sunday to clear a path for an equally unpaid-for ditcher which followed the next day. Sixteen volunteer employees of the Amarillo Water Department, along with four men from Borger, worked until dark on two Sundays to lay the pipe and install fire hydrants obtained at government surplus and given to us.

Meanwhile, the ranch boys themselves, under supervision of the superintendent—a six-foot-three, two-hundred-twenty-pound ex-football star named Jack Hardin—had mixed and poured the concrete foundation for the tower in accordance with specifications, using cement donated by the trade acquaintances of one of our most loyal and energetic directors, J. B. (Polly) Parrott. The sizable job of connecting the new water system throughout our town took care of itself when a plumber from the city of Plainview approached me when I had finished a talk before the Kiwanis Club at Tulia, offering his services at a time when plumbing was uppermost in my mind. The next weekend he appeared with fifteen plumbers gathered from all over his part of Texas to work a full Saturday and Sunday, and they returned the following week to finish the job with the help of an additional dozen plumbers from Amarillo. Men from the Public Service Company installed four thousand feet of high line and a transformer; a fellow customer in a barber shop, while I was being lathered for a shave, offered to provide cinder blocks for a wellhouse; local lumbermen put the roof over our new pump and motor; and the job was done.

That pump and motor, incidentally, became ours without purchase because the president of the Alhambra, California, Rotary Club at that time happened to be the president of the Pomona Pump Company, makers of irrigation pumps. During lunch I had been telling him about the irrigated farm owned by Boys Ranch and seeking some preliminary guidance regarding the additional pumps we would eventually buy. Later, in the middle of my scheduled speech to the club, I mentioned our recent well-drilling as an example of the manner in which the ranch had been built.

"And I'll furnish the pump," the club's president interrupted.

When it later developed that the big new well on the hill would require a much larger pump than the one mentioned, I wrote him about that fact, insisting on paying the full difference in cash.

"I don't recall saying that we would only give you a *little* pump," the president of the company corrected me in reply. "If you will quit wasting time and specify the pump you need, we'll ship it right away. Now, what have you done about getting a motor for the thing?"

In my mechanical ignorance I had done nothing about that, presuming that the motor and the pump would come in a single package. Later came another letter from this new friend of no more than an hour-and-a-half luncheon acquaintance.

"Your pump is on the way," he wrote. "I have just telephoned a friend of mine here in California who makes the big electric motors this pump requires, telling him I had just donated a fifteen-horsepower motor on behalf of his company to the boys at your ranch. It will be shipped this week from his factory. Now, will you please write him a letter and explain the work you are doing at Boys Ranch — he had never heard of the place!"

A minor portion of the total cost, four thousand dollars or so, remained beyond the farthest reach of our finagling and had to be paid in cash. Enter Bob Hope and Jerry Colonna: tickets to the broadcast of their weekly radio show from Amarillo brought in comfortably more than that figure. And Mayor Hagy, whose actions and influence had kept the project in motion at several crucial junctures, considered himself well rewarded by the privilege of touring his city as the genial host of the Hope troupe.

Boys Ranch had a water system.

BOYS RANCH GETS A WATER TOWER

Instant rapport between Amarillo's mayor Lawrence Hagy and Bob Hope sped preparations when the Hope radio troupe arrived to highlight the premiere of the Hollywood feature film *Boys Ranch* in 1946. The proceeds helped rapid expansion at Old Tascosa.

How was all this made to happen?

As the ranch took on size and solidity and became more widely known, that question was always in the minds of the friendly folks who—with the arrival of the pavement to the ranch on the seventy-mile route from Amarillo via Channing—were beginning to come to visit us in numbers upward of fifteen thousand a year.

The same frequent question was asked more pointedly by those who began to arrive from all parts of the country to study the techniques and the records of our ranch in reclaiming boys and who had stayed to study the separate phenomenon—the manner of its growth. These visitors without exception were startled to learn that Boys Ranch had been begun, maintained, and solidly established without public solicitation of any kind—that we had set up no annual budget, announced no organized campaigns, accepted sponsorship by no one in particular, and employed no professional welfare staff.

They found it hardest to believe that in plain truth we had never *asked* any man for a nickel—though I would quickly add that we had indeed taken all pains to *show* people what we were doing and make it easy for them to help if they wished—then, above all, thanked them warmly and immediately if they saw fit to help.

As the ranch grew I continued to wonder many times why it is so difficult for so many of us to understand the prime motivations of our cagy fellow Americans, who are accused all over the world of being money crazy, gadget crazy, luxury crazy. Instead, I am sure that the principal interest they have in making money is the activity they can contrive from it. First and last they like action. Mostly they do not have time to study another man's blueprinted dreams, having enough of their own, but their greatest pleasure comes from joining up and being a part of a going, progressing, rapidly moving operation. They always pay off on progress.

If our southwestern people had figured Cal Farley, for example, to be a fellow whose great ambition was to walk the streets like a pink-and-holy benefactor of mankind, the first sack of cement would never have been mixed for new construction at Tascosa. To them it simply seemed a sound idea to give those kids a home off the streets, and during the years to follow they showed a persistent eagerness to help that purpose along. More than that, it often appeared that each citizen of our sprawled-out range country wanted to know and study each new development of the ranch as it came—to discuss it, write letters about it, and make it a part of his personal business.

That warmth of personal interest, I was learning, is a valuable but two-sided coin.

In such a venture as a Boys Ranch, the public is the most relentless of taskmasters. Visiting contributors are never at all inclined to take into account the fact that the water pipes may have frozen, the assistant cook has drunk all the vanilla extract and disappeared, the tragic waiting line of weeping mothers beseeching care for boys the ranch has no room to take is longer than usual at the downtown office door, or that other parents meanwhile are badgering and threatening the management for the return of boys their own criminal neglect sent to the ranch only a few months ago—simply because they have now found a place where that healthy boy can pick cotton and earn them a little drinking money.

No matter. The boys at the ranch must remain—and we see to it that they themselves know *why* they must remain—just a little cleaner and better mannered than the children of their visiting guests. The school they attend must be not only a good standard school but an above-average school and, as soon as possible, a really model school—simply because it must stand the test of such incessant inspection—and so with nearly everything else about the place.

Finally, having muddled through all these problems and survived, the builder of a ranch for boys can address himself to still another dilemma

BOYS RANCH GETS A WATER TOWER

that time will prove only to be insoluble. This is the publicity problem of what to do with himself.

By now, whatever private life he once enjoyed is no more than a fading memory. But in his new role he is caught between the primary law that too much publicity is the quickest kind of career suicide and the equally potent fact that he cannot stay out of the spotlight and still do the job. The public tires of any face in a hurry but, of the face of a do-gooder, twice as rapidly. After the burst of public notice necessary to put across such special events as the annual rodeo, the head of the ranch quietly pleads with his editor friends to "keep us out of the paper" for several weeks.

On the other hand, there is the need for a name to trademark and personalize any project, and there is also the inbred desire of any customer to do business with the boss-man himself. Few fans know the name of the second clarinetist in Harry James's dance band; one name is all the general public can readily handle in connection with any one orchestra. And any well-wisher who contributes so much as a pair of used galoshes to the boys at the ranch seems to want to have the president and founder himself receive that gift and thank him for it.

In desperation, the head of the ranch may decide to swing the spotlight and the so-called glamor of the operation upon the head of the ranch superintendent instead of himself. Not only does public support sag immediately, but even the most level-headed superintendent — or his wife — may begin to read those news stories too carefully and start off on some tangent of his own. At best, he has little time left to get his work done.

If the ranch head squeezes into his schedule trips to Washington, Denver, or Atlanta to speak about his approach to youth problems and incidentally to obtain a little sustenance for the boys those same cities have sent to the ranch, some of the home folks tut-tut him as a national power seeker. If he stays at home, the same commentators blame him for burdening their community with "young criminals" from other states.

Certainly he has little chance to have his breast pockets reinforced for medals and his head fitted with honorary Stetson hats. Instead, he is bound to hear himself described, at one time or another, as a man who is secretly putting half of the ranch receipts into his personal strongbox or as one who is beating and mistreating the boys at the ranch or as one who, "really, now," is merely building himself a big name so he can run for the United States Senate!

At the worst of such times there is only one thing left for that man to do: go to the ranch and walk alone among the boys themselves, woolling their smart and trusting little heads, noticing how they've grown, listening to tales of the fish they've caught or the arithmetic they've conquered, and somehow drawing from them a renewed and unshakable belief in the deep-down decency of all human beings.

And people *are* decent.

Thousands of just such greathearted and spontaneous acts as those mentioned in this chapter on the part of everyday American citizens brought Old Tascosa — water hole of the Indians, plaza of the comancheros and sheepmen, bullet-punctured resort of the cowboys — back to life again as a village of boys. I am humble merely in letting my mind wander back among so many, in overalls or pinstripe worsteds, bringing a bundle of worn clothing or a four-figure bank draft, and simply asking us to take it and help a boy.

Only a few scattered examples have been mentioned here. Others who may have contributed even more generous devotion to our lads have neither had nor desired public recognition for their continuing support. From the full-stuffed hopper of a grateful memory I could fill the pages of another book this size with a mere listing of what these men and women have done. But I am sure that the only reward they sought already has been theirs in the sight of the boys they visited and watched and helped.

Nineteen forty-seven was my year of decision.

Before I could make mine, however, my daughter, Genie, made her own commitment — shaking me up no end by announcing her engagement to be married. The mere thought that my baby — my sprightly little companion on a hundred speaking trips, outings, and "circus" performances — could possibly be leaving the nest left me with an appallingly vacant feeling. It was of little help for Mimi to remind me patiently that Genie was now a grown woman and a sophomore doing well at the University of Texas, thinking quite properly about making her own life in her own way.

A bit of bleak reassurance arrived when I learned the credentials of the classmate she had chosen as her mate. He was Sherman G. Harriman, Jr., son of the same Colonel Sherman Harriman who had been my good friend and colleague in athletics during my closing days in army uniform in Europe, a career officer who had later distinguished himself in technical and other fields, and had retired as a brigadier general. When we met I found the young fellow alert, self-contained, and ambitious, a worthy son to a fine father, and try as I might I could find no objection to him.

From then on through, and for a year and more after, the wedding, I tried to fend off the unaccustomed and uncomfortable (sometimes downright unpleasant!) feeling that *I* was being sternly inspected by this Harriman fellow rather than the other way around. That was exactly the case, and when he told me in 1949 that he, too, had become fascinated with the work of the ranch and that he and Genie would like to stay on as a part of that work (and thus would not take my daughter away from me), I was the happiest man in Texas. I promptly dumped upon him, over his vehement protest of lack of qualifications, the chore of founding and editing the *Boys Ranch Roundup*, the newspaper we had long needed to keep our widening circle of friends informed about doings at the ranch. (He performed that chore with notable success thereafter for a dozen years.)

Meanwhile, I myself had come to a "turkey-track"—a three-way fork in my road—and had a tough choice to make. All three paths were tempting, any one of them offering rewards beyond what a broken-down second baseman turned tire jockey could reasonably have expected twenty years back.

First, the business. Especially since such a target was now easily within range, I could find nothing at all either uncouth or unpleasant in the idea of becoming just another one of those (so-what) Texas millionaires. Wartime shortages were past and inventories were plentiful. The whole economy was booming, and by now our busy store was a landmark widely known around a two-hundred-mile radius in three states. Without half the personal effort of former years I could readily bring home the other half of my first million plus two or three more besides, and keep some "hobbies" too. But businesses when built are no longer the great sport they were in the building. I was not yet bored, but I could crank up little real enthusiasm for sticking with Wunstop Duzzit indefinitely.

Politics? Now, that was much tougher to walk away from. I had a fascination for politics and a flair for it. I had been mentioned as, even asked to be, a candidate for mayor two or three times. In 1945 and 1946 I had been under real pressure to accept a nomination for Congress, which my most knowledgeable friends in Amarillo—and in fact I, myself—felt sure could lead to election after a relatively easy campaign. The pressure came from men including those for whom I held the deepest friendship and sense of obligation—Gene Howe, Wes Izzard, even one or two members of my own ranch board. At that time I could beg off rather easily, pointing to a dozen urgent requirements at the ranch for which solutions were not yet off the ground.

By 1947 the same friends and others were back urging me toward running for Congress, and their arguments were more persuasive. The North Texas economy, like the national economy, was lifting off like one

Co-author E.L. Howe, Cal, and a small friend on the courthouse steps in 1948.

of Wernher von Braun's captured V-2 rockets, and dozens of matters of vital importance to the welfare of our region called for the most broadly experienced representation possible in the nation's capital. When my friends kept saying, "Look, Cal, can you honestly see anyone else in the Panhandle who has experience and the long-standing acquaintanceships to compare to yours, who could do nearly a much as you can to protect the interests of this region?" it was not modesty but the record that kept me silent.

Throughout most of 1947 I pondered just where I belonged, whether I could be of greater service in Washington or on the Canadian River. True, I was known as an impatient, do-it-yesterday fellow who might go nuts in the swamps of Congress, but on the other hand aren't political skill and the talent for putting together complicated promotions like the water tower nearly one and the same thing? In that year, as through the late forties, especially after Elvon Howe's *Denver Post* story brought the story of the ranch to the world's largest magazine audience in the August 1947, *Reader's Digest*, I was flooded with speaking invitations and chose a number of them for selfish purposes. In cities from California to the East, I picked in turn the brains of at least ten close and knowledgeable friends in earnest discussions lasting half an afternoon or a full evening each, all on the subject of my congressional quandary. Their advice was valuable but not conclusive.

BOYS RANCH GETS A WATER TOWER

My decision to decline an entry into politics once and for all was marked by no particular dramatic moment. It swung, ultimately, on the improbability that the ranch could reach a state of stability and permanence with me away in Washington. Financial support would be curtailed immediately in the chorus of "I-told-you-so's" from critics who had contended all along that my main reason for getting into the boy business was to build my personal and political fame. That, I felt sure, by now could be overridden.

But I could not escape the feeling that I was the driver of a twenty-mule team pulling a wagonload of borax up a steep and narrow mountain road, holding all the reins of all ten spans in my own two hands. No other driver was yet aboard, and even if there were, the mere attempt to switch the reins at this point might send the wagon over the cliff. At best the wagon would be slowed or stalled indefinitely and might never reach the divide. Something utterly compulsive in me would not let me climb off that wagon halfway up the hill.

I sent word of my decision to my political friends and sold the Flying Dutchman Wunstop Duzzit to the B. F. Goodrich Company for something under three-fourths of a million dollars. Disappointed but generous as always, my friends at the *Globe-News* announced my full-time commitment to Boys Ranch with the front-page headline: "THE KIDS WIN AGAIN."

The cliff-hanging crisis in the life of the ranch was approaching faster than I knew at that moment.

In those years at midcentury I was traveling constantly, my concentration focused on finding resources for a major construction program at Tascosa. Most of all, I was determined to re-create a "family" atmosphere: to replace as fast as possible our converted military barracks with permanent-residence dormitories of brick faced with pink Colorado sandstone. Each of these contained spacious quarters for house parents and their own children at one end and similar quarters for the alternate house parents at the other, with recreation rooms and six residence rooms between, each of the latter furnishing study and sleeping quarters for four boys—twenty-four boys in all. The first of these residence dorms was completed in 1951, and others were built as fast as means became available.

Meanwhile, however, a change of superintendents had become necessary with the departure of the big, steady Jack Hardin. In this case I abandoned for the first, and last, time the sound theory that a boys ranch should be run by a man of rural origins and experience, persuading myself to bring in as ranch superintendent a young man of good physique, good education, and excellent credentials in the handling of groups of boys—but of urban

Preoccupied with financing and construction, Cal Farley suddenly faced a crisis in ranch discipline and recruited famed wrestler and old friend Dory Funk—now remembered as one of the most beloved of all former superintendents.

rather than farm or ranch background. The change occurred at a time when I would typically bring home to the ranch from each major trip a boy who had defeated the best reclamation efforts that a city could provide. Without realizing it, I was tipping the balance of power in the ranch society—bringing in a disproportionate number of older, tougher boys, so that the essential peer dominance of the "good" kids was weakened. And the new superintendent was proving to be, not exactly indecisive, but inclined to continue discussions rather than simply to assert control after the time for discussion of a situation had passed.

As a result, I came home from one trip to a situation in which a group of the older boys had, in effect, taken control of the ranch and were threatening to throw the superintendent into the river.

This was by far the most serious situation we had ever faced at the ranch. One organized revolt, even a half-successful one, would dry up our public support immediately and endanger the whole experiment. Drastic and swift action was called for, preferably the kind of action that would bridle and salvage the tough ringleaders one by one.

Dory Funk was a young two-hundred-pounder who had earned a national reputation and a considerable amount of money on the professional

BOYS RANCH GETS A WATER TOWER

wrestling circuit. He was headquartered in Amarillo, and I knew that Dory and his bright-eyed wife, Dorothy, and their two sons were a remarkably devoted family. I went to Dory and his wife, told them of my desperate plight, and asked them if they would move to the ranch, with Dory as the new superintendent, for three months until I could find a suitable replacement. They consented.

The insurrectionists remained uncowed at first. Dory gave several of them second thoughts by casually showing them wrestling holds, apologizing good-humoredly when his opponent began to indicate discomfort. He sustained some elaborate hazing, patiently tracing down the culprits and assigning them to standard disciplinary chores. When he heard that the team's biggest and toughest football player, whom he had banished from the field for hitting a teammate, had declared he was "gonna get me a big knife and cut Funk's heart out," he called the seventeen-year-old into his office, a hunting knife lying unsheathed on his desk directly in front of the boy, leaned back in his chair, and told the boy to "start cutting." Shortly thereafter the two walked out of that office fast friends.

Before long Dory Funk came to exemplify the "never-give-up-on-a-boy" philosophy as well as anyone who ever lived at the ranch had done. After losing his own automobile to the boy Rudy, he brought back the boy several times. One unconquerably surly, compulsive thief he finally delivered to the sheriff in Amarillo to be sent to reform school—then repented, drove twenty miles back to town to pick up the lad, and ultimately straightened him out.

Dorothy Funk and her two sons reveled in life on the ranch. Dory's departure to resume his foreshortened athletic career—not three months but three years after his arrival—was a tearful scene indeed. His wife and sons were weeping. The hundred and fifty boy ranchers were lined up at roadside waving good-bye, and half of them were shedding tears as well.

Though this experience ended happily, it had locked in place a rule we had more or less established before the "revolt" occurred: that no boy was ever to be admitted to the ranch who had passed his fifteenth birthday. Under the duress of our building campaign we had fudged on that rule to our sorrow. We never fudged on it again.

The building continued apace, helped along notably by the talents of our new superintendent, John Nickles. Coming up strongly also in the business administration of the ranch was a young man named Gene Hayman, who had come to us after World War II service in a rehabilitation center at Amarillo Air Force Base and eventually would become business administrator of the entire ranch operation.

In 1953, with major help from Amarillo realtors, our downtown Boys Ranch headquarters building was built and dedicated on Eleventh Street, facing Amarillo's largest city park.

My borax wagon—our Boys Ranch—had negotiated the steepest, rockiest part of the road and was approaching the summit of the pass.

BOYS RANCH GETS A WATER TOWER

14

A Long Visit with an Old Friend

WITH THE vigorous, sustained, and substantial support of the North Texas business and farming community, Cal Farley's Boys Ranch had taken solid form, to be sure, by the early 1950s. No longer, at least, anywhere in Texas or in adjoining states was the ranch being dismissed as a noble but harebrained idea that dollar and distance factors would bring to earth. But its future remained uncertain: Cal Farley knew too well that, should the fates decree a suspension of his own personal efforts for any length of time, the ranch would wither and die.

Permanence and institutional maturity arrived at Tascosa within an elapsed time of a few short months in 1955 and 1956. In 1954 the state highway department had at last completed the two-thousand-foot-long highway bridge over Canadian River quicksand and, in 1955, completed paving the highway from Vega to Channing past the ranch gate, opening the ranch to easy visitation and immensely relieving the heroic logistical labors that had been required to sustain the operation. Two years later that access was eased even further with the paving of that formerly horrendous back-country trail through the mesquite, the 36-mile "Amarillo cutoff" painfully remembered by thousands of earlier visitors to the ranch, not to mention the hundreds of would-be visitors frightened into retreat, or actually stranded in crossing those rocky miles, over past years.

Special legislation, pursued with great effort by Cal and his Amarillo friends, had been required to bring about accreditation of the Boys Ranch

When administrative skills were needed to bring organizational stability to the
solidly established ranch community,
Robert E. Wilson became superintendent in 1957. He and his gracious wife
Ada fulfilled that need for twenty years.

school through the tenth grade some years before, but without full accreditation or adequate facilities it had been extremely difficult to attract
or retain competent teachers, and the school situation remained Cal's
number one headache. As will be noted in more detail in a later chapter,
the solutions to both problems came in quick sequence: full accreditation
in 1954, and in 1955 the completion and dedication of the capacious,
modern, fully equipped, brick-and-stone school building financed and built
through the efforts of the United Peace Officers of America.

Still another new element equally vital to the long-range stability of
the ranch administration also arrived in 1955 in the businesslike new
superintendent named Bob Wilson of Muskogee, Oklahoma, and in his
warmly expressive, ladylike wife, Ada. Cal's selection of Wilson, a man
without any previous experience visibly relevant to the job of range boss
over a remuda of two hundred boys, no doubt raised many an eyebrow
even among Cal's widening circle of friends operating sizable business
organizations. But here again the Farley penchant for staff people of rural
background with industrial rather than scholastic or charitable-agency
experience proved intuitive. ("Now," Cal had confided to his son-in-law,
"we need an organizer.")

At the time he was offered the superintendency, Bob Wilson was
managing an Oklahoma store of the Western Auto Supply chain. In prior
World War II years, however, he had served with notable success as
supervisor of a substantial number of employees among several thousand

A LONG VISIT WITH AN OLD FRIEND

then employed at the Beech Aircraft Factory in Wichita, Kansas, where he had alertly educated himself in the basics of administration of a large and complicated organization. It was the latter experience that was to prove invaluable at Tascosa.

Says his colleague and ultimate successor, Lamont Waldrip: "When he came to the ranch, Bob Wilson had no knack of working with boys except those two essential qualities of always being fair, meticulously fair, and direct, even blunt, so that neither the boys nor the staff members ever had any doubt as to exactly where they stood with him. He applied himself to learn the skills of the boy business, and he did learn them well, but in the meantime he rendered one of the greatest possible contributions to the future of the ranch—by putting our operation in writing!"

Complexity intrudes itself inevitably into the policies, the procedures, and the organization chart of an institution like Boys Ranch, dependent upon free-will contributions from the general public. Those complexities could be unraveled or overleaped readily by the mind of Cal Farley, but the future success of the ranch would largely rest on the translation of the Farley genius into organizational terms. Bob Wilson's "Policies and Procedures" was the answer—the "P&P" which, under Bob Wilson's analytical eye, was written, tested, and proved during the twelve years remaining from his arrival at the ranch and Cal Farley's departure from the earthly scene, enabling the ranch administration to hold steady course during the years of wild national turbulence thereafter.

The following tribute came from Virgil Patterson, speaking as president of the ranch many years later: "It would be hard to overstate what Bob Wilson did for Boys Ranch. He put together a sheet structuring the duties of the staff. He drew up a complex organization chart—which works. He wrote rules and procedures which were the 'law' for new teachers and staff people but which kept the free and open spirit of the ranch. For example":

He held up the thick "P&P."

"Here are the rules which *must* be followed when a boy must be spanked.... Here are the rules for fire-safety training.... Here are the policies applying to teachers' leaves...."

"I'm a navy man," I reminded him, "and the navy runs on navy 'Regs.' What you're saying is that the 'Policies and Procedures,' Bob Wilson's "P&P," is the 'Regs' for Boys Ranch?"

"That's about it," he said.

Boy dramas and staff dramas and patron dramas—triumphs and tear-jerkers, miracles and minor disasters—these crowded upon one another

Within a few years an upsurge of support from the region brought visible permanence and architectural distinction to the remote community. The new dining hall shown here became the first of what are now more than forty structures of multicolored brick and pink sandstone selected by Cal.

as always during this period of the blossoming of Boys Ranch. It is tempting for the writer and might well be more intriguing for the reader to browse through a number of these tales, but for the present purpose of tracing an institutional and ideological continuum, two boy tragedies must suffice. The first of these calamities illustrates to what an amazing degree Boys Ranch by now had won the acceptance and trust of the North Texas public. The second was the incident which, for reasons partially obscure, depressed Cal Farley more deeply and for a longer period than his friends could then remember.

During a spring "runaway season" at the end of a school year the wanderlust gripped Buddy, a lanky fifteen-year-old who had been at the ranch for several years, doing reasonably well and causing no significant discipline problems whatsoever. Yet, this lad proved once again what every veteran staff person at Boys Ranch had learned a hundred times in a hundred ways: even after long study no one can be sure what secret tides flow deep in the nature of another human being.

Persuading another boy of a slower mind to go with him, Buddy led the way northward across the mesquite, arriving at a remote ranch home where they begged a meal, then discovered a hunting rifle mounted in the cab of a pickup truck parked outside. After ripping out the telephone and threatening the rancher and his wife, they raced away in the pickup, but the rancher found other transportation and spread the alarm.

Three patrol cars were waiting when the pickup approached Amarillo, but the runaways only clamped down the accelerator, one of them firing at the pursuing police with shells found in the glove compartment. From north to south at wild speed through the full length of the city the chase continued, with bullets flying in both directions. When it ended on a highway south of Amarillo, one patrol car and the pickup, with forty-two bullet holes in its cab, lay wrecked in a barrow pit. Buddy's companion had been killed by a police bullet, and the rookie officer driver of the wrecked patrol car died soon thereafter from the runaways' rifle fire.

The ranch, staff, and resident boys alike were stunned. The Panhandle community was aghast. Nothing remotely approaching the seriousness of a crime like this had occurred in the more than twenty-year existence of the ranch. News media played the event in large type across the region.

"We waited for the storm to break over our heads," Virgil Patterson remembered. "We waited for the newspapers, the law-enforcement people, the state officials, to demand radical changes in the ranch rules or perhaps even closing the ranch.

" 'Maybe we'll have a Boys Ranch next year and maybe we won't,' Cal said grimly one day as the young murderer was shipped off to prison. Worst of all, we waited for a flood of hand-wringing letters from dear friends of the ranch who no doubt were feeling that we had somehow let them down."

The storm never broke. The flood of letters never came, but almost all that did come were warmly *in support* of the ranch. "I can recall especially one letter we received about this matter," Virgil Patterson said, "and that was a sympathetic letter from the sheriff of Dallas County. 'Considering the kind of tough cookies you are willing to accept and try to straighten out, Cal,' that sheriff wrote, 'the wonder to me is that something like this hasn't happened long before now.' "

Weather forecasts were ominous on Thursday, March 21, and all day Friday, March 22, 1957, warning of the approach of a late "blue norther," one of those howling blizzards that occasionally rip across the high plains turning ranchers' hair gray in worry for their cattle. Though spring had arrived on the calendar, Superintendent Wilson and his staff decided to batten down the ranch against a big winter storm.

Disappointment was thick at the dining hall that deceptively quiet Friday evening as weekend recreational plans gave way to special work assignments necessary for protection of livestock and ranch equipment. Hadacol dormitory was deepest in gloom as the announcement came that the scheduled Saturday bus trip to Amarillo, eagerly awaited by Hadacol boys in their regular rotation, had been canceled. To one of these boys the news was a crushing blow: he was in love, and he had a long-sought date to take his girl to a movie in Amarillo on Saturday night.

Chester A. Simpson was a strong boy and a good boy. He played football, rode saddle broncs, and in only twenty months had caught up a full year's deficiency in his schoolwork so as to be scheduled for honor roll that spring, and was tractable if a bit stubborn in his work assignments. Other ranchers and his teachers generally liked his openness and honesty. That midnight, even as the advance fingers of the storm stirred curls of dust around the courthouse, Chester put on his entire wardrobe of shirts — five of them, one on top of the other — pulled his winter cap down over his ears, stuffed some previously hidden bread and cheese into his jacket pocket, crossed the river bridge, and set forth to walk the thirty-six miles of the "back" road to keep his date with his girl.

The storm was a bad one — one of the worst of the decade.

Snow blown horizontally on fifty-mile winds closed all highways in the area, and the big blow lasted a day and a half, drifting cattle into clusters in the fence corners. Then the temperatures dived well below zero; some cattle froze.

As soon as search parties could stir, more than two-thirds of the men and boys of the ranch set out to find Chester Simpson, and another major search effort was mounted from Amarillo. Every foot of the length of that unpaved trail was traversed, and areas to the left and right were scanned from the air, all with no result.

On the following Monday, the third day, a range rider searching for calf casualties of the storm reined his horse to look more closely at what appeared to be a human figure hanging halfway across the top wire of a fence. It was Chester. Exhausted and lost several miles south of the automobile road, he had frozen to death only a dozen miles from his goal. A news photographer's picture of his supremely tragic figure, his right shoulder draped on the top wire, his right arm in five shirtsleeves hanging down on the Amarillo side, poignantly told the nation the story of that blizzard of 1957 in the following week's issue of *Life* magazine.

Cal Farley was devastated. Weeks later he had still not shaken off his depression, writing in a letter to me at Miami that "Losing that boy, that way, makes me want to quit."

Time and the visibly rapid progress at the ranch, however, improved matters. From here on, in truth, his work at the ranch would be a downhill pull. Most of the major items on his lifetime agenda of the 1940s were rounding toward completion or were already accomplished.

Except one: the book—this book.

The book was to be his statement, over his own name, not merely to the southwestern region but telling the nation what he saw as his own role and that of his Boys Ranch in contributing to a better future for America. The book project had been stalled at dead center seven years for a sequence of reasons, some pertinent here.

The braiding of the Farley and Howe lifelines had begun in the fall of 1946 when the latter young editor, chosen upon his return from Pacific aircraft carrier duty to launch a new four-color rotogravure magazine *Empire* for the then strongly resurgent *Denver Post*, had first heard about a fellow named Cal Farley at Amarillo, Texas.

This Farley fellow, as the word had arrived in Denver, was a champion athlete who had built a highly successful retail business by staying on the radio and in the newspapers with no end of wrestling and baseball chatter. Then he had launched, without support from any public agency and without a fund-raising effort of any kind, his wild idea of salvaging homeless and delinquent boys by putting them on a ranch at Tascosa, a ghost town forty miles from nowhere across a quicksand ford in the Canadian River, and hoping they'd straighten out. So far, the cockamamie scheme was still afloat.

The young editor had already assigned himself to put a torch to the drowsy Denver Chamber of Commerce by writing and publishing two *Empire* stories about how the master community builder Stanley Draper had built Oklahoma City. From there he was booked to report Wernher von Braun's first liftoff of a captured German V-2 rocket at White Sands proving ground. This Tascosa ranch ought to make a good colorful feature. Amarillo was more or less on the way from Oklahoma to El Paso, so why not drop off and see this Farley on the way?

He did, and the young editor's story about Boys Ranch at Old Tascosa became the first story ever reprinted from the *Denver Post* by the *Reader's Digest*, which then as now claimed the world's largest circulation by any magazine, and was followed in the next five years by a dozen more *Digest* stories or other topics from his fledgling *Empire* magazine.

This young editor's first visit to Tascosa was soon followed by another, and another, until the interchange of Howe and Farley ideas became continuous. Often he arranged his own field trips to intersect Cal Farley's, trying to satisfy Perfectionist Cal's insatiable appetite for advice on, say,

A favorite family photograph of Cal and Mimi . . . reflecting the several peaceful years spent in residence at Tascosa after the ranch was built.

his speechmaking technique, in return for Cal's uncanny critique of which stories had rung true and which not so true in the pages of *Empire*.

The idea of a book recounting Cal Farley's flavorful background and analyzing the unique Boys Ranch philosophy had crystallized by 1949 in the minds of both men. Newspaper and magazine stories by the scores, radio and civic group appearances by the scores and hundreds, Cal Farley had discerned, were not enough to assure the deeply committed, day-in, day-out support Cal now required as the sole breadwinner self-assigned to satisfy the ravenous appetites of 140 boys, 42 saddle horses, 120 beef cattle, and assorted pigs, chickens, and pet dogs then already constituting the resident population of Old Tascosa. Only a book that was detailed enough to nourish and satisfy the minds of those thoughtful patrons already on his team, and attract others, could assure that kind of support. "I need that book," he said, and a contract was signed.

For the young editor the timing was nearly impossible. He was approaching a climactic stage of launching his *Empire* in new format and in its own new rotogravure printing presses in Denver. Concurrently, he was in charge of preparing three elaborate special publications incident to the opening of the *Post's* new publishing plant, including a four-color history of the *Post* itself, and a collection of regional tales from his *Empire* magazine to be published at New York by Doubleday in 1950.

For the next two years he faced, at best, a killer schedule. Later he was to wonder endlessly what mystic power within the Farley message caused him to try to fit Farley's book nonetheless into that schedule. During the

A LONG VISIT WITH AN OLD FRIEND

ensuing months he managed somehow to visit the ranch several times and to record and transcribe more than eighty hours of interviews with Cal and other prime sources of Boys Ranch information. By the fall of 1950 he had prepared and reviewed with Cal in final draft some four hundred pages of manuscript. But troubles loomed.

Cal's designated biographer had maintained his active duty status in the U.S. Naval Reserve. Before the first five issues of his new-format *Empire* magazine had rolled off the *Post's* new four-color presses in the fall of 1950, he stood already under summons to report for Korean War duty in the Office of Naval Intelligence at the Pentagon. Chances were good that a strong plea by the *Post* might gain his release from this involuntary recall by the navy, but in a rending decision he chose not to protest those orders.

The Farley Boys Ranch book was a major factor in that decision to "scour clean" from the *Post*. Working from a base at the Pentagon, the young editor felt sure he could more handily finish the book and negotiate a desirable publishing contract.

He was in error.

Carrying his manuscript from publisher to agent to publisher, he soon learned that both his thesis — the Boys Ranch formula — and his central character, Cal Farley, were merchandise frightfully déclassé in the intellectual climate of that time. It was, perhaps, a regional diary destined to rest in a few hundred rural bookcases. A subsidized chronicle from the vanity press massaging the Farley ego and that of his major contributors, perhaps. "This Farley fellow, now, does have a certain color to him; his bucolic slapstick is a caution. But — a *serious* book about a small-town automobile tire salesman — a *Rotarian*, no less? Surely, my cow-country friend, you jest."

Typically, a faint crinkle of amusement would begin to intrude upon the studied tolerance of the publisher's face.

The harvest of well-manicured scorn garnered from this tour of New York publishing houses solidified further the young editor's resolve to earn his living in some fashion other than writing upon his release from navy duty.

First, in a gesture hardly common among writers, he responded to Cal's immediate need by volunteering the recordings of those eighty hours of his Farley interviews as an aid to a contract writer who could and did produce, in 1959, the regional book needed for distribution to past and potential Boys Ranch donors. Second, he carefully stowed in his files those four hundred pages of manuscript, the interview transcripts and other materials, and hunkered down to try to survive the winter of the western American's discontent.

It was a long, long winter.

Retreating to the corporations and ultimately to the East Coast, he kept in reasonably close touch with Boys Ranch through those years, sending contributions as he could. Gaining success but little satisfaction and much travel weariness from his battles with the corporate bureaucracies in New York, he switched course once again when, in 1964, he seized an opportunity to become an English professor in what was rapidly becoming "the world's largest community college" at Miami, Florida.

Now it was 1965, and the now not-so-young editor was a guest of Cal and Mimi Farley's for what would be the last time in their apartment at Tascosa. It was our longest and quietest visit ever — two uninterrupted days and evenings of earnest talk about boys, the ranch, and the West, to be sure, but mainly about the growing troubles of our country — and only the passage of time would remind me a hundred times how prophetic that conversation would be.

I recall having arrived with two concerns of long standing, on both of which Cal promptly set my mind at ease. One of these involved a conversation many years before — in 1947 or early 1948 — when Cal had come to Denver, bought me a lunch, and asked me, as one of a dozen close friends to whom he had posed the same question, whether he should accept a nomination and almost sure election to Congress from the Panhandle District. "No," I had said flatly, surprised by my own antipathy toward that idea, and had worried ever after if my repugnance had helped to crystallize a decision he might later have regretted. "Not at all," he now at last reassured me. "Politics is the reflection of what goes on in our homes and schools, and *that* is what I'm worried about."

This was a brooding Cal Farley I had not seen before. Only when we strolled around the ranch did he slide back into his old self, showing me with special pride the two newest dormitories. Faced with the distinctive pink sandstone from Lyons, Colorado, which long since had become the prevailing decor of the ranch, each would accommodate twenty-four boys and two families of dorm parents occupying apartments at opposite ends. These dorms, Cal explained, would allow the ranch for the first time since its earliest days to approximate a true family atmosphere for its charges.

He spoke with satisfaction of scholastic achievements of the high school class lately graduated and of the broadened understanding of the core

The Farley clan in the early 1960s: Cal, Mimi, Genie and her husband Sherman G. Harriman, and their two children Michelle (Shelley) and Cal II.

philosophy of the ranch that he had finally got through to most of the leadership of Texas. He mentioned new buildings and programs that would be installed in due time but without his past urgency. Like a man surveying his masterpiece essentially finished, he was now preoccupied, not so much with his Boys Ranch, but with his country. And he was filled with foreboding over the course his nation was taking.

Mimi Farley was, I recall on this visit, being her happiest self ever, busy as a commodity pit trader, with letters and phone calls to and from her departed boys and their wives and even a grandchild or two, inspecting scratched fingers, and bestowing all manner of motherly affection on the worshipful troupe that followed her every step when she left the apartment to walk to the dining hall, or to the site of the new elementary school that would bear her name.

We talked at some length, of course, about the book—*this* book—and

TWO THOUSAND SONS

I had to make rueful confession of the obvious, that I was still not in a position to take on any major writing project. Having to live as an assistant professor on less than one-third of my New York earnings, and having to contrive as well while teaching a full schedule to take the graduate courses necessary to legitimize my position, I would need awhile to begin to put the book back on track. Cal was sympathetic, even casual about it.

"When the time comes around right for your book, you'll know it," he said. "Meanwhile, believe me, we need all the people like you we can get in our college and university classrooms." Then, as an afterthought: "When you do get the book out, don't forget to give the sports editors a shot at it."

Mostly, it seemed, Cal wanted to pick my brains. He quizzed me briskly to get my fresh-from-the-East-Coast viewpoint on just about the whole spectrum of national affairs.

What about the creeping paralysis of our national will in foreign affairs — the top-level dementia that had tried to establish in Korea the absurd principle of war without victory and was even now, in 1965, beginning to send Americans into another shooting war in the Southeast Asian jungles? I could only speculate, as the former official correspondent of the *Denver Post* aboard the press ship *Appalachian* at the Bikini atom-bomb test sites, that this paralysis was a syndrome of our guilt complex over possession of the A-bomb.

What's going on in Hollywood, anyway?

Having enjoyed a wide and happy acquaintanceship in the film capital, Cal was deeply perturbed about certain trends of the 1960s in the entertainment industry that he saw as threatening the welfare of our youth. A series of immensely popular films like *The Graduate* climaxed a surge of films teaching millions of youngsters' contempt for parental authority, irritating Cal's businessman's sensitivities in the process by deriding every visible practice of American capitalism. The even more popular *Easy Rider* and its retinue of films were powerful, persuasive primers in experimentation with hallucinogenic drugs and sexual promiscuity. So also were the Beatles' recordings, not to mention those of other, more nauseating gorgons arising to populate the rock-music subculture and batter our youth with gut-busting stereo sounds that in time shattered earbones and damaged learning capacity.

"Why are we doing these things to our own kids?" Cal asked quietly.

With that, we were off again on the theme that had been the most recurrent in our many philosophizing sessions over the years. "We've been so busy putting this country together," Cal had said so often, speaking

Cal typically kept his grandchildren in high good humor.

always as an ordinary businessman, "that we've let our schools and our big media get away from us. Now we're in real trouble."

As far as the colleges were concerned, I told Cal, the American tradition as we knew it was in a worse way than even he had imagined. Having just completed my first year of teaching in a college classroom, I was still in shock, still trying to make myself believe the ferocity with which the American higher education establishment had assaulted every element of the American tradition in the years following World War II. Under the rule of the relativists, it seemed, every standard practice, every code of behavior, every "traditional" value stood subject to individual judgment, if not mockery. Even the rules of grammar and language basic to instruction in my English classes apparently were no longer in force. *Webster's Third New International Dictionary*, the only new unabridged dictionary to appear in a generation, had refrained from labeling as nonstandard any collo-quialism, dialect, slang, or other idiomatic usage, no matter how esoteric, on the theory that "If it's in use, it's a word, and who are we to judge whether its meaning is generally accepted or not?" My own and many other colleges had launched major new programs to instruct whites as well as blacks, for credit, in the jargon of the black ghetto. Though labeled by

Hayakawa and others of our most learned linguists as an obviously colossal economic and social folly, bilingualism as an official policy already was drawing swarms of advocates.

History was a forgotten subject: In my own classrooms I was already greeting freshman students who were not sure at all just whom their own fathers had been fighting with or against in World War II. On campus in the social sciences, as in our politics, the Era of the Underdog Overdog was in full swing, in which every legal and social amenity was to be extended to every splinter minority while the native American, lest he commit the mortal sin of prejudice, had been clamorously conditioned by our school systems not to assume any clear identity. "Remember those ethnic jokes, Cal, that use to be responsible for maybe half the laughs on the air during your radio days? Well now your typical American kid is forbidden even to tell one lest he stir in another person an indignation he himself is never entitled to indulge in. Baffled and yapped at for what he is from all sides, this young person arrives in my classroom not knowing *who* or *what* he is."

And religion? A dirty word. Madalyn O'Hair and the United States Supreme Court had already served upon God formal notice of his eviction from the educational process.

"I sure could've done just as well without *that* report," Cal muttered.

Shortly after breakfast on the following bright, cool morning, Cal and I swung back into our favorite conversational romping ground of all, the mass media. From his days of youthful vagabondage my friend Cal had developed an uncannily sure intuitive perception of the media game— print, film, radio—and during his earlier merchandising days had served with humor and competence as a sometime roving correspondent for Gene Howe's *Amarillo Globe-News*. Our own head-to-head note swappings on these subjects over the years had been numberless, and by 1965 I had adopted as my academic specialty intensive studies of the media tidal wave that then was engulfing American society. Had he lived through the 1970s, I am sure that he would have ranked as one of our most penetrating and sophisticated analysts of an inundation still uncomprehended by all too many who claim expertise in this realm.

This time I had brought him especially good chomping fodder from two important new books I had discovered in my first year of teaching. One of these was Daniel Boorstin's *The Image: A Flood of Pseudo-Events*, an insight into the mass manufacture of "soft" news stories to amuse the reader or viewer and to serve various commercial and other purposes. Boorstin characterized the media age as calling for the mass fabrication also of personalities — that is, "celebrities," — most of which "human pseudo-events" have few qualifications for fame except that they suit the immediate purposes of the media. My students, I told Cal, entered college more sophisticated in such media realities than their parents probably ever would become, and they devoured revelations like Boorstin's so eagerly that I already was cranking media studies into my regular syllabus.

The other book I was itching to talk about was a thing published in 1964 called *Understanding Media*, which was then making famous an obscure English professor from Toronto. ("Not another English professor, please," Cal protested. "Lord knows you're obscure enough.") His name, I said, is Marshall McLuhan, and he has blocked out the theory that the media revolution, particularly with the arrival of the electronic media, would bring more radical change, more social and political disruption, more quickly, than did the Industrial Revolution, the Scientific Revolution, or any of the other revolutions all the way back to Gutenberg and maybe beyond.

"Big statement," Cal commented, then added, "but the way things are shaping up, maybe he's right. Remember way back there when once in awhile you would swing the weight of the *Denver Post* around, I told you once you were using more power than you knew what to do with?" I remembered. "Offhand, I'd hate right now to be a Mr. Big, even a president, who'd need to steer my ship upwind against any big blow the media might set on."

He talked on, hoping but doubting that American parents, teachers, politicians, and business minds would think to shelter American kids just a bit from the onslaught of the all-pervasive media. He worried particularly about television and its hypnotic effect, its capability of keeping them in trancelike suspended motion for hours, simply detached from the real world. He stared into a darkening future — seer that he was — and saw with a clarity I could only recall and reconfirm again and again over ensuing years, that our America just then was a river raft already swept into Cataract Gorge, with many miles of white water yet to negotiate and, hopefully, a divine boatman to get her through.

Our English Department in Miami, I was reminded by Cal's talk about TV, that year had adopted George Orwell's *1984* for required reading campuswide, and no teacher had been more diligent than I in explicating what some reasonably sane critics were still calling "the most important single book of the twentieth century." That, in turn, reminded me that I had brought along for Cal's edification a most intriguing "revision" of the Big Brother threat published in 1964 by another writer who would rapidly become a favorite of mine, Malcolm Muggeridge. I fished out the excerpt and read it, as follows:

Orwell's Big Brother was a somber, frightening figure. How instead were he urbane, kindly, enlightened? Orwell envisaged the telly as an instrument of terror and oppression. How if it were the Proles' great joy and solace, making manifest for their delight all their hopes and desires . . . whole multitudes gazing with narcissistic enthrallment at their own image?

Orwell . . . failed to envisage the collectivity becoming its own tyrant . . . fabricating its own lies, falsifying its own history, partaking of its own mysteries, with the priestly advertiser presiding—eat this! wear this! desire this! Ah, the paradise that awaits us in 1984! Orwell imagined a Victorian melodrama, but it's a musical. . . . We're liberated, mate: sex-happy, affluent, educated (any amount of education, more and more); we're healthy, wealthy and wise. We can fornicate without fear, eat without obesity, live without tears. For every ill a pill. Tranquilizers to overcome angst, pep pills to wake us up, life pills to ensure blissful sterility. I will lift up mine eyes unto the pills from whence cometh my help. It's Technicolor, it's VistaVision; a spectacular . . . "

I was just winding down that peroration, as I recall, when Mimi bounded in with sandwiches and some sarcasm to the effect that we two masterminds had better break off our gab marathon and eat a bite or I would ride hungry with the ranch staffer in whose car I was due shortly to hitchhike to the Amarillo airport to return to the Atlantic seaboard combat zone.

In another very few minutes they walked me to the door of the apartment and I well remember studying them a moment as I said goodbye—Mimi's joy of living showing lively in every line, Cal as trim and straight and jauntily dressed, with as much of the look of the eagle as he had had twenty years before.

"With that shine you've got on those shoes, I need sunglasses," I told him.

"Go back there and mow 'em down," he said.

It didn't cross my mind that I might never see either Cal or Mimi again.

Came another January and another and Mimi was felled by a heart attack. She rallied gamely and cheerfully but, being still quite weak, was taken to a hospital in Houston for specialized attention. She had returned in mid-February 1967, when Cal made an overnight trip to a banquet at Fort Stockton, Texas, at which the state's Optimists were honoring the "Ten Outstanding Young Men of Texas." One of the ten college students was Tommy Alvarez, a recent graduate of Boys Ranch, and Cal felt

A LONG VISIT WITH AN OLD FRIEND

obligated to be there as a stand-in so that Tommy, too, would have a "parent" to introduce when the other honorees asked their parents to stand up.

He returned to Amarillo on a Saturday so as to be on hand in the white ranch chapel the next morning when members of his prize winning Boys Ranch chapter of the Future Farmers of America were scheduled to conduct the worship service. Louie Hendricks, veteran Boys Ranch publicist and spokesman, recounted the sorrowful events of that morning as follows:

Cal stood on the steps of the chapel building, as many boys of all ages passed before him, all smiling or waving a greeting as they walked inside with their dorm parents. Some wanted to chat, and two brothers, Carl and Allen Crouch, stopped to tell him their grandfather was in the hospital and ask if he would go see him. To keep up with all the things he had to do, Cal kept a note pad handy and wrote reminders to himself. Checking on the boys' grandfather went on the list of "things to do."

Only a few minutes remained before the services would commence. Cal walked inside the building and seated himself in one of the pews near the back. Sitting on the row directly in front of him, Gary Pearce would become the last boy ever to hear his voice. Cal leaned forward and asked, "How ya' doin', Gary?" The soft tones of the organ prelude drifted over the assembled boys and staff. Sixteen-year-old Paul Puschnig was giving the invocations. Cal closed his eyes.

Seated beside him was Lavon Adams, high school teacher and football coach. "Mr. Farley has gone to sleep," he whispered to his wife. "No," she replied, "he is not asleep." In an instant, men were lifting Cal from the pew, and carrying him to the chaplain's office, where efforts were made to revive him. The services continued with the congregation singing "Glorious Is Thy Name." So suddenly did it happen, the boys were not aware that Cal's great heart had stopped its beating, yet they sensed something was wrong. He was carried to the Ranch ambulance, and at Amarillo's Northwest Texas Hospital death was attributed to a massive brain hemorrhage.

The boys first learned that the founder had died when the Ranch chaplain made the announcement before the noon meal in the dining hall. They walked back to their dorms in silence, their food untouched. That night they returned to the chapel for a memorial service, and as two of them were leaving the building, one scanned the stars in the sky and said, "I'll bet he's already getting another Boys Ranch started up there."

A life lived in incomparable personal style with clear and clean and unwavering focus on the welfare of his America had ended in the same style cleanly, suddenly, in the presence of three hundred of his two thousand

Death came to Cal Farley cleanly and suddenly on February 19, 1967 in the presence of three hundred of his two thousand sons during Sunday morning service in the white frame chapel. Ranch boys in solemn procession to services at Amarillo's largest school auditorium led a mourning in which the whole Southwest joined. Mimi died just one month later on March 19.

sons, in the house of the God he had acknowledged a hundred times as having been with him every step in the building of his Boys Ranch.

In Amarillo, Genie and Sherm Harriman went directly from the emergency room to Mimi's apartment. Genie's account: "Mimi was resting on her bed, heavily sedated because of her very bad heart. She knew something was wrong and asked, 'Is it Pawpaw?'

"Over there in the emergency room," I told her. "I swear I felt something like a hand on my shoulder and heard Dutch Mantell's voice saying 'Irish, vat took you so long?'

"It must have been the right thing to say. Mimi bounced back into her old self and took charge, telling us whom to call, who should be pallbearers, what suit Cal should wear. She got out Cal's Rotary district governor's pin for him to wear and his Boys Ranch service pin for us to give to our son, Cal.

"Most of our ranch family, and even her doctor, feared that in her condition Cal's death would simply overwhelm her, but all of us underestimated her great strength. She bore up well both during and after

A LONG VISIT WITH AN OLD FRIEND

the funeral, still calling her own shots, and when the ranch board the next day named her president of Boys Ranch she was deeply gratified and proud to exercise that prerogative in the days that followed."

In the *Amarillo Globe News* later that week its editor, Wes Izzard, long one of the tallest figures in Texas journalism and an intimate Farley friend for decades, delineated the Cal Farley legend in this tribute:

Three things there were that made Cal Farley great. He had a God-given insight into what makes boys tick. He had a powerful sense of dedication that drove him to do something about those boys in whom the ticking was off-beat. And he had an instinctive grasp of the mechanics needed to do this job on a big scale — organization, salesmanship.

The world is full of men endowed with one of these gifts. There are a few who possess two of them. But rare indeed is the man who has all three.

Cal Farley was a persuasive man. It was hard to say no to him. He had a talent for making others see the boy problem as he saw it. . . . It was just that his earnest common sense and concern were eloquent and unanswerable.

Those of us who knew Cal through the years found him a warm and witty friend, as well as a dedicated hero of the wayward boy. He could have been a great sports writer or radio personality. He attended the World Series several times and sent back to this newspaper stories that rivaled the baseball tales of Ring Lardner. And some of the most colorful sports broadcasting ever heard over an Amarillo station was wrapped in the excited, knowledgeable voice of Cal Farley.

"It is a time of shock for his friends. But the mourning need not be for long. While his quiet counsel will be missed — perhaps desperately, for a while — his job was all but finished. He had carried the building of Boys Ranch to a point from which it can go on indefinitely.

The region and the nation should be grateful that he was spared for this. He had achieved an immortality few men attain.

Operational reins of the ranch were handed to Virgil Patterson as executive vice-president. There was no hesitation: Cal, with typical foresight, had passed the word privately, not to Virgil Patterson, but to key board members Lawrence Hagy, Harold Dunn, and Jay Taylor: 'When I'm gone, let's give Virgil Patterson a shot at running the place."

Mimi declined quietly, always cheerfully, and on March 17, 1967, exactly one month after the passing of the man whose utterly devoted and amazingly effective helpmeet she had been, Mimi Farley closed her eyes, too, for the last time on this earth.

In Florida I had received word of Cal's death in a letter from Virgil

Patterson addressed to all regular supporters of the ranch. Shortly after Mimi's death I received from Genie and Sherman Harriman a letter remarkable both as an expression of wrenching bereavement and as a pledge of filial determination to carry on Cal's work. And that's what they did, settling without even a short respite into their separate and now much more demanding duties in the administration of the ranch. So also rallied the board members and the other key men on the ranch staff who in more than a decade of practice had developed into a fast-break team: Ranch Superintendent Wilson, School Superintendent Rattan, and Business Administrator Gene Hayman.

At its first meeting after Mimi Farley's funeral the board installed Virgil Patterson as president and adopted a declaration of fidelity to the vision of the Farleys that still hangs in an outsize frame on a wall in the visitors center at Tascosa.

Quivira 1985

An Indian of soaring imagination led the first white man into these plains in the year 1540. The victim was that stubborn Spanish gold-hunter Coronado, who followed a nimble-tongued native he called "The Turk" into the region later to be termed El Llano Estacado (The Staked Plain), hunting the fabled land of Quivira. This aboriginal ad-man filled his client's ears with wondrous word-images of "a river to the East that is two leagues wide, with fish as big as horses."

"Great lords," he told the Spaniards, "travel on this river in huge canoes, with sails and twenty rowers on each side. These lords sit on the poop under awnings; on the prow of each boat is a golden eagle. These lords take their siesta under trees on the branches of which are hung tiny golden bells that make music for them as they doze. The people of this country eat their meals from wrought plate, and drink from bowls of pure gold."

Several months under The Turk's guidance brought Coronado no profit and only one ultimate pleasure—that of permanently silencing his guide's golden tongue by stretching his neck with a rope. That done, he wrote disconsolately to his king in Madrid:

"I reached some plains so vast that I did not find their limit anywhere I went, although I traveled over them for more than 300 leagues. And I found such a quantity of cows [buffalo] that it is impossible to number them.... It was the Lord's pleasure that, after having journeyed across these deserts seventy-seven days, I arrived at the province called Quivira, to which the guides were conducting me, and where they had described to me houses of stone, with many stories; and not only are they not of stone, but of straw, and the people in them are as barbarous as all those I have seen and passed before this.... I have done all that I possibly could to serve Your Majesty and to discover a country where God Our Lord might be served, and the royal patrimony increased, as your loyal servant and vassal...."

15

Mission Improbable: A Homing, A Hegira

SPACE... capital S. Miles and miles, as they say on the Alaska Highway, of nothin' but miles and miles. Peter Hurd country. Charles Goodnight country.

Topping Raton Pass on this bright, calm March day, I felt a sudden hurtful hope for the lift in spirits which always before, on this pilgrimage so familiar so many years ago, had occurred upon first sight of the grandiloquent sweep of the mesas and plains of northern New Mexico. Today only a few puffs of cumulus speckled the limitless pastures with shadow, and off to the southwest one scrawny raincloud was managing a bit of a sprinkle—a pygmy compared with the magnificent two-mile-high black thunderheads which will cruise in stately procession across these skies come summer.

A suggestion of spring was discernible, the barest hint of green on the gentle slopes after a wet winter; 1985 should be a good year. At Raton I turned east, trying my best to enjoy sweeping my eyes fifty miles north and south of Highway 87 on a crystal afternoon, and not succeeding at all. Heading into John Steinbeck country, I suddenly realized that my trip thus far was less a homing than a hegira, a retreat in combat fatigue from Washington, D.C., where sophistries are stacked upon pious sophistries like flattened automobile chassis piled in a salvage yard, and institutionalized policies visibly bankrupt a generation ago are still defended with glassy-eyed stridency and desperation by their incarcerated partisans.

Heading back to Texas to fulfill a contract after thirty-five years, I

189

acknowledged for the first time, as the wheels turned, an apprehension, a deep doubt within me that the awesome thing which had drawn me here again and again as a young editor could possibly remain now as it then was. After all, the glistening promise of those unforgettably confident years just after World War II had never materialized in the careers of most of us swabs returning from Europe or the Pacific. And as to the national scene? Well, the wheels seemed to sing to the meter and caesuras of G. K. Chesterton's prayer of a century ago as the miles rolled by:

> O God of earth and altar, bow down and hear our cry,
> Our earthly rulers falter, our people drift and die,
> The walls of gold entomb us, the swords of scorn divide,
> Take not thy thunder from us, but take away our pride.
>
> From all that terror teaches, from lies of tongue and pen,
> From all the easy speeches that comfort cruel men,
> From sale and profanation of honor and the sword,
> From sleep and from damnation, deliver us, Good Lord.

My pickup whined through the TO Ranch, one of those several spreads of 200,000 acres each which constitute the cattle economy here. For perhaps the tenth time I admired the TO headquarters at a distance from the highway — an impressive array of well-painted buildings complete with private airstrip — and for the tenth time resolved to contrive to strike up an acquaintance with the no-doubt impressive owners of such a layout. Not a cow or a steer had I seen for miles: still on winter range somewhere, I supposed. Then at considerable distance I saw a herd grazing. A herd strange in color, unmistakably diminutive in size: by slowing down, I made out about seventy-five antelope.

Approaching the town of Clayton, a county seat and the only significant cluster of population within two hours' drive, my spirits began slowly to rise, for a reason obscure to anyone not a writer. In a book of mine once long ago I had written about Union County, an article with a lead that achieved a rhythm I was proud of. Now, even as a writer who had stalked unrepentant out of that calling three and a half decades ago, I could still recite and did recite aloud the words of that lead (writers do that, you know), savoring their cadence:

"Union County, New Mexico, is an expanse of buffalo-grass and endless, lonely arroyos once highly favored for their privacy by manufacturing bootleggers of the prohibition years. As large as all Connecticut, it grows chiefly the more drought-resistant species of cedar, piñon pine, beef steers and people. Wheat grew, too, until the dry years came and northeastern New Mexico literally blew away...."

I had then proceeded to tell, in that article, how the rancher-school teacher Raymond Huff, the "Cal Farley of Clayton," had earned his own immortality as "The Man Who Saved Union County" when Northeast New Mexico and adjoining sections of Oklahoma, Colorado, and Texas had become in the 1930s the center and focus of a grim new Gehenna called the dust bowl.

As big blow followed big blow through 1933, 1934, and 1935 until dust had drifted to the windowsills of farmhouses and cattle died or were shot by the herd by ranchers who could not watch them starve, County Superintendent of Schools Raymond Huff had set his jaw against the elements and decided that, desperate as they were, Union County's ranchers would not join those wind-routed thousands already streaming westward past Cal Farley's Amarillo filling station department store along Route 66 in the tragic exodus memorialized in John Steinbeck's *Grapes of Wrath*.

Returning from Denver with a small allocation of federal relief funds, Ray Huff was bound, furthermore, that no leaf-raking, mock-work program would insult the souls while feeding the bodies of these work-hardened rural people. Instead, they would build from Union County materials a new school plant to be proud of while emulating the Pilgrim fathers of Plymouth Rock in rotating parsimoniously, to each family in turn determined most desperate at the moment, the paying jobs that would put food on the table and keep a roof over their heads.

First they built a gymnasium that would seat 3,000, its walls of adobe dug at the edge of town, employing only four skilled workmen: a plumber, an electrician, a concrete finisher, and a superintendent who taught ranchers and townspeople their trades as they went along. Then Raymond Huff outlined his "dream school"—three remodeled grade buildings, a new high school, vocational and agricultural facilities, machine shops, athletic field, meeting rooms, even a blacksmith shop—all with a bond issue of only $60,000 to be retired in six years without any increase in the county's school taxes! In pure shock, the school board gave way to Ray Huff, a medium-sized man who looked like the honorable but harmless cashier of a country bank. Numbly also, it endorsed Huff's decision to avoid false economy at the outset, hiring the Southwest's best architect in his field to draw up master plans for a harmonious cluster of Spanish-style buildings with patios between, and a landscaped schoolyard enclosed by a heat-absorbing stone wall.

MISSION IMPROBABLE: A HOMING, A HEGIRA

A force of 300 to 600 men from all over the county was employed on the project under supervision of only a dozen or so skilled foremen. In time the aid was rotated among nearly six thousand men, boys, and girls in a county of barely 10,000 souls.

Using Union County's hard pine, high school students under tutelage of a Spanish-American woodcarver-virtuoso cut out, carved, and finished chairs, desks, tables, doors, and woodwork for thirty classrooms. A tanner was brought to town, and the ranchers donated the hides of their slain cattle to make heavy, practically indestructible interlaced seats and backs for the chairs. Another Spanish-American virtuoso taught students and parents to convert discarded farm implements, automobile fenders, and scrap iron of all sorts into heavy, ornate door hinges, curtain rods, locks, keys, and even the upholstery tacks that went into the furnishings. Still another taught Clayton's girls to wash, card, weave, and dye from native herbs the wool from Union County sheep they fashioned into heavy draperies that covered all classroom windows. From Montenegro came Miles Gjonovich, who found in Union County a deposit of pottery clay "equal to the best in Europe" and set up a pottery department in which nearly half the school enrolled, generating what is still a lively market to tourists along Highway 87.

Good times had returned in 1939. When the United States entered World War II, Union County sent no less than 600 skilled workmen to the war production plants, almost every one of whom would have been termed "unskilled" in 1936. Union County's taxpayers owned an educational plant valued at $756,000 (prewar). And rancher-schoolteacher Raymond Huff could say that not a single family to his knowledge had been compelled by destitution to leave Union County. "They stuck, they changed the face of our district, and they got back on their feet. We simply tried to do the best we could with what we had."

And in Amarillo, not far away, Cal Farley continued to study intently for his own purposes what Raymond Huff had done.

On this quiet Saturday evening I turned six blocks off the highway to drive slowly, twice, around the sprawling campus of the Union County School System, rendering an interior salute to the spirit of the new long-departed Raymond Huff still present, somehow, in those charming patios at this vesper hour.

Past Texline, the improbabilities of my latter-day mission to Tascosa floated a bit more comfortably in the highly improbable ozone of the Panhandle. Passing a roadside historical marker memorializing the intersection of Highway 87 with the Goodnight–Loving trail, I lost touch with the twentieth century for ten whole minutes as I retrieved from memory the unbelievable exploit of Charles Goodnight and his beloved elder partner, Oliver Loving, in trailing for the first time in 1866 several thousand head of cattle 1,000 miles from South Texas through bloodthirsty Comanche country, along the Pecos where not another native living animal but rattlesnakes could survive, on one infamous crossing keeping both men and cattle awake and moving for three days and nights across 80 waterless miles—all the way to the tall green grass of Wyoming, thus opening to the beef business an insatiable northern market and giving first real substance to America's most durable frontier legend.

Soon this Panhandle had become the land of the improbably huge cattle spreads, mostly—except for Charles Goodnight's 1 million acres—financed and managed by tycoons from faraway bases like Boston or London or Aberdeen. Their brands were famous worldwide: the LX, LS, the Frying Pan, and the LIT later purchased by Lee Bivins, who used as his ranch headquarters the stone courthouse at Tascosa where, still later, in 1939, Cal Farley housed the first six residents of his new Boys Ranch. Here also was that biggest and most improbable ranch of all, the XIT, which came into being because, far away in Austin, the Texas state capitol buildings had been destroyed in a fire. The state's shrewd tribunes, smiling slyly behind their hands, slickered a group of Chicago entrepreneurs into constructing a new state capitol in exchange for 3 million acres of Panhandle land listed in the last previous census report as "absolute desert, unfit for human habitation." With a massive transfusion of British money the XIT fathered dozens of hip-slapping Texas tales centering around Messrs. Babcock and Campbell, the first a planner who brought big-business practice to the cattle business (and earned immortality for his fastidious refusal to eat his meals over a campfire fueled by buffalo chips, which became known thereafter as "Babcock coal"), the second the XIT's first manager, Barbecue Campbell, who ordered fence staples, door hinges, even cigarette papers in carload lots. (As regards the fence staples, at least, such purchases were not overenthusiastic: the XIT's western fence line ran arrow straight, it was said, without a jog or a bend for 150 miles!)

Even here in this implausible land chances seemed slim indeed for the success of my present search. I was, after all, exactly in the role of an anthropologist following a fragmentary trail and hoping against hope to unearth a lost civilization, a native American culture extant and at a pinnacle of global prestige only forty years ago, now altered and so far erased that it stands today in the daily comprehension of students in my college

194 classrooms as curiously remote as the Gladstone-Disraeli-Kipling days of Victorian England.

A foreboding of violent change, of a rising tidal wave threatening the fundamental welfare of American youth, I remembered too well, had preoccupied a brooding Cal Farley through the two days of my final visit with him nearly 20 years before. Now it was 1985, the year after *1984*, when by George Orwell's bleak prophecy not only all the joys of a free society, but all memory that those joys had ever existed, might well have been battered from the modern mind by massive information machines driven by tyrants. A tidal wave indeed has inundated America during those intervening years, altering and eroding our basic social and political institutions. My present errand was to determine whether, if at all, Cal Farley's remote village had coped with that change, had ridden out that wave.

Through the decade before that visit and the two decades after, I had never been out of touch with the ranch at Tascosa, either as a regular contributor as my means permitted, as a diligent reader of the Boys Ranch newsletter, as a correspondent, and as a passing motorist-visitor now and then. But this would be my first opportunity in more than thirty years to spend several days with the boys and their dorm parents, visit the chapel and schools, and talk at some length with those responsible for management of the village Cal Farley had created.

My doubts and apprehensions had tumbled back upon me in full force as I reached the ranch gate at Tascosa on this Saturday evening in March, 1985 — then on impulse drove past it a few hundred yards to check, in the twilight, whether any water was visible in the red quicksand bed of the notorious Canadian River. Could it be possible that this small, self-sufficient, remote community, supported and carefully managed for a single purpose, might somehow have escaped inundation by the media tidal wave and other storms of violent change which, over the past thirty-five years, had wrought the cultural devastation I myself had observed from coast to coast?

Were that lost civilization of traditional America still alive here in recognizable form, I was certain already that Cal Farley's Boys Ranch would supplant the XIT in *my* mind, at least, as the most improbable ranch in the Panhandle.

Water *was* flowing in the Canadian, a rivulet, at the middle of a ten-yard-wide band of raspberry-red wet sand. More than enough damp sand, I warned myself, to have made crossing at this quicksand ford doubtful even had I driven my burly four-wheel-drive of today on the unpaved forty-mile "short" trail through mesquite from Amarillo to Tascosa during those years before this sinfully convenient highway bridge was built in 1954.

There was no traffic, and I listened a long minute to the quiet, hearing nothing but the distant yapping of coyotes far, far off in the echoing hills south of the river. Rather suddenly a curtain parted, and my battered urban soul could begin to soak up the richest of all nourishment these flinty uplands provide.

Silence.

Pure silence. Eloquent silence.

Solitude.

Something there is about the human spirit that demands for its survival a handhold on infinity. Only in solitude can we get our heads screwed on straight and begin to communicate with the cosmos. Solitude — space, silence — was formerly the ambience of the frontier: loneliness often to the point of desperation. More recent generations have sought it earnestly — on the salt water, the shorelines, the peaks, the fishing streams, the lakes, in the timber. But now noise is the one ubiquitous constant in our lives. (Twenty years ago — the contrast forced itself upon my memory — the fat yellow subtropical moon moved still with some quiet nightly majesty through the palm fronds and telephone wires of my south Florida backyard to the hum of an occasional passing automobile. Now the roar of the traffic river barely slackens at 3:00 A.M., and a dozen firewagon or police sirens shriek through my bedroom every night.)

So thoroughly programmed are we to the clangor of our industrial existence that it seems we must overlay the inescapable with the discretional noise. We seek, it seems, no longer to escape, but to prolong, distraction — to avoid quiet thought. We fight traffic all week in the hope of getting away to the beach — and then carry along blaring stereo receivers. We drive hundreds of miles and spend hundreds of dollars for camping equipment to fish in a solitary lake at timberline — then can't eat the fish without watching the evening news on our portable TV set. We jog around the park to get back to nature — wearing headphones that keep our skulls ringing with rock music. The first person ever to seek ardently the tranquillity of a Japanese garden carrying a transistor radio, I have long suspected, was a modern, wired-for-sound American with noise-glazed eyes.

Already, it occurred to me, my mission improbable had turned up one reassuring answer: certainly no resident of Tascosa could have much of a problem finding all the solitude necessary to the soul bent on learning to live with itself.

Floodlights now suddenly illuminated the tall stone pylon on the hill behind me marking the entrance to Cal Farley's Boys Ranch—an impressive spire visible for miles across the valley.

I parked at the base of the pylon and studied the text of two large bronze plaques, one summarizing the colorful history of Tascosa as a wild-west cowtown, the other the origins and growth of the Cal Farley ranch. The pylon itself, it was noted, had been erected in 1964 by the Phillips Petroleum Company in memory of Thomas C. Craig, one of two officers of that company (the other: L. E. Fitzjarrald) who had served on the board of directors of the Farley ranch.

A Saturday cops-and-robbers epic flickered on the tube as I knocked at the door of the ranch superintendent's quarters—the same well-appointed two-bedroom home where I had stayed during my unforgettable two-day final visit with Cal and Mimi Farley in 1965. The ranch boss who admitted me, Monty Waldrip, was a big man in frame and voice, as had been most of his predecessors I remembered warmly as my hosts here in former years. Our exchange of greetings was appropriately brief: I asked the superintendent to save me two hours of visiting time during the forthcoming eight days of my stay; his genial wife, Frances, admonished me firmly not to neglect to interview Melba Brown in her tiny pink house behind the chapel, the cheerful, motherly Melba now preparing to retire after her fiftieth year of teaching Tascosa's first-grade students; then I betook myself to guest quarters as comfortable as any triple-A motel.

In the dining hall for Sunday morning breakfast—the only meal of the week served cafeteria style—I was again in familiar, though notably better appointed, surroundings. Kitchen equipment of polished metal showed no signs of second-hand origin. On the serving tables one chose first a plate containing eggs—one, two, three—every one of which was produced, I was told, in the ranch henhouse; picked bacon strips from a huge pile produced on the ranch hog farm; biscuits or toast from the ranch bakery; milk in half-pint cartons ("How many would you like, sir?") from the large Boys Ranch Holstein herd.

Choosing at random an unoccupied seat at one of the circular tables in the bustling dining room, I was again overwhelmed as of old at the instant friendliness, the eagerness to communicate, and the simply flawless courtesy extended to any visitor by the boy residents of this ranch even at this most informal mealtime of the week. Noting two or three white shirts and neckties at my table, worn by boys who for choir or other

After the Farleys' deaths, plans for a new non-sectarian chapel in their memory took top priority. Principals at the ground breaking on February 16, 1972 were Genie Farley Harriman and veteran ranch directors Lawrence Hagy (at left) and J. Harold Dunn.

reasons needed to be early at the chapel, I was reminded that my open-necked sport shirt, even with jacket, would not be at all proper at the 11:00 A.M. service. My breakfast dispatched, I took a leisurely stroll back to the apartment, gospel hymns echoing crisply in the clear Texas air from the chapel carillon, to don a fresh shirt and tie.

The chapel, centerpiece of the ranch, is an imposing structure of pink-and-buff Colorado sandstone topped by a towering white steeple above a portico supported by four tall columns. It stands atop three tiers of steps on the hill alongside the courthouse, and its expansive foyer of handrubbed wood paneling opens into a sanctuary seating perhaps 600, facing a choir stall large enough to accommodate the 60 voices soon to lead the morning service. To the west a smaller portico gives access to a capacious Christian education building, a more lately built companion structure also of Colorado sandstone, from which a stream of Boys Ranchers, everyone in jacket and tie and well-shined shoes, was emptying into the chapel as I arrived for the morning service.

I sought a seat in the rows occupied by boys of the Anderson home, with a pair of whom I had chanced to have breakfast and who had insisted I be their guest. After a call to worship by the choir, a responsive reading

MISSION IMPROBABLE: A HOMING, A HEGIRA

led by Matthew Rice, one of the ranch boys, a brief prayer and doxology, came the offering—before, rather than after, the sermon as I had considered customary. A well-scrubbed rancher chosen by rotation, Mike Hysmith, spoke in his own words a brief formal welcome.

As the pipe organ's full diapason bulged the walls of the sanctuary in "My Hope Is in the Lord," the first of several hymns, I was suddenly beamed in a time warp back over the decades to the Sunday worship rituals unvarying throughout my childhood. That aura of an all-but-forgotten past only deepened as the young chaplain, the Reverend Ralph Nite, after recounting a sardonic anecdote or two from his life in the United States Armed Forces, settled into an earnest, verse-by-verse explication of Psalms 127 and 128, drawing from these texts a persuasive formula for lasting and productive happiness at work and in the God-fearing home: "Unless the Lord build the house, they labor in vain who build it...."

Americans, he said, seem not to understand the proper place of work in our lives. Deriding on the one hand those who won't work and make welfare a career, he was equally critical on the other hand of those "workaholics" so totally committed to their tasks that they lose their families and other true pleasures: "It is in vain that you rise up early, to go late to rest, eating the bread of anxious toil; for he gives to his beloved in sleep...."

Though pleasure-mad and inclined to flock like a herd of goats toward "self-actualization," Americans don't understand pleasure too well, either, he admonished his young charges, stressing that many of the deepest satisfactions derive from work well and happily done.

The sermon was not short. As this muscular six-footer proceeded phrase by phrase to translate for his audience of formerly homeless boys the psalmist's prescription for a normal, truly happy home, referring to the miracle of birth as exemplified in his own firstborn infant daughter, I began to study that audience as he touched visibly responsive chords of pure male challenge in the passage:

"Like arrows in the hands of a warrior are the sons of one's youth. Happy is the man who has his quiver full of them! He shall not be put to shame when he speaks with his enemies in the gate."

Traces of animal restlessness were discernible, to be sure, when the minister dipped without simplification into a complicated theological analogue. But only traces. Soon it came through to me that the young man in the pulpit spoke in the matter-of-fact assumption that the Scriptures, if earnestly and forthrightly discussed in educated-adult terminology, will reconcile themselves and challenge and penetrate minds like these, almost all of them having arrived here at an educational level months if not years behind their chronological age. ("My job is to teach the Word of God straight and whole," he said to me later, "not to run it through a strainer.")

And, mostly, the message was getting through. Though under some obvious constraint in their Sunday jackets and ties, these healthy young males maintained a posture of attentiveness quite convincing even to the skeptical eye of a visiting college English teacher. Was this the rigid "attention" of a military school? In part, perhaps, but only in part.

After the service I learned how remarkably this Christian education program has been expanded and strengthened during the previous decade, now numbering as active participants most of the 150 adult teachers, administrative staff members, and their families living in the ranch community.

The Sunday vesper service is a songfest. The music ministry now features three choirs. The well-trained regular chapel choir some years ago recorded a Christmas cantata with the Amarillo Symphony Orchestra of a quality deemed worthy of national distribution to friends of the ranch. More recently it has been supplemented by a children's choir and an adult ranch choir that fulfills numerous engagements around the region, especially during the Christmas season.

Fond of quoting the maxim of semanticist S. I. Hayakawa—"English is used for two purposes: one is to communicate, the other is to impress others with how much you know"—the Reverend Ralph Nite declares flatly, "If the audience is bored, it's the speaker's fault." He works hard to draw illustrations with strong boy appeal from his experience in the military, as a licensed small-plane pilot, as a scuba diver and skier. The saddest element of his ministry is the unjust burden of guilt carried like a yoke by most of the boy residents at the ranch, of whom he counsels privately perhaps a dozen or more each week. "Almost all of our boys come from broken homes," he says, "and a majority of them tend to put blame on themselves, sometimes to their own severe detriment, for their parents' separation."

Most remarkable, not only in providing ranchers a firm basis of belief in a nihilistic age, but also in helping to restore these castoffs to normal social confidence is the Bible Memory Association (BMA) program in which the rancher commits to memory and recites to a monitor 8 to 15 prescribed Bible verses each week to a total of 150 verses in a year. Though an entirely voluntary activity, BMA offers inducements that seem to be persuasive indeed; in 1985, 250 ranchers of 350 enrolled were rewarded,

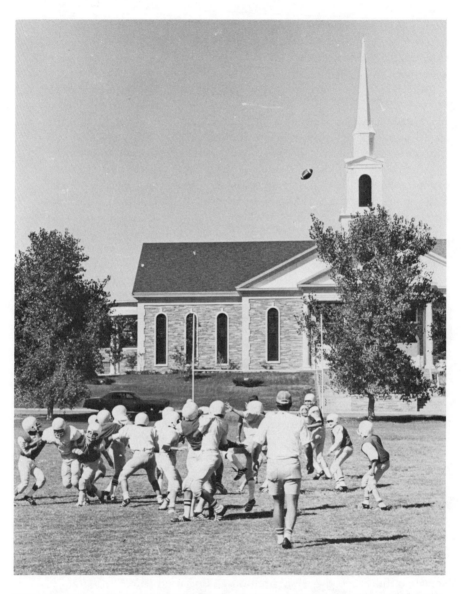

Architectural and instructional centerpiece of Boys Ranch, the magnificently equipped chapel dedicated in 1972. A Christian education annex was added shortly after its completion.

Ranchers and staff members both participate in the elaborate cantatas presented both at Tascosa and in Amarillo each year, the climax of a well-rounded music program at the ranch.

in groups of 50, with a week in the fellowship of boys and girls from all over the United States at a large summer camp operated by the Bible Memory Association at Ringgold, Louisiana. An additional thirty top performers in a three-year BMA program went to a camp at Atlanta — with a coveted side trip to Opryland at Nashville!

Outside in the sunshine I accepted the offer of a ranch alumnus — now a traveling sign painter, portraitist, and ceramic artist stopping off to enjoy a standing invitation to all former ranchers to visit the ranch for a few days or longer — to lead me across the highway along the trail to the Magenta Farm and the Cheyenne Ranch. (Magenta Farm? The name, I learned, uses the most precisely accurate designation of the color of the Canadian River sand.) This farm and ranch, comprising 3,100 acres, had been the last acquisition before Cal Farley's death. At the ranch, quarter horses and registered Hereford cattle are bred for show purposes and a herd of beef steers is pastured.

Under tall cottonwoods a rancher and his parents, out visiting him from town, were munching sandwiches and tossing plugs into one of the two

MISSION IMPROBABLE: A HOMING, A HEGIRA

202

large fishing lakes in a scene straight from a Fred Gipson vignette. I drove on down the river road, stopped and, still in my churchgoing shoes, walked through the mesquite to where the sand was damp. There I sat down on a cottonwood log, whittled long on a twig, and reflected upon the morning.

Dimly, from another era utterly remote, I could recall having been required to master the Shorter Catechism as a lad in a strict Presbyterian home—before American youth began to be deprived of *any* fixed belief even while in other lands this identical sort of instruction was being adopted en masse in the service of the religion of totalitarianism.

This morning and every morning, as we know, hundreds of millions of youngsters are drilled from infancy to recite when they begin their day in the schoolroom their supreme motto: "Death to the imperialists! Down with Amerika!"

Should *our* catechisms now be revived?

No doubt, I decided, that might be just as well.

A boy, so we are told, is inclined to eat.

During the next few days at Tascosa I was thoroughly reeducated in the unlimited instructional potency of that most marvelous civilizing implement of all time, the dinner table.

Here at least it would seem to be still true that, if offered plenty of good food, the most tumultuous young male animal of our species becomes uncharacteristically amenable to the prerequisites under which that food is provided—even including standard etiquette. At Boys Ranch the capabilities of dining hall instruction are polished to a level of sophistication I have not seen elsewhere.

Meals are served family style at circular tables of eight by ranchers whose work station at the dining hall requires them to see to it that empty serving bowls are promptly refilled, more milk cartons and bread supplied, until the diners are satisfied. As I invite myself to sit down at a vacant chair at one of the tables assigned to the Veigel Home I am welcomed, first, by a color postcard photo of that home addressed to any visitor and held in a wire clip at center table—a photo on which has been typed the given names of six to eight of the ranchers who live there. I introduce myself, and hands are extended in turn around the table.

None of the generous mounds of food, I note, are disturbed until announcements are completed from the stage microphone, recognizing by name, each with lively applause, every winner of a trackmeet race or other achiever of merit for that day—these announcements made, not by adult staff members, but by appropriate rancher teammates themselves. A rancher then comes to the microphone from that week's "spotlight table" to ask the Good Lord's blessing on the assembly, and from that moment the devastation wrought upon those comestibles would gladden the heart of Generals Sherman and Patton or other scorched-earth practitioners—any adult visitor, however, being scrupulously and insistently persuaded to take the first portion from each serving bowl.

Ranchers at table seemed consistently and alertly responsive to my questions about their activities, politely curious about my own errand, and above all full of ardent pride in *their* ranch. More than once, when I was still in lively exchange with a boy or two when the meal was finished, I was embarrassed to notice every other lad waiting in silence to be formally excused.

Tables meanwhile are being cleared with military dispatch. Back in the kitchen, Chef John Kinkade (a retired U.S. Navy cook whose girth bespeaks good eating indeed) and his top lieutenant, Bill Harner, are watching with hands on hips while food scraps are put in barrels for the hogs, other food and milk are being stored in the large walk-in coolers, dishes are fed into giant washers by ranchers who somehow make the job look as if they were warming up on the baseball field. Within twelve minutes the job is done, the rancher-crew departed to their next activity, the dining hall and kitchen scrubbed, quiet and ready for the next meal. I inquire of one of the kitchen supervisors what secret formula provides the motivation impelling these muscular outdoor western males to execute so rapidly the "menial" chores of preparing, serving, and cleaning up after meals.

"Ask one of those boys," he suggested, and I did, stopping a fast-paced, dark-haired passerby from New Jersey to repeat my question.

"That's easy," he said briskly, more or less over his shoulder as he went about his business. "We fellows in the kitchen crew earn the most money... and we get the best food... while it's hot."

I strolled back to my quarters trying without success to recall any dining occasion in my recent memory during which I had been accorded comparably unfailing courtesy, or eagerness in both the talking and the listening components of good conversation, or pure and simple efficiency in meal service.

Even before a newly arrived boy resident is served his first meal, however, in that transcendent instructional lyceum, the dining hall, he has been launched quite emphatically in yet another integral element in his educational syllabus.

At Cal Farley's Boys Ranch today, as in its earliest years, a rancher begins within the hour of his arrival his transformation into an arrant free-enterprise capitalist, an irreducibly profit-motivated entrepreneur, an earner and conserver of his resources, a payer of his bills and selector of his own charities, a bargainer and a businessman.

Thorough training and discipline in personal economics could be expected, of course, in the program of a ranch founded and built by merchants, bankers, oil producers, corporate executives, and the like — all inclined to a trace of forgivable militancy in defending as honorable the term "businessman" during the decades when America's elite looked upon that breed with delicate distaste. Even the most ardent free enterprisers on the ranch board, however, underestimated the by-product in dignity, in "getting a boy's chin up," that often accrues from the mere process of opening and managing his own account at the ranch bank.

Admission of a new boy — one of the approximately 100 the ranch can accept from among more than 1,200 applications taken annually — is a process in carefully planned cordiality. He is welcomed by Jim Dillingham, program manager, one or more resident boys of his own age, and one or more members of the junior and senior staffs, in a brief discussion during which he reaffirms his pledge made earlier by himself and his sponsors that he will stay at the ranch through graduation from high school, and is given a durable, hip-pocket-sized booklet covering the rules of life at the ranch, written in upbeat, nonmilitary language. Next he goes to the ranch bank, where he meets Ranch Business Manager Herb Schroeder, signs a signature card, watches his laundry number being cranked into the computer as his account number, and is issued a checkbook with which he can write checks at the store and snack bar up to the amount of his first month's pay for his job assignment ($25 at seven years and under, $30 for older boys).

At the "country store" a few steps away the new arrival is issued his first quota of clothing without payment, but he is aware that replacements and frills must thereafter be purchased from his own funds at ranch cost. A savings account is encouraged. (Some boys have accumulated enough money to purchase their own automobile on graduation.) Loans are available from the bank at 5 percent interest for the purchase, say, of a feeding or show animal in the agriculture program — and the bank can even offer insurance on the animal if the purchaser chooses to pay for it!

To the starting minimum a longevity increment of 5 percent is added at the end of each succeeding three months in the boy's stay at the ranch. Thus, after a number of years, senior boys can build to pay and allowances of up to $115 a month. Certain more difficult or less desirable jobs offer a pay differential—cook's helpers, for instance, who sometimes have to report for work at 5:30 A.M., draw a base pay of $55 in winter and up to $70 in summer. Boys appointed after elaborate investigation to "junior staff" positions as assistants to adult supervisors, draw a pay bonus of $10 in third-class rank, $15 in second, $25 in first.

The bank is the busiest place on the ranch during the half hour before boarding time as bus passengers eligible for their every-third-week recreational trip to Amarillo draw authentic greenbacks for their outing. Senior supervisors especially, including Herb Schroeder, take understandable pride in enumerating a respectable list of highly successful businessmen among alumni of Boys Ranch.

From the earliest days when Cal Farley often taught wrestling holds to his first boy residents on a mattress spread behind a potbellied wood stove in the sorely overcrowded Old Tascosa courthouse, the ranch developed on the basis of a policy that might be stated: "Let the boy and his needs create the policy."

This "no rules or guidelines"* principle, which proceeds from one specific situation to the next without reference to patterns and practices accepted as standard elsewhere, continues even yet to run deep.

Superintendent Monty Waldrip recalls, for example, how the "brother" system came to be established in the dormitories. Until that time the "standard" practice of housing boys of comparable age together had been followed—the younger ones in McCormick Hall, the adolescents in Boot Hill dorm, and the senior boys in Hadacol. ("When it arrived from the Dalhart Air Base we 'hadacol' it something!") Then in 1958 half a dozen boys ranging widely in age developed an ambulatory but highly contagious disorder and had to be strictly isolated. They were lodged in two rooms in the residence where Monty and Frances Waldrip, as dorm parents, could bring in their food and assure their segregation from other ranchers. When the time came for the six boys to return to their former dormitories, such mutual attachment had developed among themselves and with the Waldrips that they stayed, and soon thereafter the policy of assigning boys of all

---

* This is the title of a compact history of the ranch developed in 1970 for distribution to donors by Louie Hendricks, veteran ranch publicist and spokesman known to hundreds of local audiences throughout the Southwest.

MISSION IMPROBABLE: A HOMING, A HEGIRA

ages (except the five- to eight-year-olds) to all dormitories was instituted ranchwide.

In a manner of speaking, Superintendent Waldrip himself is another embodiment of this *sui generis* principle. Following the Farleys' death, the board, knowing how deeply the support of the ranch had depended upon Cal's constant presence in the public eye, and taking respectful note of the nonpromotional background and personality of the new president, Virgil Patterson, nonetheless ignored the suggestion of seeking a widely known "name" as ranch superintendent upon the then approaching retirement of Bob Wilson. Continuity instead remained the decisive consideration, and when Wilson retired in 1976, ranch affairs held perfectly steady course under the strong, quiet, genial, and thorough twenty-year veteran, Monty Waldrip.

Esthetic goals in permanent construction were set high and early. Down the road apiece at Clayton, as Cal had noted well, Raymond Huff had proved that people even in desperate need will labor in better heart toward making a product with style that evokes permanent pride. Cal thus wanted no part of a notion too prevalent among enterprises dependent on freewill public contributions, namely that only by ostentatious frugality and mediocrity can cries of "waste" by a certain type of giver be avoided. Instead, he elected early as the basic decor of the ranch the distinctive pink sandstone he had learned from Denver friends is quarried at Lyons, Colorado, on the Boulder-Estes Park road. This and other design details required for optimum livability as well as beauty were passed along to the top-ranking Shiver-Megert firm of Amarillo responsible over the years for most of the site planning and architectural work at the ranch.

Even these demanding esthetic goals always had to be achieved in obeisance to the distinctive needs and purposes of the ranch. Clayton Shiver, senior partner of the firm, once grumped ruefully to Monty Waldrip: "You fellows out here at Tascosa have 'adapted' our buildings so much that I can't recognize our original plans in a one of 'em."

Not always, however, did the purely distinctive have a clear track to approval by the ranch administration. When a number of unusually generous gifts had provided a fund in hand of $850,000 for the purpose and it was time to plan with some magnificence a new chapel that would serve as the centerpiece of the ranch, the architects outdid themselves in submitting several spectacular designs, some of them as futuristic in style as, say, that of the Air Force Academy chapel at Colorado Springs. Traditionalists on the ranch board balked, however, and Virgil Patterson sent back the plans with the notation, "It's just got to have a steeple."

The imposing chapel that was dedicated in 1972 has, indeed, a tall white steeple.

Such "adaptations" in no wise prevented the present-day Boys Ranch from achieving national recognition with some frequency as an architectural showplace—a repute guarded carefully for many years by the veteran ranch construction foreman, M. C. (Bo) Vandergriff.

Contributing immeasurably to the daily pervasiveness of the original ranch philosophy is the continuing residence here of Cal and Mimi Farley themselves. The Farley Memorial Gardens, expansive in quiet beauty with meticulously tended L-shaped formal flowerbeds, greet the visitor near the ranch gate in the space adjacent to the Old Tascosa courthouse, the chapel, and the visitors center.

A clean marble headstone bears the inscription: "If you want to see what Cal and Mimi Farley did, look around you." Between the gravestones and the roadway is a statue of Cal Farley walking, his right hand on the shoulder of a lad of perhaps twelve. An anecdote from Sherman Harriman well illustrates how the ranch administration set aside rigid custom even in such a solemn matter as this statue in order to adhere most faithfully to the maxim Cal Farley himself had lived by and had demanded of his associates: "Never will we fail, in anything we plan or do here, to ask first the question, 'How will this help our boys?' "

Endless consultation and effort throughout the entire ranch family had gone into planning the gardens and the statue, the selection of Clyde Doney of Durango, Colorado, as the sculptor, and the completion and casting of this most appealing pair of strollers, the man figure standing almost exactly at the five-foot, five-inch stature of Cal Farley himself. Then came the question, upon which the family preferences of Cal's only daughter, Genie, and her husband, Sherman Harriman, quite properly should be decisive: Should the statue be cast in the customary "heroic" proportion— one and one-half times life-sized? The cost would be an additional $15,000.

"Talk about a tough decision," Sherman Harriman reflects.

The statue would be the cynosure of the ranch, first focus of the attention of its 25,000 or more visitors each year, and if the statue created in their minds an unexpectedly puny image of Cal Farley, well. . .?

With much trepidation all around, the $15,000 that would have recast a bigger-than-life Cal Farley was pumped into routine boy needs—a decision that was justified promptly and in rarely satisfying fashion. The Harrimans, Monty Waldrip, and other staff members took unusual pains to study the developing bond between the statue and the boys themselves. Time after time a boy rancher passing his mentor's bronze memorial, after

MISSION IMPROBABLE: A HOMING, A HEGIRA

furtive glances had assured him he was not being observed, would measure himself sidewise over his shoulder alongside Cal Farley himself and depart with a swing to his gait that translated clearly, "Well, if he could do all this, reckon I can do something too."

So far, so good.

Just twenty-five years before this visit of mine to Tascosa, John Steinbeck's *Travels with Charley in Search of America* across the breadth and depth of our land had ended in disappointment and frustration: the America he had known was no longer to be found. The new America was one suddenly unsure of itself, uncharacteristically contentious and volatile, teetering in visible alarm on the lip of its then imminent plunge into the electronic revolution, the "McLuhan Revolution," or whatever one wishes to call the turmoil of the sixties and seventies.

Thus far my own mission improbable into the Texas Panhandle — without Charley the poodle — was turning up signs of greater promise.

16

Education for Manhood

*S*UI GENERIS DESCRIBES most accurately the remedial, vocational, and academic educational programs in place at the core of today's Boys Ranch operation. Any veteran teacher from the public schools is startled to observe the elaborateness of these programs, their professional sophistication, and above all the tenacity with which they are applied.

"Over the years we have learned that our boys require much more time and counseling than the average public school is able to provide," Superintendent of Schools Garland Rattan tells his teachers. "Our classes are necessarily smaller, and we can never give up on a boy regardless of the situation."

How's that again?

"We can never give up on a boy regardless of the situation."

Can a school system like this exist?

It does, here at Tascosa.

Under Superintendent Rattan's direction, these programs reflect in a hundred respects his endless philosophical discussions with Cal and Mimi Farley during their quieter later years when they were privileged to live a greater portion of their time among their boys at the ranch. Having arrived as a teacher concurrently with the opening of the first modern permanent school building in 1955, Garland Rattan has been in fact a primary guiding influence in development of the program.

Prior to 1955, schooling at the ranch had been an exercise in

209

improvisation that had brought Cal Farley many of his most painful frustrations. After The Texas State Board of Education had established Boys Ranch as a new independent school district in November 1942, twenty-six boys and their teachers moved into a then new gym-dorm-school building adjoining the courthouse.

Rapid growth, however, presented constant problems. With the closing of the Dalhart Army Air Force Base after World War II, buildings were transported to Tascosa to become dormitories. The former base hospital was converted into a school building. The situation remained desperate, however, since the ranch school remained unaccredited and thus ineligible for state aid. Cal Farley and Amarillo area leaders twisted legislative arms doggedly until in 1947 the state legislature passed an amendment permitting nonsectarian Boys Ranch to become the first of several special-service independent school districts allowed to receive state aid though lacking in taxable property within their boundaries.

Accreditation through the tenth grade was awarded in 1948-49, but full accreditation through the twelfth grade was not accomplished until 1955, an interim period during which several of the by then nearly two hundred boy residents of the ranch had to complete their high school work at Channing, twelve miles away. Meanwhile, the sheriff of Hartley County, Gene Collins, had led in organizing the United Peace Officers of America, who undertook as their first project the financing and construction of a permanent Boys Ranch school building.

In the fall of 1955 the ranchers and their teachers moved into a spacious, fully modern brick-and-stone building, and the then fully accredited ranch school for the first time was adequately quartered.

"There was never any question," said Garland Rattan, "that accreditation and the completion of the UPOA school building stood clearly in Cal Farley's mind as the point at which his place in the country for homeless and wayward boys had ceased being a crazy experiment and had reached maturity as a permanent institution. The way was cleared at last for the ranch to complete its growth and to develop and refine its programs."

Some hint of the extent of this development can be seen at a glance in the following chronological listing of expansions of the Boys Ranch school campus since the 1950's:

1962 — Natatorium (indoor swimming).
1963 — Cal Farley Gymnasium.
1964 — Agriculture Building (classroom, shops).
1965 — Vocational Education building
1966 — Mimi Farley Elementary School

1967-68 — Remodeling and expansion of UPOA building.

1969 — Remodeling of Agriculture building to accommodate farm mechanics. Remodeling of shop facility, adding auto body shop.

1970 — Elementary school addition.

1971 — Band Hall.

1972 — Vocational Education building remodeling and expansion.

1973 — Farm machinery repair building, also Scott Junior High Gymnasium.

1974 — UPOA building renovation; also, all-weather track surface provided.

1975 — UPOA building addition (new wing).

1977 — Football stadium, pressbox, concession stand rebuilt.

(Next in order for the 1980s, as resources permit: Auditorium-Theater; Fine Arts Center.)

Enrollment in the ranch school has more than doubled, the number of teachers more than tripled, in the thirty years since 1955. The school year 1984-85 saw a system accommodating 112 elementary school students (kindergarten through sixth grade), 102 junior high school students, and 212 senior high school students—a total of 426, of which 36 were children of resident staff members. Professional faculty numbered 52, supported by 6 teacher aides, 4 office secretaries, and 2 part-time staff.

"Support had come in so generously from Texas and from all across the country," Garland Rattan mused, "that Cal and Mimi themselves happily saw the day arrive when few boys indeed were being lost, as had happened in the earlier days, simply because our ranch staff was too overworked or underqualified to give them the special attention they needed."

(His remark recalled immediately the last letter Cal had patiently written to the boy-genius Rudy, who had run away from the ranch seventeen times and now, even while serving his fourth hitch in a federal correctional institution, had written at length yet once more to Cal proclaiming his abject repentance. "I shall always think," Cal wrote back, "that if we had had the staff of people at the ranch when you were here that we have today, you would not be writing me from that address.")

Strengthening and expansion of the curriculum began with the 1955-56 school year to include vocational and special education; remedial classes; and some electives in business, speech, and journalism. Quality programs in other areas were added gradually until now the ranch school curriculum incorporates a complete range of subject offerings from basic skills through the arts, besides a remarkable variety of vocational and technical courses.

During the 1960s the ranch school developed a college preparatory track alongside its highly regarded terminal program in vocational and technical

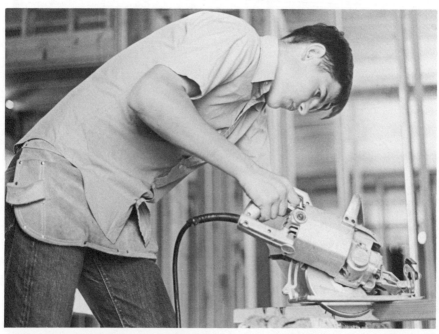

Building meticulously on the basis of twelve years of close personal association with the Farleys, Superintendent of Schools Garland Rattan has created and now directs a fully accredited instructional program in remedial, vocational, agricultural, and academic disciplines that is widely studied and emulated.

studies, and in recent years 10 to 15 percent of the ranch graduates have gone on to earn bachelor's degrees, taking advantage of the several four-year scholarships the ranch can now offer to colleges and universities in Texas and elsewhere. (One of the first of these degree candidates was Bill Sarpalius, a 1968 ranch alumnus who now serves as a Texas state senator for the expansive Panhandle District). Another 15 to 20 percent of recent graduates have gone on to advanced technical training at area and regional vocational and technical schools where they take six to eight quarters of study in such courses as welding, saddle-making, building trades, meat processing, computer science, and range management.

Full-scale interscholastic competition began with the admission of Boys Ranch to the University Interscholastic League in December 1962. In the Farley tradition these contests are sought at the ranch with an ardency focused first on the educational and character-building benefits they can provide. To these boys, who had been shunted early in life into the backwaters, there comes a precious sense of joining the mainstream at last merely in running a race or standing at a lectern in competition with students from the "big-name" schools of Amarillo and other Texas cities.

EDUCATION FOR MANHOOD

Their motivation is of the highest, and they are well aware that, should they return to the ranch with so much as a fifth-place ribbon in their particular event from an area, regional, or state competition, that achievement will be accorded a sincere and resounding accolade from their peers, house parents, teachers, and other ranch staffers. (This type of recognition is greater and more conducive to further effort, an outside observer must regretfully speculate, than was probably accorded to the student champions in the same event in their more distracted city environment.)

Superintendent Rattan's remarks on the values of competition to teachers and students have a flavor of their own:

"Competition," he says, "helps you keep control of your emotions, your actions, your language. It eliminates fear of failure; you get a rubber bottom so that when you're knocked on it you come zinging right back up again. It teaches you to set visible, concrete goals. It teaches you to prepare instead of repair, to act instead of react, to pounce instead of being pounced upon, to look for that little edge and take advantage of opportunity when it comes. It teaches you commitment, a positive get-it-done attitude, determination to do what you've set out to do."

Though competing more often than not as distinct underdogs in area, regional, state, and national competitions, these highly motivated ranchers have earned awards that in both variety and quantity constitute an astonishing record, especially in individual as opposed to team events. The wrestling and track-and-field teams, for example, have maintained consistent championship caliber in regional and state competition, the Boys Ranch wrestlers having brought home their first state championships in 1968 and 1969. In 1985 the trackmen rocked the dining hall with their announcement that the crosscountry team had won its first state AAA championship. Among a total of thirty-five area, regional, and invitational competitions sponsored by the Future Farmers of America in 1984-85, ranchers scored first seven times and second twelve times. In the 1985 Vocational and Industrial Clubs of America state contest, four ranchers won individual awards. In the district literary meet Boys Ranch entrants ranked second overall, winning two debate events besides the one-act-play contest.

The baleful upsurge in functional illiteracy decried across the nation over the past decade has intensified emphasis upon, and experimentation in, remedial education at Boys Ranch. Since the mid 1970s the ranch has greatly expanded its testing and counseling services and has given priority attention to expansion of its basic skills program: reading, writing, spelling, arithmetic. Ingenious modifications of the vocational curriculum for the greater general benefit of slower students ("dull/normal") or for those who have never learned how to learn have produced promising results and are continuing.

Students other than the slower "dull/normal" lads who need remedial work are placed in one of four administrative categories. These are:

1. *Resource students.* These students' problem is simply that they have fallen behind the standard scholastic level for students their age. Almost all new admissions to the ranch are initially so classified; on average, new admissions are twelve months behind their normal grade level in school.

2. *Learning disabled students.* These boys must learn the fundamental elements of the learning process before they can become receptive to standard instruction.

3. *Learning disabled/emotionally disturbed students:* Boys in this category began to arrive in notably increased numbers during the violent social unrest and multiplying family disruptions of the 1960s; their numbers are still disproportionately high. They are not usually combative but often are very difficult to reach.

4. *Learning disabled/emotionally disturbed students with behavior problems:* These are the toughies who test the disciplinary "fences" of the ranch — usually intelligent, resentful, truculent or scornful, impervious to most adult approaches. With some exceptions these are the "wildcats" Cal Farley decreed would always be admitted in manageable proportion to his ranch when they could be placed nowhere else except in incarceration.

Offering by far the greater challenge to the supervisory and instructional staff, boys in the latter two categories are being reclaimed in rising proportion as the staff has developed in size and experience. Failures do occur with some frequency, of course, but those failures continue to be more than counterbalanced by the quiet minor miracles accomplished with some other students.

If the remedial programs at Boys Ranch merit intensive study by specialists, the vocational education programs stand as perhaps even more remarkable in their field, both in variety of offerings and in the innovativeness of techniques employed.

Having begun in 1939 with the 120-acre site of the old ghost town of Old Tascosa, Boys Ranch had grown considerably in land area before an opportunity arose in the mid-1960s to buy 3,100 acres west of the highway. In what was to be his last major acquisition for the ranch, Cal Farley spread the word to all friends of the ranch how greatly the agricultural and vocational training activities of the ranch would benefit through acquisition of the Magenta Farm and the adjoining Cheyenne

Ranch, with its fishing ponds and ranch headquarters facilities. He sought many small contributions, some covering less than the cost of 1 acre, and 1,400 loyalists responded, their checks coming in from almost every state lying between San Diego, California, and Bangor, Maine. That purchase completed, later bequests made possible the purchase in the 1980s of another 6,600 acres from the Bivins family, which had donated the original Tascosa site. Today the ranch encompasses over 10,000 acres excellently balanced between cropland and range land suitable both for production of foodstuffs to help make the ranch self-sustaining and for training its charges in the widest possible variety of agricultural skills.

Under the guidance of John Sharp, farm and ranch manager, four full-time faculty members, and ten adult supervisors, the widely admired Boys Ranch agriculture program is as impressive in its boy-building as in its production of food to meet the needs of this isolated community of nearly 500 residents.

These needs are sizable: four beef steers averaging 1,100 pounds each, ten 220-pound hogs, 850 gallons of fresh milk, and 5,250 eggs are consumed each week in the dining hall, plus appropriate vegetables—all produced and processed on the ranch through the efforts of the 150 boy ranchers who elect to participate in the agricultural program. To feed the livestock, 35,000 bales of hay are produced on the ranch, and 100,000 pounds of grains are purchased raw and mixed scientifically in the ranch micronizer.

Thus, on any day, one may see boy ranchers working and learning at almost any type of farming and ranching activity, from breeding and grooming registered show cattle and quarter horses to managing range or feedlot, to repairing power machinery, to mending fences. Each hour of their regular instruction in, say, the processing of meat or milk, is combined with a two-hour laboratory, so that on leaving the ranch each boy is fully trained, on modern equipment, to move directly into regular employment in one or more specialties.

Nearly one-third of the 150 boys in the "ag" program work under the supervision of Jim Phillips, horticulture manager, who is responsible for the 7-acre ranch garden; for mowing and grooming the 25 acres of lawns, playing fields, and flower gardens; for taking care of the orchard, lakes, and fish in the ponds around the ranch; for the transplant area, 2 greenhouses, landscaping, sewage disposal, and tree trimming. Hard and demanding work as it is, the horticulture program has been expanded and refined in recent years because the magic of growing things evokes a spark of interest in some listless boys not otherwise readily stimulated. They find satisfaction in tending and transplanting the 15,000 seedlings and shrubs bedded in the greenhouses in the spring, achievement in presenting to the throngs of tourist visitors a panorama of meticulously groomed lawns, and dignity in being permitted to tend the formal flowerbeds in the Farley Memorial Gardens.

Other vocational education is arranged so that the ranchers have the opportunity to choose, and to develop marketable proficiency in, almost any one of the multitudinous skills and services needed for daily operation of the compact ranch community. Concurrently with their technical instruction by the vocational instructor, auto mechanic trainees, for example, are assigned for regular "lab" work (typically ten hours a week) under the staff supervisors responsible for keeping the ranch's fleet of seventy vehicles in operating condition.

Those favored few designated for the most envied assignment of operating tractors, bulldozers, and earth-moving carryalls do so under the gaze of D. A. Prichard, ranch maintenance supervisor, who protests with a trace of a smile that "It's not true—quite—that we have leveled whole hills around here just so more boys can taste the triumph of operating this big equipment." (Comments Ranch Director Hagy: "Our boys, like many other boys, would rather push dirt around with a bulldozer blade than drive a Cadillac at the head of a parade.")

The automobile body repair and painting shop typically finds twice as many regular jobs waiting for its trainees than there are ranch graduates to fill them. Demand most often exceeds the supply, also, for ranchers skilled in the building construction trades—carpenters, plumbers, painters, electricians who as trainees have effected most of the upkeep of the ranch buildings. Under the uncompromising oversight of their teachers, over a two-year period these ranchers also have built, from the foundation up, a complete three-bedroom, two-bath house which, after it has been officially certified as complying in every respect with the Amarillo building code, is auctioned and hauled away.

Elsewhere throughout the ranch community is evident the eminently practical strategy of training young men intensively in skills which, first, help the ranch operate economically and, later, enable them to earn an honest dollar in the general economy. At the dining hall, students are instructed, evaluated, and graded on their performance in bakery work, meat-cutting, food preparation, and warehousing. At the ranch laundry, the medical clinic, the ranch store, and the ranch bank, other students are measuring themselves, and being measured, against standards reliably represented to them as prevailing in comparable endeavors out there in

218 the "real" world. Whether accepted with or without enthusiasm, these are lessons not lost on young minds previously initiated into the calamities of antisocial behavior.

Basic skills and job-oriented schooling necessarily had preempted most attention and emphasis during the first three decades of the growth and development of the ranch. By 1970 the ranch had arrived at a stability and a level of financial resources permitting a new concentration on "standard" academic excellence. Sooner than most of their teachers had hoped, the ranchers began to achieve distinction as measured by impressive numbers of awards in the University Interscholastic League's literary, debate, poetry, journalism, speech, and music contests.

A "defeat" the whole ranch took to heart occurred, for example, when in 1984 the Boys Ranch one-act play failed to place in the district UIL contest, interrupting a record during which for thirteen consecutive years the ranch players had placed first in this event in the district and had won five area and four regional contests and two state titles. That setback was promptly erased, however, when in 1985 the one-act players sailed through area and regional competition to place fourth in the state. Applause and ranchwide accolades comparable to the homecoming of a championship football team greeted the actors, as had been accorded the nine boys who qualified for the regional literary contest in 1983, to bring home the top district award for the first time ever.

The computer age has arrived at Tascosa. By 1985 sixteen computers were in place in the elementary school and twenty more in the high school. With computer training fully cranked into the curriculum, the computer labs, like the two school libraries, are kept open all summer for voluntary practice and study.

In 1979 specialized instruction and an accelerated curriculum were provided for gifted ranchers of unusual linguistic or mathematical talent. The planned construction of a new auditorium and a new fine arts building during the present decade cannot but add further impetus to the drive for academic excellence in the Boys Ranch school system.

What is the philosophical infrastructure of this instructional program at Cal Farley's Boys Ranch? A recent and typical briefing by which their superintendent greeted teachers at the opening of a new school year answers that question with a clarity and candor all too rarely heard elsewhere in an educational establishment afflicted with terminal obfuscation.

"The purposes of education, I believe," Superintendent Rattan declared, "remain about the same in my view as they were stated in a textbook I studied many years ago. They are (1) to pursue the truth; (2) to teach organized, disciplined, systematic subject matter; (3) to hand down the cultural heritage of the race; (4) to help the individual realize his own potential; and (5) to insure the survival of our country.

"I believe that we do have a very fundamental school system here at Boys Ranch. We never left the 'basics,' never wandered from the pursuit of individual excellence. Reading, writing, arithmetic, responsibility and respectability are emphasized. Our students have tests and homework. Their assignments are expected to be done on time and when they are not, we see to it they are completed through a coordination with the house parents that duplicates the teamwork between teacher and parents existing in the one-room country school Cal Farley attended as a boy in Minnesota.

"Failure slips are routed daily to house parents whenever students flunk a test or miss an assignment, and teacher-parent conferences occur promptly when a student's schoolwork starts to slide. Often no more than a quick interchange at the dining hall is enough to correct an incipient problem, but more detailed conferences occur routinely as required. We stay on top of the situation. Restrictions are applied as the house parent deems appropriate — most often the immediate banning of all television viewing, followed by withdrawal of such more important privileges as that of recreational trips to the city.

"Our students attend pep rallies and assemblies complete with the pledge of allegiance to the American flag, the singing of our national anthem, the school song, and prayer. They are taught good manners, courtesy, and respect for their elders. They dress within a pretty strict code. They get old-fashioned A, B, C, or F grades (no D's) and they are spanked for serious misbehavior in the school as elsewhere in their life at the ranch."*

This formula is, as Garland Rattan never wearies of illustrating, a Cal Farley formula in every respect, refined to make good use of up-to-the-minute teaching techniques and equipment.

"Cal Farley's recipe for rearing boys," he reminds his teachers, "was

---

* This spanking rule was the subject of considerable controversy for a number of years. Eventually the ranch administration demonstrated to the satisfaction of Texas state welfare authorities that spanking as a last resort in disciplinary situations is a necessity, at least in the circumstances applying at Boys Ranch, and that the rule can be safely maintained under the following rigid controls: The spanking can be administrated for cause by any dormitory parent or other designated staff member only in the presence of another adult as witness, and only after carefully reviewing with the boy the reasons for this punishment. The adult may use only the plain leather belt he is wearing, doubled, and may administer no more than ten swats to the buttocks. He then must place immediately in the permanent ranch files a detailed report of the incident.

simply this: Mix some incentive for doing right with an expectation of punishment for doing wrong; add a generous dash of love and recognition, and you have a boy headed in the right direction."

Thus, the academic and vocational procedures in these classrooms and shops are integrated meticulously with the other three agendas in progress at the ranch, namely, physical conditioning (i.e., athletics); social development, centering in the dorms and the dining hall; and spiritual development, centering at the ranch chapel—where Superintendent Rattan himself, incidentally, aids the successful launching of his high school seniors into the world outside by discussing prerequisites for a happy and productive home and family life in a Sunday school class each week.

As a guideline for the operation of his schools the superintendent repeats often to his teachers St. Paul's admonition to the Thessalonians: "Prove all things; hold fast to what is good." Then he adds: "After we determine what is good and change what needs to be changed, we must consider individual differences in all the personalities involved. We must never forget that learning takes place much better in an atmosphere of warmth and security, and we should develop a degree of careful 'touchingness' in our association with students, especially the small ones and the shy ones. I still have and use a *Reader's Digest* reprint Cal Farley gave me years ago entitled, 'The Magic of Being in Touch.'*

"Cal never failed," he continues earnestly, "to stress how important recognition is to all children, and we watched how, at every step as he walked around the ranch, he always waved and spoke, or mussed a boy's hair or dropped a hand on his shoulder with his friendly kidding humor so that even his usual greeting, 'Hi, how ya doin'?' made a boy feel good."

The briefing for Boys Ranch teachers takes on a new directness:

"A program like ours calls for a different approach from what might work very well elsewhere. We must look beyond the mess someone else has made and see the potential in every single boy. We must remain flexible and *never* quit trying until we find the key that opens up each boy's mind to the learning he is capable of. We must never 'run past them too fast'—

---

* A member of the Boys Ranch School Board deplores actions by public school administrations, harried by recent media flurries over "child abuse," banning all physical contact between teachers and students. "The American child grows up in a public school environment that is cold and hostile enough at best. Now, instead of concentrating on the *only* ultimate answer, namely, more careful teacher selection, these administrations are further depriving even the little ones of those gestures of warmth almost as indispensable as good food to their healthy development."

that was Cal's way of saying it—because the boy who's hanging back not saying anything is the boy who needs you most.

"Cal cautioned us always to gear down our teaching as individually necessary for the slower kids, always remembering that they'll make fine, productive citizens in their own place and at their own pace. And their loyalty is unquestionable. 'The sharp ones,' Cal would say, 'may be more fun, but they'll be running the ranch and you, too, in about three days if we don't watch out. They don't need half as much help as the slower boys.'

"I prefer to believe," the superintendent concludes, "that this school system, as part of the whole Boys Ranch program, is Christianity in action."

And the latter terse summation is an aperçu this correspondent, for one, would not choose to dispute.

From their eyrie in the supernal realms Parson Weems, William Holmes ("Eclectic") McGuffey, Horatio Alger, and those few other notable pedagogues who shaped the mentality that built America no doubt smiled warmly to see their precepts so creditably embodied in the thirty-three high school seniors who, on May 20, 1985, marched in cap and gown at the thirtieth commencement of the fully accredited Boys Ranch High School to receive their diplomas from the hand of Cal Farley's daughter, Genie Harriman. Half of these seniors were A and B honor roll students, and five were National Honor Society members. The thirty-three had received a combined total of 114 years of vocational training while living at the ranch an average span of 6½ years. Several had taken pains to speak or wave a warm retirement good-by to Melba Brown at her little pink house.

President Reagan did not happen to call, but these boys, and this school system, were clearly almost exactly what he had in mind as he stumped the country during that spring of 1985 urging various high school and college graduating classes to claim the rewards of the work ethic and the personal moral code integral to the American tradition.

Superintendent Garland Rattan wonders meanwhile, with good reason, just who the truly underprivileged adolescents in today's American schools *are*: his students at Boys Ranch, every one of them from a disrupted if not even a destitute childhood environment—or the overindulged, sports-car-driving, physically flabby students of the typical affluent suburban high school who are being thrust by impatient parents, sophisticated movies and television shows, and gut-busting rock music into an "unknown territory of adulthood" before they are mature enough to handle its challenges.

EDUCATION FOR MANHOOD

"Here," he points out, "our boys grow through these adolescent years with the time and opportunity to adapt themselves to the radical transformations their bodies, minds and emotions are normally undergoing."

He echoes precisely Neil Postman's thesis,[*] terming America's first television generation a "lost generation which has not matured by integrating concepts and values into a well-defined sense of themselves, but by picking up bits and pieces to form a 'patchwork self.' And like a house of cards, an identity that has been patched together can collapse under merest stress. Again, the statistics are familiar: teenage suicide, drug and alcohol abuse, increased sexual activity, streams of runaways from home. These are the grim fruits of 'hurry up and grow' seeds sown in childhood."

[*] See his *The Disappearance of Childhood*. Delacorte Press, New York, 1982.

17

"It's the Kid that Counts"

FTER FORTY-ODD YEARS, the influence of Cal Farley the athlete is clearly visible the year-around, not only at Tascosa, but on all the courts and playing fields of Amarillo, a city now grown past a population of 150,000. In fact, one might comfortably assume that, largely because of that beneficent influence, residents throughout the spacious Texas Panhandle can count themselves exempt from the dismal conclusions of recent nationwide studies of the physical condition of American youth—findings that, in the words of one national news magazine, "our kids are less fit now than at any other time data has ever been taken."*

At the ranch, Athletic Director Roger Waldrip, Superintendent Rattan, and their ten teacher-coaches continue to press for every one of the multiple benefits to be gained from athletic competition. (One veteran Boys Ranch coach, LaVon [Lefty] Adams, had been named Texas AAA "Coach of the Year" in 1984.) All are constantly reminded that "raising boys is our first responsibility."

"Interest in athletics is not common among new arrivals," said Roger Waldrip in his twenty-first year as athletic director. "These boys are—almost all of them—poorly developed and sloppy and flabby when they arrive here, having lived mostly on junk food. They are woefully inexperienced in athletic games of any kind, with poor eye-hand coordination;

* *Newsweek*, April 1, 1985, p. 24.

thus, we have to start pretty much from ground zero in developing any team sport.

"First of all, we have to create an interest. A boy is not assigned to any specific sport but is offered a wide variety of choices. We coaches and the house parents then keep the pressure on him until he understands that he must choose one regular athletic activity. After that, it may take as long as six months for his growing competence and competitive spirit to begin to take hold."

He explains how the Boys Ranch two-phase system fulfills the Cal Farley thesis that every healthy boy should have a generous exposure to athletics in some form. Year-around interscholastic competition is carried on in football, basketball, wrestling, track, and cross-country. In football, for example, each of five teams — seventh grade, eighth grade, ninth grade, junior varsity, and varsity — plays an eight-game fall schedule against other schools in the district.

Meanwhile, boys not of interscholastic skill level are occupied just as diligently in another year-around program of intramural competition between dormitories, featuring volleyball, basketball, wrestling, track, and softball — the latter encompassing an overfull 230-game schedule during summer vacation months!

"Don't think for a minute that we deemphasize victory or tolerate excuses for not winning," Roger Waldrip stresses. "These kids have been losers all their lives, and they *must* learn the taste of winning at something. But it is equally important that they learn to win the *right* way. That's why, whenever a championship trophy is awarded in intramural competition, a sportsmanship trophy is also awarded, on the basis of detailed observation.

"At the end of every game each of the three umpires turns in a signed slip rating the sportsmanship of each competing team on a scale of zero to ten. That sportsmanship rating covers, besides the courtesies required in the sport, such factors as dress (a flying shirttail is a no-no), attitude (a sulky face after an umpire's decision won't do), and hustling — team spirit. At the end of the season the [team with the] highest cumulative score wins the trophy. And, although we don't say a word that might deprecate victory, our boys don't fail to notice that at Boys Ranch our sportsmanship trophy is always ever so slightly taller than the championship trophy awarded at the same time.

"Public school athletics tend almost irresistibly to gravitate toward pleasing the parents whose pride demands that their offspring outscore benefit to the player himself."

And ranch teams are greeted with highly unpredictable reactions when, after the end of every interscholastic game, they invite their opponents to join them in a brief prayer at midfield!

So far, so very good, I am musing to myself. In no element of the program at the ranch have I discerned any significant deviation from the Farley track, the Farley system. But surely, I am guessing, that string has got to break when I shift focus downtown, where the crosscurrents of rapid growth to metropolitan status could hardly have failed to blur or erase Amarillo's classic distinction as a compact, salty, flavorful "family" of Texans so many years ago.

That apprehension seemed by way of at least partial fulfillment when I drove to the Maverick Club, a structure almost roofed by the overpass of an interstate east-west highway, now adjoined by a brick-walled natatorium built since my last visit quite a few years ago.

Clean and spacious, obviously use-worn as always, the gyms do not support the volume of boy traffic that prevailed in the Maverick Club's early unlicensed years. When Ralph Dykeman constituted the entire paid staff, he and whatever volunteers he and Farley could recruit kept several hundred youngsters off the streets. Present state regulations—requiring well-paid civil service supervisors to be on duty every minute the doors are open and providing facilities for the admission of girls as well as boys—add up to a cost factor that sharply reduces the daily hours of the club's availability and shifts its function toward that of a day-care center. Still, the club is well supported by the business community and continues to serve an "indispensable" function in these unfashionable downtown districts.

I returned downtown on an errand I had subconsciously postponed for fear of what I might find out. I walked unannounced into the *Amarillo Globe-News* and inquired for Putt Powell, who had written a memorable "sports obituary" after Cal Farley's death and who was the only remaining Amarillo sportswriter familiar to me from former years. Putt was at his typewriter, and he was cordial to the idea of a new book reexamining the Farley legend, especially if that book did full justice to Dutch Mantell, the seditious Luxembourgian whose dismaying face stared down at us from a front-and-center position among the pictures on Putt's office wall.

I showed him that that solemn obligation had already been fulfilled in

my manuscript and asked him how things go today with the Maverick Club and Kids, Inc.

"Just fine," he said, and conducted me to the office of Garet von Netzer, a young managing editor recently graduated from the sports desk and also, Putt disclosed, a recent president of Amarillo's Kids, Inc. With the fervor of a proud father and a fitness zealot, von Netzer spun for me a remarkable story.

"In Amarillo, 'It's the kid that counts,' " he said. "That has been the motto of Kids, Inc., all the way, and we have lived up to it."

For the first ten years after the citywide program had begun as the Amarillo Recreation Association, Ralph Dykeman as administrator and Cal Farley as promoter had kept Kids, Inc., growing without paid staff. In 1947 football was added to the original softball competition; basketball, shortly thereafter; by 1956, the organization was given a charter under direction of a citywide committee. The program continued to grow.

"Cal was always concerned," Garet von Netzer said, "to keep the focus on the program, not so much on the star players, as on the 'little guys' not blessed with star athletic talent."

To hold that course he persuaded Earl Smith, one of the outstanding early graduates of Boys Ranch, to become the first full-time director. In

The late Ralph Dykeman, revered as the young man recruited by Cal Farley to build the Maverick Club and later Kids, Incorporated, the nation's preeminent municipal program of youth athletics in which today 4,500 parental volunteers keep more than 15,000 Amarillo youngsters in organized play the year round.

1963 Kids, Inc., began to become the neighborhood program it is today, with teams for the different sports being chosen from the same elementary, junior high, or high school districts. Earl Smith was ably succeeded by Jim Brock in 1973, and Brock was succeeded in 1983 by Gary Abramson, a former West Texas State volleyball coach.

Present-day figures are impressive.

Today's year-around Kids, Inc., program commands the willing and loyal exertions of a small administrative staff supported by more than 4,500 volunteer adult coaches, officials, and supervisors who lead 1,100 teams through league play annually, involving as many as 18,000 Amarillo youngsters from kindergarten age through high school! The most demanding of these volunteer jobs are those held by the 65 members of a so-called Roundup Club, each member being responsible for recruiting parents and other volunteers to keep the teams of one neighborhood school community operating.

From September to late October, league play is offered in tackle football (grades 4-6, boys), flag football (grades 2-12, boys and girls), cheerleading (grades 4-6, girls), and soccer (grades K-6, boys and girls). Next comes basketball (grades 3-12, boys and girls) in gymnasiums provided by the Amarillo Independent School District for a rental fee. After the Kids, Inc., season ends, both boys and girls in four age groups—6-7, 8-9, 10-11, and 12-13—may play in "Little Dribblers" basketball leagues under a franchise operated by Kids, Inc. Youngsters below the fifth-grade level play the game with a youth-sized ball and goals eight and one-half feet high instead of the regulation ten feet. Volleyball for boys or girls in grades 3-6 and "coed" in junior and senior high school, plus indoor soccer, round out the winter season.

Spring offerings are limited to track and soccer for both boys and girls in grades K-6.

Then it's summer, and a boisterous, buoyant preoccupation seems to take over the whole city of Amarillo as midget warriors, visored and valiant—swarms of them, *three hundred fifty squads of them*—carrying their war clubs, converge for mortal combat on the city's more than 175 diamonds. Triumph and heartbreak, tense drama and comedy, training in sportsmanship and tenacity and eye-hand coordination—and, above all, adult-youngster comradeship in richest measure—occupy most of the summer weeks, with a fillip of bowling and summer basketball offered as "dessert" for those few young athletes and their parents and coaches who are not happily exhausted when the softball championships are at last decided.

The rewards of sports competition, as Cal Farley insisted so long ago, are equal for all participants so long as the skill level of the competing teams is held in reasonable balance—so long as "it's the kid that counts." Still just a bit worried about the answer I would hear, I asked Garet von Netzer whether Kids, Inc., still adheres to the simple Farley dictum which keeps the program on track and minimizes the almost inexorable adult urge to make *victory*, not the kids' welfare, the central aim.

"No," he replied, "Kids, Incorporated, never did and still does not permit open sponsorship of a single team by any commercial firm. Several scores of commercial firms do support the *program*, you understand, but the teams' jerseys all bear noncommital names—Panhandle, for instance—that give no clue to the comparative level of play going on in that particular league. A partial exception is our USSSA softball league, but that involved last year only thirty-eight teams."

"Is any other city in the country as seriously involved in fostering the physical and emotional health of its youngsters as Amarillo is?" I asked.

"Well, if there's another city devoting as much effort and enthusiasm to organized youth athletics and offering half as large an overall program as our Kids, Incorporated, plus a number of other programs sponsored by our YM-YWCA and others," he answered, "I just don't happen to know where that city is."

Moving contentedly toward the door, I paused for a reminiscent moment, recounting how Wes Izzard had told me more than once in earlier years how the *Globe-News* had learned to capitalize on an amazing intensity of reader interest in these neighborhood competitions by assigning some of its top sportswriting talent to the sandlots, meticulously publishing the box scores, and at the peak season devoting as much as half a page daily to coverage of Kids, Inc., games. "Tell me candidly, Garet," I asked, "aren't your readers today at least as curious to know how well their own kids' teams are doing as they are to read stories reporting breathlessly from two thousand miles away that yet another seven-foot basketball player who's already making a million a year is refusing to play until he makes a million and a half?"

"That's a leading question for sure," Garet von Netzer said, laughing. "For your answer you'll just have to notice how much sports-page space we routinely devote to our Kids, Incorporated, competition."

An outstanding program. An amazing program, setting me to pondering several large questions.

What are the inner secrets of Kids, Inc.'s, sheer size and vitality? Why, after forty years of preeminent success, hasn't this program been more widely emulated in other communities? Has it ever, in fact, been duplicated elsewhere? If not, why not?

I began to inquire. Ralph Dykeman, the former young insurance man who had joined forces with Cal Farley to start both the Maverick Club and its "across-the-tracks" offspring, Kids, Inc., was then still alive but in rapidly declining health, unavailable to tie to the present day the philosophical threads he had woven so eloquently for me many years ago. (Ralph died a few months later.) Others were available, however, both old-timers and younger loyalists, and from them gradually came some answers.

First, I had to salute once more the distinctive character of these Panhandle people. They were "different" in earlier years of our century, and they retain in the 1980s a flavor of their own. They are a breezy people in a breezy land, a sardonic, patriarchal people whose natural parental instincts gain strength from a land that remains "healthfully bigger than the people on it."

But surely those parental instincts are alive and well in scores and hundreds of other American communities where they are not given the organized citywide momentum that Kids, Inc., provides. Why Amarillo, not often elsewhere? Amarillo of course once heard a Cal Farley doggedly, passionately, incessantly proclaiming that "it's the kid that counts," insisting that every youngster needs to learn from participating in physical games with others of comparable skill the rudiments of victory, of teamwork, of maturity. But after forty years it seems more apparent than ever that the Farley thesis could never have crystallized in lasting institutional form without the vision of broad-gauged, ink-stained editors like Gene Howe and Wes Izzard who put the full reportorial and promotional power of the *Globe-News* onto the sandlots day after day, season after season, in the process overcoming the inertia and economic distraction endemic to American parents so that Amarillo's fathers and mothers learned how the richest of all joys are to be found on those same sandlots with their own kids. Only thus was a tradition born.

How had Amarillo held its focus on the "little guys," the youngsters deficient in athletic talent or perhaps not before attracted to physical exercise at all? How, in other words, had Amarillo deflected the almost irresistible gravitation of a hotly competitive society toward overstressing victory with deemphasis of the character-building demands of team play — the "my kid can beat your kid" syndrome? On this point the key was unmistakable: Cal Farley's original hard-line policy against commercial sponsorship of individual teams, thus linking league success to the downtown cash register, in the main has been held intact against pressures particularly strong in the past decade toward more and more citywide and regional headline-seeking competition. Those pressures have been accommodated, as mentioned, in the USSSA softball league and also in the Little Dribblers, who compete after the close of the Kids, Inc., basketball season. Merchants in general, however, support the program as a whole; the necessary additional dollars formerly raised by citywide solicitations of the Girl-Scout-cookies type have been raised instead in recent years by highly publicized major events featuring professional teams. Thus, the program stays on track.

At core, however, the scope and dynamism of Kids, Inc., derives from its nonprofessionals, its volunteers, its Round-Up Club. That's the categorical opinion of Gary Abramson, the executive director who himself constitutes fully one half of the full-time staff of paid physical education professionals in charge of the whole giant activity! (His assistant, Lee Stinsman, is the other half.)

"Never anywhere else, I think, was there a more successful demonstra-

tion of American voluntarism than in this program," he declares. "Here
in Amarillo it is the volunteers who recruit the volunteers, the parents
who recruit other parents. Each one of the fifty-four members of our
Round-Up Club fulfills the demanding job of finding the coaches for the
teams of one of our elementary, junior or senior high schools, then finding the officials for league games and in general selling the idea of volunteer
service. The results are monumental, enlisting the energetic services of four
thousand five hundred adults who shepherd the eleven-hundred teams
through their paces. One of them, our current president Dan Lynch,
overtaxes the large computer at his office with the massive chore of preparing playing schedules for all leagues."

Other employees on the astonishingly small paid staff number only ten,
headed by the motherly Phyllis Squyres, the business manager, with
twenty-four years' service; her assistant, Karon Spear; and Edna Bryant,
fund-raising manager.

Typical of the troops in this volunteer army is Tom Reyman, owner
of a building supply business, who was coaxed twenty-five years ago into
becoming coach of a team on which his six-year-old son wanted to play
and has never since wavered in his loyalty to Kids, Inc.

"Teaching," says Tom Reyman, "is what it's all about. If a kid can learn
responsibility and sportsmanship, the winning of ball games will take care
of itself. Learning responsibility to themselves and to the team applies here
and now, but also to their daily lives and to the future. Face it, we live
in a competing world, and these kids need to learn how to perform individually and as a team to a hundred and ten percent of their potential.

"This program isn't just for the athletically gifted kids; it's for every
one of them. I treat 'em all just the same. In twenty-five years now I've
seen so many lost or clumsy or unsure-of-themselves kids grow through
this program into vigorous citizens of our own or other towns that I'm
sure of one thing: we simply must continue to draw our youngsters in
large numbers into Kids, Inc."

From all visible evidence Tom Reyman's wish will be fulfilled, though
for a time in the early 1980s that outcome was shadowed with doubt. A
shift of mood was noted in Amarillo as in much of the rest of the nation,
a climate of parental preoccupation, defensiveness, and rancor ascribed by
seasoned observers, on the one hand, to the rapid exodus of homemakers
to jobs in the marketplace and, on the other, to the soaring divorce rate—a
confluence not at all conducive to happy parent-child relationships. From
a peak of 18,000 youngsters in 1981 Kids, Inc., activities, enrollment

dropped off sharply to 11,000 two years later. Coaches and staff were being increasingly badgered with protests of unfair treatment and other interference, mostly by parents either relieving their own frustrations or reflecting guilt over their recent inattentiveness to their children.

A vigorous new administration, however, generated a strong rededication to the original Farley principles, and enrollment bounced back to 13,000 youngsters in 1985 and to 15,000 in 1986. As of this writing, Amarillo, Texas, retains its glistening repute as a place where the pure joys of parenthood are a highly visible element of civic life, a place where "it's the kid that counts."

18

The Process Hums

M Y SEARCH MISSION by now was winding down. My eight-day visit to Tascosa had extended itself into a full-scale investigation, and a conclusion as remarkable in the history of personality-dominated human institutions as is the Tascosa community itself had crystallized in my mind. Here in this spring and summer of 1985, eighteen years after Cal and Mimi Farley had departed the earthly scene, their by then more than 3,000 sons were being nurtured and matured in a pattern almost exactly as if those years had not elapsed — so nearly so that an eye like mine closely familiar with this ranch since its early days could detect no significant change except the welcome one of vastly improved services and facilities.

That rare continuity, it now seemed clear to me, had been achieved by a ranch organization combining two primary elements: family, and friends.

At the Cal Farley Boys Ranch headquarters, a spacious one-story building faced with pink Colorado sandstone and fronting on Amarillo's largest municipal park, the Farley process hums from 7:30 A.M. often until well into the night, as ranchers here for their regular in-town recreational trips or for medical visits play billiards or browse in the library while waiting to board their bus to return to Tascosa. It is from here that the Farley family influence effectively exerts itself in ranch affairs on an hour-by-hour, day-by-day basis.

Gene Farley Harriman (here, more often, Genie) inherited her father Cal's unrelenting energy and sense of purpose to a striking degree. At headquarters she remains, with her former song-and-dance partner of early Flying Dutchman Circus days, Marilyn Cornelius Van Ausdall, closely involved with the direct-mail operation, now under direction of Business Administrator Gene Hayman. Built meticulously by Cal over many years into six-figure national size that now requires as operating space most of the capacious full basement of the headquarters building, these homespun, twice yearly letters to friends of the ranch until quite recently had accounted for the bulk of the ranch's operating funds. Diligently trained by Cal in the supreme importance of a prompt and sincere "thank you" for all expressions of interest or for financial contributions, she receives all mail and personally composes or supervises answers to every one of the hundreds of letters received each year which merit the "family touch."

Even more demanding is her administrative function in preparing the in-depth progress reports and evaluations required semiannually by Texas state regulations on each boy in residence at the ranch. With her husband, Sherman, and his two assistants, Forrest Baldwin and Terrell Thomas, she aids in preparing nearly 800 evaluations each year. From interviewing the boys and the ranch staff—a duty requiring her presence at Tascosa about two days each week—she gravitates with warmth into Mimi Farley's role of providing some of the innumerable motherly touches vital to the morale of the boy animal.

(When I acknowledged rueful neglect of the Mimi Farley legend in this chronicle, she responded in all good cheer: "Mimi was used to that. Boys Ranch is and must be a male-dominated society." I predicted that on another day Mimi and Genie would share fully with Cal in a more personal biography.)

A well-spoken good listener of quiet charm and often penetrating wit, Genie is seldom reachable evenings at her home telephone. More likely she is involved in rehearsal or a planning meeting of the Amarillo Little Theater Group, of which she is a loyal long-term director and is especially proud of the group's size (numbering several hundred) and its solvency. During this particular spring season, both were on stage during a sellout run of *The Bells Are Ringing*, finding that raucous comedy an especially salutary antidote to the poignancy that characterizes their daytime labors.

Or...

On another evening Genie Farley Harriman may well be attending a dance class, a diversion she has not often neglected since those days in the 1940s and 1950s when she and Marilyn Cornelius Van Ausdall and Vesta O'Dell Orr constituted a feature attraction in tours of the Flying

Dutchman Circus from California, to Yellowstone Park, to Toronto, to the farthest reaches of Texas. "I used to be quite sure I had tap-danced in every church basement in the Texas Panhandle," she remembered, "and afterward the three of us exhausted brats would fall sound asleep in the same bed in a drafty hotel while Daddy sat up somewhere telling the grownups about Boys Ranch."

Or...

She is frequently away from Amarillo fulfilling the role of surrogate parent upon a special occasion in the life of a ranch graduate — a university commencement, say, or a wedding. A most special event of this one recent spring was the wedding of Soapy, who had been committed to the ranch as a boy of nine by his presumed mother, an Indian "princess." Soapy early declared to Genie with amusing solemnity that he liked her but couldn't let himself "get close to anybody," set records in rodeo and several other sports at the ranch, sailed out of the ranch school with honors through a university degree in business administration, chose instead (partially in favor of his rich singing voice) to enter the ministry, attracted and stirred a dynamic young congregation in a large and remote Texas city, and now — with Genie at his side — was giving his ring and his name to his helpmeet for life.

She is busy in some family project with her daughter, Shelley, and son-in-law Bob Sloger, or perhaps off in Dallas with her son, Cal, a computer expert, and her daughter-in-law, Phyllis, teaching her four-year-old grandchild to tap dance.

Or...

If she is at home, she likely is fussing in the "doll room" with her floor-to-ceiling display of dolls, or riffling through, and adding to, her scrapbooks and other Farley memorabilia, which rival in scope the Farley collection at the Panhandle Plains Museum at Canyon, Texas.

"I have a tough question for you," I said to Genie on a day when she was stuffing boy evaluations into files at the ranch headquarters. "Summarize for me in five minutes how the so-called collective psychological profile of boys admitted to the ranch has changed over the years."

She answered: "In the earliest years most of the boys were undernourished, many of them from desperately poor circumstances. Mere food did wonders for them if they had not already been too well trained in stealing. During the war years and through the fifties physical want was a less frequent factor than parental neglect. Mama had gone to work in the factories during the war and was still employed outside the home. The divorce rate was climbing, and the child was increasingly being brought

THE PROCESS HUMS

236 up by the television set but, at the same time, could plainly see alongside his perhaps tumultuous existence a stable order in which success could be earned.

"In the sixties that order fell apart. Our incoming boys who'd seen little but disorder and violence on television and in the streets, and had known nothing resembling a normal home, began to arrive with real and deep emotional problems. Saddest of all was the burden of guilt they carried, blaming themselves for their parents' problems.

"One of the unforgettables was Jules, who had come to us at five years of age from a mother sincerely concerned for his welfare. For seven years he had given us no trouble and had developed fairly well, but I had been puzzled as to why his schoolwork periodically suffered while he went through a period of profound, impenetrable depression. More or less by chance, I asked him one day; 'Jules, do you know why you came to Boys Ranch?' 'Yes, Miz Harriman,' he said, with the face of felon making a clean breast of things after many years, 'I set fires in our house.' When I finally persuaded him after much effort that his mother had given him to us, *not* as punishment for his 'crime,' but because she was desperately fearful for his safety during her working hours when he had to be alone in the house, his problem was solved.

"Finally, in the seventies and the eighties, when we began to get the children of the 'flower children' and the peace marchers and the Woodstock crowd, we were confronted with youngsters some of whom had never observed at close hand an adult who had a marketable skill or worked regular hours at a job, children who furthermore had such a sketchy acquaintance with school that their fundamental learning patterns had never developed; they had never learned *how* to learn. We began also to admit a larger proportion of mixed-up boys from upper-middle-class or affluent homes, and more boys from fathers whose wives had walked out on their families 'to fulfill themselves.' The emotional problems of these boys are something *else*, more complex and difficult to penetrate, I would judge, than any in former years."

Whatever the problem, the solution remains the same: control, rewards or punishment fairly dispensed for right or wrong behavior, commendation and recognition, an atmosphere of affection. "We continue to bump into some painful letdowns," Genie Harriman said. "But much more often this formula brings these boys out of the woods in good shape, sometimes with little or no special effort on our part."

She held up and read from an evaluation she was about to file: "Lester is the son of professional parents, both away from home during the day and unpredictably into the evening as they build their separate practices, leaving Lester footloose around their swimming-pool residence on a mountainside above Denver. When he came to the ranch just over a year ago, he had been expelled from school as a twelve-year-old of 'severe immaturity, negative self-image, extremely willful—a severe discipline problem.' In the past year he has been disciplined at the ranch only four times, in the worst instance having taken four swats for breaking plates while arm-wrestling with another boy in the dining hall. He has worked very hard to catch up his schoolwork 'and will make the A and B honor roll in the final quarter.

"We don't have any idea what really straightened Lester out," Genie continued. "Those four swats on the rump? Just the orderly atmosphere of the ranch? But he has seen the light and is such a different person that we're only hoping that by the time he leaves here his parents will have seen a bit of light themselves."

In his office near the front of the headquarters building Sherman Harriman puts on one of his four hats, that of president of the Boys Ranch Independent School District, to explain in detail the expansion of services and the dozens of subtle alterations effected over the past dozen years in both academic and vocational programs in order to meet the needs of the boys of the 1970s and 1980s.

Counseling and testing have been constantly expanded. Basic-skills instruction in reading, writing, and arithmetic has been intensified and kept at "state-of-the-art" levels. Experimentation in the vocational curriculum is constant as refinements are sought to meet specific needs of each of the four categories of students mentioned in Chapter 17.

"What about television, the 'plug-in drug'?" I asked.

His answer reaffirmed those of Superintendents Waldrip, Rattan, and others I had quizzed regarding the hypnotic fantasy-box now recognized by more and more educators as perhaps our most all-pervasive hindrance to the educational process: at Tascosa, television is no serious problem at all.

"Television-viewing is the first privilege to be taken away when a boy falls behind in his schoolwork. Other than that, we have not found it necessary to impose any ranchwide policy regarding television upon our dormitory parents. Our boys have relatively little time at best to sit in front of the TV. What with their schoolwork, their homework, their athletics, their ball games, fishing, and other recreation, their time is pretty well occupied in more active pursuits from breakfast to bedtime."

As secretary to the board of directors, Sherman Harriman is responsible

THE PROCESS HUMS

238 for recording directors' meetings, keeping records of weekly executive committee actions, and guiding the organization through sometimes impenetrable thickets of institutional, regulatory, and legal requirements.

Under his third hat as director of admissions, Sherman had to assume more than eighteen years ago the responsibility Cal Farley had regarded as posing the severest test to all the judgment, experience, and intuition in his own arsenal, a responsibility constantly confronting questions like these: Which boys have the greatest need, coupled with the best potential, among the literally hundreds of worthy applicants seeking admission? Which troublemaker or high-octane "wildcat" should be admitted and which prejudged just a hair beyond the line of possible reclamation? What is the present tone of the ranch community? Can we accept any more 'incorrigibles' without tipping the balance against law and order? If so, how many?"

On the basis of applications, each incorporating some forty pages of parental affidavits, school records, biographical summaries, questionnaires, reports of physical and psychiatric testing, and so on, Sherman makes preliminary selections and books airline passage for himself or one of his assistants to Shreveport, Orlando, Milwaukee, Houston, Portland, Sacramento, or Albuquerque to conduct personal interviews of all pro- spective ranchers. After returning, he makes his final decisions, and new ranchers arrive to start a new life at Tascosa.

(He relates sardonically that, after thirty years in the ranch administra- tion and several years as director of admissions, he had been officially designated as "not qualified" under a new Texas law requiring a master's degree in social work for the latter position. Considerable time and money spent for legal fees had to be consumed to obtain a waiver.)

Finally, as administrative manager, he performs executive duties as one of the three persons — along with Ranch Superintendent Monty Waldrip and Business Administrator Gene Hayman — in charge of the daily opera- tion of the ranch. In that capacity he has labored successfully toward a strong upgrading of the ranch staff in training and education, and has in- stituted a system under direction of a ranch veteran, Carroll Powell, in which each staff member is kept current with fifteen to thirty hours of in-service training each year.

Most taxing are the emergencies, which invariably peak when the sap runs strong in trees and humans in the spring and early summer. On this particular day a sheriff calls from San Angelo, in central Texas, a fifteen- hour drive distant.

"We have a young fellow here who stole a car last night, and we burned

Sherman G. Harriman.

a little gas chasing him about sixty miles down the road toward Waco. Says his name is Alton and that he ran away from Boys Ranch three days ago. Know him?"

"Yes, sure do," Sherman Harriman says. "Good student, most of the time. Plays line backer like a Sherman tank. Rides nothing but bulls in our rodeo. But every spring when school is out he's got to take off. Last year he only got as far as Childress. When we get him back and he takes his punishment, he has been, so far, good for another year. But I admit he's stretching us a little thin."

"Shall we send him on down the tube?"

"No, I guess not," says Sherman Harriman after a pause. "He's still got possibilities. Let's see, it's three o'clock. I'll have a car and a driver at your office at eleven tomorrow morning to pick him up."

The next call is from a tearful mother who is not requesting but demanding release from her written agreement to leave her son at Boys Ranch until his graduation from high school.

Sherman's questions are rapid, skillful, long-practiced. Is this a mother who's not doing so well herself and needs to try to make a breadwinner out of her muscular young offspring? Well, no. Is she in the middle of a fit of remorse for what she didn't do for this boy but hasn't yet straightened out her own life? That's more like it.

"We've had a problem with Roger smoking after the last two Christmas vacations when he went home to visit you. He brought cigarettes onto

THE PROCESS HUMS

the ranch, but he told another boy he'd smoked marijuana at home. That true?"

After an ambiguous, resentful answer, he reaches for a file from a side drawer in his desk.

"Mrs. Matheson," he says, "your Roger is a high school sophomore now, and he seems to be taking better hold of his studies and his life in the last few months than he's ever done before. We've had some trouble with him, as you know; he doesn't have to toe the line when he's with you, and no boy likes to learn self-discipline. We have completed applications from perhaps two hundred other boys who'd like to be in Roger's place, but our experience shows there's a ninety percent chance we'll lose all the progress he's made if he goes home to you now."

More pleas, more tears, ending in threats. Sherman reaches into another file drawer and tries one final tack. "Mrs. Matheson," he says, "I'm holding another file. It's half an inch thick. It contains nothing but letters from mothers exactly like you who persuaded or forced us to send their sons home before we felt our job had been done. Every one of these mothers is pleading with us now, some desperately, to take their boys back — and that sort of pitch-and-toss game we simply cannot get into. Let me read a couple of these letters at random."

He reads. It is of no use. He puts down the phone with a sagging face.

"Three years and ten months of hard concentration by a dozen more-than-competent, determined people, down the drain. She's got an expensive lawyer and another one of those judges — there are a lot of them nowadays — who's interested in keeping a clean desk and maybe running for the legislature. We've lost her boy."

His secretary opens the door and says, "Mr. Patterson called *again*. He's impatient for the Executive Committee minutes."

"I think I'm about burned out on this job," Sherman says.

Digging deep in my papers, I smiled at him. "You said that to me, let's see, thirteen years ago next October 2, remember?" I held up a 1972 diary containing the notation: "Fast roll from OK City, the panhandle 'green and golden.' Long, reminiscent chat with Wes Izzard at the *Globe-News*. To dinner with Sherm and Genie, he just back somewhat relieved from two and a half hours with his doctor, after having chest pains."

Clearly a job — four jobs — for which an advertisement seeking a replacement for Sherman Harriman should read: "Heavy responsibility, long hours, much travel, endless intrusions on personal time, modest salary, little hope of promotion, minimal organizational or public recognition.

Big event of the year at the New Tascosa . . . the all-boy ranch rodeo which draws 12,000 enthusiastic and loyal fans to the ranch arena each Labor Day weekend.

Rewards, if any, will derive from exercising superlative diplomacy, judgment, urbanity, patience, management expertise, and a will as flexible and unbreakable as a Damascus steel blade in the cause of salvaging otherwise homeless and aimless and potentially destructive American youth."

Like his spouse, herself comparably equipped with vertebral steel, Sherman keeps his footing under these responsibilities through balancing diversions, first and foremost thespian, elsewhere in Amarillo. Over the years he has developed a true actor's felicity of enunciation and verbal restraint advantageous across the spectrum of his activities. (His all-time favorite role on stage, he says, was that of Dr. Einstein in *Arsenic and Old Lace.*)

As an ardent western history buff, he is a past president and has served for sixteen years as a director of the Panhandle-Plains Historical Museum at nearby Canyon, Texas, ranked as one of the top ten museums of its type in the nation. He is a Rotarian, a Mason, a Shriner, and a member of the Archeological Society who took special interest in helping organize a corral (chapter) of The Westerners, that amiably contentious comradeship of amateur experts who meet monthly to hear a member's hour-long paper

THE PROCESS HUMS

produced over months of labor on some obscure and otherwise unrecorded aspect of western history, then to wrangle far into the night over its merits and deficiencies.

Thus has Cal Farley maintained, in absentia, a strong family influence on the day-by-day progress of Boys Ranch.

Cal Farley's personal friends, and clear proof of their faithfulness, are amply in evidence inside the spacious reception area of the visitors center at Tascosa. On the wall beside the main window of the ranch bank hangs a document enlarged to fill a frame four feet square. The text is more than that of the eulogy adopted by the ranch board in its first meeting after the death of the Farleys. It is a pledge, in moving language, to hold the ranch to a course true to the methods and aspirations of its founders.

In a small frame nearby are individual portraits of members of the present board of directors of the ranch—and here again a visitor long familiar with ranch affairs finds cause to salute the toughness of fiber this adamantine landscape breeds in both its chaparral and its men. In amazing proportion the same team of Amarillo businessmen and ranchers who helped Cal Farley build his ranch are still present and active, eighteen years after Cal's death, keeping that ranch on track.

Senior in years is Lawrence Hagy, mayor of an upsurging young city named Amarillo during the late 1940s, partner of Cal Farley in dozens of private encounters in cajolery and public promotions of Boys Ranch, at eighty-six, still in his office at nine sharp each morning, still dapper and jovial, still directing daily operation of his oil business, and still staying current in his numerous other affairs, including Boys Ranch.

Somewhat younger was Virgil Patterson,* eighty-two, the banker who succeeded to the executive vice-presidency, then the Boys Ranch presidency, following the Farleys' departure. As his designated successor Cal had chosen a personality as home-rooted as Cal had been restless traveler, as private and unpromotional as Cal had been constantly in the public eye. In his role as a community-building banker, Patterson had been perhaps proudest when, as reward for his sponsorship of the High Plains Agricultural Research Center, a new and successful strain of soybean had been named in his honor.

"I was surprised and, frankly, a bit stunned," he says, "when I learned at the first meeting of the board after Mimi Farley's passing that I had been chosen by Cal to take over operation of the ranch. But as time went

---

* Mr. Patterson died on May 4, 1986.

on I began to realize that, in an accelerated number of trips with him to Tascosa over the previous two years, Cal had been preparing me for the job. One of his last 'instructions' to me, I can't forget, was this:

" 'Running a place like this is simple if a fellow wants to take bows and keep the do-gooders and the press and the public and everybody happy: all he has to do is to accept only the *good* boys who are merely homeless, and leave those wildcats alone. They're trouble! Problem is that when you do that you're running just another boys' home. Everybody loves you, but then those wildest colts—who've got the greatest capacity to become real leaders if they're properly broken to ride—have got simply no place else in this country that I know of to go, except to reform school and become pros in crime.' "

A skipper who ran a taut ship, Patterson took greatest satisfaction in creating, with members of the board, the Boys Ranch Foundation as a depository for the wise investment of larger gifts and bequests beyond those exceeding the immediate needs of the ranch. With the foundation in existence, the ranch administration has been able to effect a large expansion of instructional and other staff and also, during the Patterson regime, construction of the ranch chapel and Christian education building; eight dormitories, each housing twenty-four boys and two dorm-parent families; plus a splendidly equipped clinic, besides also nearly doubling the capacity of the high school.

Patterson also chaired an eight-man executive committee which—*on each of the 998 consecutive Fridays between Cal Farley's death and this writing*—has met (with Ranch Superintendent Waldrip, Business Administrator Hayman, and Secretary Harriman) for a two-hour luncheon and business meeting at the Boys Ranch headquarters in Amarillo. Dominating that committee at this writing are four of the six octogenarians still serving on a Cal Farley's Boys Ranch Board of Directors that includes in its membership nearly all of Cal Farley's original colleagues in the Tascosa experiment. The full board meets quarterly.

At a meeting of this executive committee on March 29, 1985, I presented to my old friend Harold Dunn, then eighty-two and failing, a faded carbon of a long, despairing letter I had written to him in mid-1952 recounting in detail my barren eighteen-month sojourn carrying the first manuscript of this book—then entitled "Six Hundred Sons"—on the round of New York publishers and reaching this bleak conclusion: "Harold, the main problem is that I just can't seem to make Easterners believe that a place like Cal Farley's Boys Ranch really exists."

THE PROCESS HUMS

244

General Superintendent Lamont Waldrip, ranch boss since 1976, visits with one of his proteges under the gaze of Cal's statue in the well-groomed Farley Memorial Gardens. The Old Tascosa stone court-house, beyond, now houses the Julian Bivins Museum.

"What's the secret? How have you done it?" I asked my towering and most thoughtful host, Ranch Superintendent Monty Waldrip, in parting. "Just by thinking through Cal Farley's philosophy to its best application today," he replied, "and then hanging tough, even in such unpopular areas as staff dress code and attitude."

Older eyes all too familiar with the inexorable deterioration time brings to human institutions may well find in this latter phenomenon the most unlikely of all tributes to the stature of Cal Farley. Prophets, after all, are seldom honored at all or, at best, are honored only with reservations, by their peers who lived with and knew them microscopically. Strong and successful men, even when extending that honor, can rarely resist bending an enterprise to their own patterns after the founder is gone.

The fact that these seeming inevitabilities have not occurred at Tascosa is a final reason why Cal Farley's Boys Ranch has cruised from the late 1960s to the mid-1980s relatively immune to the social turmoil that has

TWO THOUSAND SONS

infused and disrupted every sector of American life during those years,
on a course as straight as the western fence line of the XIT.

My homing, my hegira is complete.

As the square nose of my pickup pulls onto Highway 87 and starts its
seven-hour slow climb back toward my high lonesome place in the Sangre
de Cristos, my transmitter is sending loud and clear on the celestial CB:

Coronado...

Coronado, good buddy, wherever you are, eat your heart out.

Quivira is here after all. You missed it, by four hundred years. My lost
American civilization is alive and well. My Quivira is intact, with treasure
hugely greater in value than all the gold plate and tinkling bells that Turk
fellow was telling you about.

Right here on El Llano Estacado.

Ten-four.

THE PROCESS HUMS

Epilogue: 1986

A Memorandum to Cal and Mimi

T THE MIDPOINT of the current decade your ranch at Old Tascosa stood fulfilled, as I have reported, without a blemish discernible to the casual eye. The personal legend of the Farleys, in the hearts of your friends surviving on Planet Earth from your own generation and mine, and in memories of your by now three thousand sons, still stands as a memorial to an earlier Texas spirit. You'd be surprised and I think startled, Cal, old friend, to cruise today's pavements of the Southwest and hear how often and frequently your name is invoked, how many artificers of how many worthy causes now wrap themselves routinely in your prophet's cloak.

Friends you have still by the thousands across Texas and the West. Those you did not know are often your friends for their own purposes as of yore, but those who knew you have built, with their bequests, an amazing community beside the Canadian River quicksand. Where you and Maud Thompson scrounged boy-vittles in thousands of Mason jars from warmhearted ranch wives, your boys now harvest from the ranch's own ten thousand acres all the meat, milk, and vegetables their dining hall can use. The schools, gyms, chapel, stadia, staff residences, and dormitories now comprise a multi-million-dollar physical plant that overwhelms the credibility of the first-time visitor to these high plains.

Money is on hand also, from Boys Ranch Foundation revenues, to 247
support not only this plant but a well-paid instructional and supervisory
staff of 150 as well, with enough left over to assure completion by mid-
1987 of an enviably fitted new auditorium and fine arts center under construction as this is written. The ranch faces still a problem or two, but
money does not seem to be one of them at the moment.*

It was reassuring to hear all three of the new officers installed after
the death of Virgil Patterson in 1986 declare their faithfulness to Farley
principles. The new president you will well recall, Cal, as one of Maud
Thompson's first family of boys at the Old Tascosa courthouse. He is Roy
E. Turner, who carved success as an Amarillo masonry contractor and has
served diligently since 1974 as Boys Ranch treasurer. His first few months'
work at the ranch helm has assured the staff and the local public that the
interests of the boy ranchers themselves will remain front-and-center as
his primary policy focus.

The newly elected president of the Boys Ranch Foundation, L.
Raeburn Hamner, Jr., is a recently retired banker and long-term ranch vice-
president who acknowledges deep concern for the sound long-range
financing of the ranch, as does Joe K. Howell, the certified public
accountant named as the new ranch treasurer.

Of priority concern to the officers and to the four new ranch directors who in 1986 brought an infusion of vigorous younger blood into
the ranch administration (C. Coney Burgess, Harold Courson, Troy Mays,
and Christopher K. Storm, all prominent businessmen in the immediate
North Texas area), is the problem faced today in the Eighties by all
charitable institutions which, like your Boys Ranch, depend for their bread-
and-butter operational income upon the freewill gifts of a great many small
donors. Those well-trained in your school, Cal, remember that you had
built your downtown retailing business on the little guy, the working stiff
who had to watch his pennies but would pay his installments somehow.
Thus you had put the fate of your ranch primarily in the hands of "little
guys," an army of small givers whose focus was more on the spirit of the
place than upon their own immortality and thus would permit you to keep

* Author's Note: At press-time for this book comes word that the Farley ranch has
confronted in its own fashion today's disproportionately inadequate facilities for the care
and education of homeless and delinquent girls. As of April 1, 1987, Cal Farley's Boys
Ranch underook the financial support and administration of a nearly insolvent Girls Town
USA, pledging to provide for up to 150 young women within Girls Town's four existing
facilities at Austin, Lubbock, Borger, and Whiteface, Texas. Installation of girls in residence
at Tascosa is not contemplated.

EPILOGUE

the ranch on track. Now that generation of givers is largely gone, and nothing short of a full-scale campaign of public reeducation will rebuild that army.

In parting for now, Mimi and Cal, I report a message imparted during my visit on the fourth floor of the Amarillo National Bank Building, early in the month before this epilogue was written, with the giant among your *friends* and the towering patriarch of the Cal Farley's Boys Ranch Board of Directors, Lawrence Hagy. At eighty-seven, still hale and hearty in frame, still magnificently unscrambled in mind, still confronting head-on the challenge of hard times in the oil business, still deadly in the daily gin rummy game at his club, Lawrence grumbled as I entered, "Howe, you'd better get this book out soon or we'll all be dead.!"

"Tell your readers for me," Lawrence Hagy said, "that never a man set up a better program to make good men out of underprivileged or straying boys—never a man set up as good a program—as Cal Farley did. Boys who live there are really among the most fortunate kids of our time. The ranch will need real leadership at home and real help quickly from its friends elsewhere when the need comes. Keeping this ranch on track will take some doing.

"But it's got to be done."

Ten-four.

E.L.H.

Appendices

(Earliest records being no longer available, there may be omissions or errors in the following listing.)

Members elected in 1939 or shortly thereafter:

Mrs. Julian L. Bivins
Oliver Bivins
Ralph Dykeman
Cal Farley

James Farwell
Roy Poole
Dr. B. M. Puckett
Jack Roach
Dr. R. Thompson

Dr. John Vaughn
George S. Vineyard
Chanslor Weymouth
Thomas Wingate

Additional members serving by the end of 1949:

Lyle Blanton
Arthur Chesher
T. C. Craig

J. Harold Dunn
Lawrence Hagy
Gene Howe
Robert Lindsey

J. B. Parrott
Virgil Patterson
Jay Taylor

Members elected in 1955 and thereafter:

B. T. Ware, 1955
Pat Babb, 1958
Clayton Heare, 1958
Ted Y. Lokey, Jr., 1958
Tom Morris, 1958
Frank A. Paul, Jr., 1958
Donald Rowe, 1958
S. B. Whittenburg, 1958
W. N. Barrick, 1959
L. E. Fitzjarrald, 1961
C. E. Robertson, 1961
R. H. Fulton, 1965
L. Raeburn Hamner, Jr., 1965*
W. D. McLean, 1966

Robert Veigel, 1966
L. P. Gilvin, 1966
Julian Bivins, II, 1970
Tom Herrick, 1970
Wales Madden, Jr., 1970
E. C. Sidwell, 1970
Dr. Harold Brown, 1973
Fred Emeny, 1973
John Greer, 1973
James Hickerson, 1973
T. F. Smith, 1973
Max Thurber, 1973
Wayne Watts, 1973
Jack Freeman, 1976
Glen Lemon, 1976

Ray Vahue, 1976
Robert E. Wilson, 1976
Avery Rush, Jr., 1977
Bill Sutton, 1977
Roy E. Turner, 1977**
Joe Kirk Fulton, 1979
E. C. Petree, 1979
Kermit Albertson, 1980
Joe K. Howell, 1980
G. D. Milner, 1982
Harold Courson, 1986
Troy Mays, 1986
C. Coney Burgess, 1986
Christopher K. Storm, 1986

* Elected in May 1986 as chairman of the Cal Farley Boys Ranch Foundation.
** Elected May 1986 as ranch president, succeeding Virgil Patterson.

All photos are from the Cal Farley's Boys Ranch file or from the private collection of Sherman G. and Genie Farley Harriman, except as follows: Putt Powell on page 96 and Lamont Waldrip on page 244, both from the *Amarillo Daily News*; portraits of Robert E. Wilson and his wife Ada on page 167, and of Garland Rattan on page 213, from the respective families.

INDEX

Farley, Dave, 25, 30; Frank, 24-26; Genie,
see Harriman, Genie; Jenny, 25-26; Joe,
25, 29, 30, 31, 33; Kossuth, 25; Margaret,
25; Mary, 25; Mimi, 9, 59, 60, 61, 63, 64,
65, 72, 76, 93, 94, 96, 159, 176-177, 181,
184, 185, 196, 207, 211, 233, 234, 242;
illus., 173, 176
Farley Memorial Gardens, 207, 217; illus.,
244
Farley statue, 207; illus., 244
Farwell, James, 248
Fincher, Mabel (Mimi), 59-60; see also
Farley, Mimi
Fitzjarrald, L. E., 196, 248
Flanagan, Father Edward, 197
Florance, Edward (Ted), 34, 55
Floyd, Pretty Boy, 81
Fort Worth Rotarians, 133
Flying Dutchman Circus, 82, 150, 234, 235
"The Flying Dutchman of Amarillo, Texas,"
see Mantell, Dutch
Flying Dutchman Wunstop Duzzit, 10, 18,
59, 69-76, 77-82, 160, 162, 191; illus., 79
Football, 34, 45-46, 78
Fort Worth and Denver Railroad, 59
Frederickson's Store, 26-27; wife, 25
Freeman, Jack, 248
Fulton, Joe Kirk, 248
Fulton, R. H., 248
Fundy, Johnny, 48
Funk, Dorothy, 164; Dory, 22, 163-164; il-
lus., 163
Future Farmers of America, 182, 214

Galloway, Emmett, 101
Gehrig, Lou, 14
Gene, 131, 134
George, 131-133, 134
Gibbons, Mike, 50; Tommy, 50, 51
Gilliam, Philip B. (Judge), 18-21
Gilvin, L. P., 248

Gipson, Fred, 138, 202
Gjonovich, Miles, 192
Goodnight, Charles, 189, 193
Greer, John
Globe-News, 102, 109, 125, 146, 162, 179,
184, 229, 230, 240
Goodrich, B. F., Company, 162
Goodrich, Colonel David, 48, 66, 74
Goodrich tire agency, 65-66, 74-75
Gotch, Frank, 30, 55
The Graduate, 177
Great Depression, 97
Greer, John, 248
Guthrie, Ignatz, 89

Hagy, Lawrence, 102, 151-152, 154, 155,
184, 217, 242, 248; illus., 156, 197
Hamner, L. Raeburn, 248
Hardin, Jack, 154, 162
Harner, Bill, 203
Harriman, Cal II, illus., 176, 178, 183, 235;
Genie, 9, 98, 150, 159-160, 183-184, 185,
207, 221, 233-237, 240; illus., 151, 176,
197; Michelle, illus., 176, 178; Phyllis,
235; Shelley, 235; Sherman G., 159-160,
183, 185, 207, 234, 237-242, 243; illus.,
176, 239
Hawk, Wilbur, 69
Hayakawa, S. I., 199
Hayman, Gene, 164, 185, 234, 238, 243
Heare, Clayton, 248
Hendricks, Louie, 182, 205 ff.
Herman (Big), 139-141
Herrick, Tom, 248
Hickerson, James, 248
High Plains Agricultural Research Center,
242
Hill, James J., 33; Walter, 33
Hillville High School, 110
Hope, Bob, 153, 155; illus., 156
Howard, Floy, 98; Gib, 98
Howe, Elvon, 161, 172-181; illus., 161
Howe, Gene, 9, 69, 90-91, 146, 160, 179,
230, 248
Howell, Joe K., 248
Huff, Raymond, 191, 206
Hugel, George, 55, 56

INDEX

Two thousand sons

has been published in a first edition
of five thousand copies.
Designed by A. L. Morris,
the text was composed in Bem
and printed by Sherwin/Dodge, Printers
in Littleton, New Hampshire
on Warren Olde Style.
The binding, in Holliston Mills Roxite
was executed by New Hampshire Bindery
in Concord, New Hampshire.

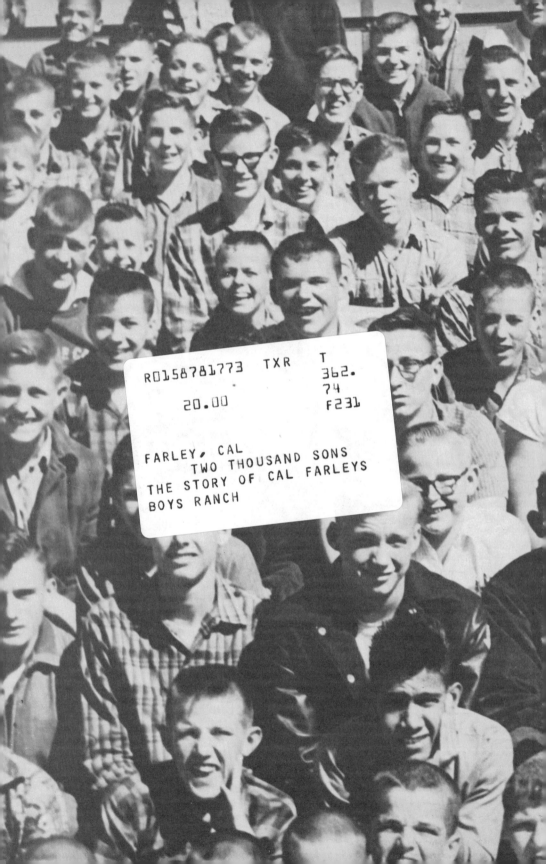